THE PREMIER GUIDEBOOK FOR BUSINESS GLOBE TROTTERS

ebiZ Guides

MOZAMBIQUE

2004

CREDITS

We would like to offer special thanks to:

(Without their collaboration this guide could not have become a reality)

Hon. Luisa Dias Diogo, Minister of Finance, and especially Mr. Gabriel Fabião Mambo, National Director of Treasury, Hon. Hélder Monteiro Muteia, Minister of Agriculture and Rural development, Hon. Dr. José Chichava, Minister of State Administration, and especially Dra. Claudina Maria S. José Mazalo, Assistant to the Minister, Hon. Carlos Morgado, Minister of Industry and Trade, Hon. Fernando Sumbana, Minister of Tourism, Hon. Castigo Langa, Minister of Mineral Resources and Energy, Hon. Dr. Leonardo Santos Simão, Minister of Foreign Affairs, Hon. Cadmiel Filiane Mutemba, Minister of Fisheries, Hon. Roberto Colin Costley-White, Minister of Public Works and Housing, Hon. Tomaz Augusto Salomão, Minister of Transport and Communications, Mr. Liam Mc Kenzie, General Manager of Mozline, Mr. Manuel Amaral, Managing Director of Mocargo, Mr. Walter Carreira, Chairman of STA, Mr. Arturo Esposito, Operations Director of Pestana Hotels and Resorts, Mr. José Esteves, General Manager of Mogas and Mr. Manuel Couceiro - General secretary, Mr. Erasmo Cardoso Muhate, Director of the Cotton Institute, Mrs. Clementina Machungo, Director of the Institute of Caju, Mr. Peter Correia, CEO of Mcel and especially Mr. Stanley Henning - Commercial Director, Mr. Salvador Adriano, Managing Director of TDM, Mr. António Souto, CEO of GAPI, Mr. J.C. Strauss, General Manager of Matola Cargo Terminal, Mr. Chambal, Director of Diname, and of course to all the people who made a special effort to take an active role in the elaboration of this book. We have felt very welcome in Mozambique and will keep a great memory of our stay.

PRODUCTION

Producer: Pascal Belda

Advertising agency: DBB Moçambique (Maputo)

International Project Direction: Corinne Semaille

Local Project Direction: Laurence Diebold

Associate Production: Gabriel Adam, Fernanda Varas, Romina Perez

Our Local team: Dorcia Leidovina Manjate, Sesinando Acacio Pereira

Researchers: Helio Macanga, Gabriel Adam.

EDITION

Written and edited by: eBizguides

Pictures: eBizguides

Charts: DDB

www.ebizguides.com

Architecture: Andrés Sbrancia and Armando Resino

Art Direction: Andrés Sbrancia

Design and Layout: Andrés Sbrancia

Printed by: Imprenta Las Vegas

Printed in Spain - E.U.

Legal deposit: M - 33905 - 2004

ISBN - 84 - 933978 - 1 - 4

Index

Did You Know?

* Did you know that Maputo, Mozambique's Capital City, was once called "Lourenço Marques"? Maputo was founded in the late 18th century in a region visited (1544) by the Portuguese trader Lourenço Marques after whom it was named. In 1898 the capital was transferred from Mozambique Island (Ilha de Moçambique) to Lourenzo Marques - subsequently the city grew to become an important port serving the South African goldfields, as well as an industrial centre. The establishing of the railway concreted its importance and under the Portuguese influence, Lourenço Marques became one of Africa's most beautiful and fashionable cities. After Mozambique achieved independence in 1975 Lourenço Marques remained the capital and was given back its original name, Maputo.

*Did you know that the World and Olympic 800 metres champion, Maria de Lurdes Mutola, is from Mozambique? Maria de Lurdes Mutola was born on the 27th of October 1972, in the suburb of Chamanculo, in the outskirts of Maputo City. She began playing sport, particularly football, in her childhood, and tried to get into the boys' football championship, since at the time women's football was unknown in Mozambique. When she was not allowed to play in the men's junior football matches, at the age of 14 she began to practice athletics. In 1988, she benefited from an Olympic solidarity scholarship for third world countries and went to live in Oregon, in the United States, where she attended and concluded high school. From then on she became Olympic and World Champion in the women's 800 metres. Today she is part of the Athletes' Commission of the International Olympic Committee and was recently appointed in Maputo as a United Nations Development Programme (UNDP) Youth Ambassador.

* Did you know that the small island "Ilha de Moçambique" was, in the sixteenth century, a port of call on the route from Europe to the East Indies opened by the Portuguese navigator Vasco de Gama? The little island of Mozambique, which lies four kilometres off the coast of Africa just opposite Madagascar, was for hundreds of years a major centre of intercontinental maritime trade. It was occupied by Arab merchants from the tenth century until the end of the fifteenth, and in the sixteenth century it became a trading post on the sea route from Europe to the East Indies. In 1507, the Portuguese built a fortress on the island where the Customs House stands today. A later fortification that has survived is the fort of St. Sebastian, which was built between 1558 and 1620 and is inspired by Italian Renaissance military architecture. Arab, Indian and Portuguese architectural influences are blended in the port of Mozambique and in 1991, this island harbour was placed on UNESCO's World Heritage List.

* Did you know that artists from Mozambique designed an unusual throne, which was made of details of weaponry and presented it to the Pope in 2002? This unusual gift was dedicated to the 10th anniversary of signing the peace agreements between the Mozambican government and the RENAMO opposition movement in Rome on October 1, 1992. The agreements put an end to the long civil war in Mozambique. The designers of the throne are members of the Maputo Art Society who have been working on the project within the framework of a campaign aiming at transforming armament and weapons into peace instruments. The campaign has been carried out by the Christian Council of Mozambique since 1995. When the campaign was launched, the local population handed in over 270,000 items of weaponry in exchange for agricultural instruments, construction materials, tractors and sewing machines.

TANZANIA
ZAMBIA
MALAWI
ZIMBABWE
SOUTH AFRICA
MOZAMBIQUE CHANNEL
CABO DELGADO
NIASSA
NAMPULA
TETE
ZAMBEZIA
MANICA
SOFALA
INHAMBANE
GAZA
MAPUTO
Mozambique
International boundary
Province boundary
National capital
Province capital
Railroad
Road

Mozambique Fact File

Land Area:	799380 Sq. Km including the various islands across Mozambique.
Population:	18.4 million people.
Population Growth Rate:	1.9%.
Capital City:	Maputo.
Main Cities (Province):	Beira (Sofala), Chimoio (Manica), Inhambane (Inhambane), Lichinga (Niassa), Matola (Maputo), Nampula (Nampula), Pemba (Cabo Delgado), Quelimane (Zambéiza), Tete (Tete) and Xai-Xai (Gaza).
International Airports:	Maputo, Beira, Chimoio, Nampula, and Pemba International Airports.
Main Ports:	Maputo, Beira and Nacala Ports.
Climate:	Tropical and sub tropical, with a cool season from May to August and three climate zones.
Lowest Point:	Indian Ocean - Sea Level.
Highest Point:	Monte Binga 2.436 m.
GDP:	3.9 billion USD.
GDP per capita income:	197.4 USD.
Governing System:	Multy Party Democracy - Republic.
Languages:	Portuguese is the official language and there are 13 main national languages.
Measures:	Metric system.
Fiscal Year:	January 1st to december 31st.
Time:	2 hours ahead of GMT.
Currency:	Metical.

C F M

GENERAL INFORMATION

INTRODUCTION

Throughout the world, Mozambique is often associated with the images of war, floods and droughts, famine and poverty. These are sad but true parts of the country's history. Nevertheless today these images do not fit the new reality. With the abundance of water resources, a high agricultural potential, considerable mineral resources, the abundance of cheap energy and the will to move forward, Mozambicans are putting the past behind them and are rebuilding their country. Mozambique is truly an amazing country full of hidden treasures and today it has become widely accepted that it has more development potential than many African countries.

Historically Mozambique has always been a melting pot where people from all horizons meet. Originally occupied by the ancestors of the Bushmen, it was invaded by the Bantu peoples in the first centuries of our era. Later, Indian and Arab navigators opened various trade corridors and ports on the country's coast where they would export gold, iron and copper from the Kingdom of Zimbabwe. In 1498, the Ilha de Moçambique, off the coast of Inhambane, became a port of call on the route from Europe to the East Indies opened by the Portuguese navigator Vasco de Gama. And in the late 1890s Portuguese and British Charter Companies settled in the Northern Provinces of Mozambique. This has made of Mozambique a fascinating destination characterized by a strong multiculturalism embedded in a diversified colonial architecture.

Despite all these movements, Mozambique has managed to keep a foot in the past. In fact Mozambique's landscape has remained exceptionally salvage and unharmed. With a spectacular 2500km-long coastline and crystal clear waters, Mozambican beaches are amongst the most beautiful in the world and places such as Ilha de Moçambique have been placed on the UNESCO's World Heritage List. In the interior of the country, bordering Zimbabwe, Zambia and Malawi, the landscape is characterized by extensive tropical forest settled above mountains picks and plateaus. There are many regional variations across the whole country and for nature lovers, Mozambique offers a wide range of spectacular sites.

While it has kept one foot in the past, Mozambique has the other in the future. Since the 1990's Mozambique has been one of the world's fastest growing economies, and successful economic reforms have managed to attract a number of dynamic and modern businesses. In fact a great number of investment projects have been taking place these last few years as businessmen from all over the world have come to understand and appreciate the opportunities that lay untapped in Mozambique.

Ministry of Public Works

HISTORY

From the Bantu People to the Arab and Swahili Era

Long before the Portuguese colonization, which began in 1498 with the arrival of Vasco de Gama, Mozambique was already inhabited for thousands of years by different ethnical groups with diversified origins. Originally occupied by the Bushmen ancestors related to the Khoi-san people, Mozambique was then invaded by the Bantu-speaking peoples, who migrated along the centuries from the Niger Delta region and established themselves some time during the first centuries of our era. The Bantu peoples, also called the Early Iron Age people for their more advanced skills in agriculture and especially in iron working, lived in small chiefdoms which sometimes developed into states or kingdoms. Thus early Mozambique and the whole region was occupied by various groups such as the Karanga or Shona and the Kingdom of Monomotapa in regions of Zimbabwe, the Maravi or Malawi in regions of Malawi and Zambia, the Yao chiefdoms in Northern Mozambique, and the Nguni with the Kingdom of Gaza in Southern Mozambique. Meanwhile, by the 10th century, Arab traders began to arrive along the East African Coast and through the flourishing trade and intermarriages with indigenous people, the Swahili language and culture was developed. The Arab traders slowly created an extensive commercial network with Kilwa, near present-day Tanzania, Sofala near present-day Beira, and various ports and settlements along the Mozambican coast that were ruled by local sultans.

The origin of the name Mozambique (Moçambique in Portuguese) is not certain, but according to tradition, it is derived from Musa Mbiki or Musa Malik, the name and title of the sultan of Ilha de Moçambique when the Portuguese arrived there in 1498.

The Portuguese Arrival

The Portuguese first arrived in Mozambique in 1498 when Vasco de Gama landed in search of a potential supply point for Portuguese traders on the route from Europe to India. The Northern coast of Mozambique thus became a crucial strategic point for the Portuguese empire and their presence rapidly increased. In fact the existence of a flourishing trade in gold, silver and ivory with the interior convinced Portugal to gain control over numerous trading posts originally managed by the resident Arabs traders and a conflict for supremacy ensued. In 1505 the Portuguese conquered the Sofala trading post, near present-day Beira, which served as the main link between Kilwa, the hub of Arab trade in East Africa, and the inland gold mines. Two years later they established themselves on Mozambique Island (Ilha de Moçambique) after dislodging the Arab sultan. The following year the Portuguese built the Saint Gabriel (São Gabriel) fortress on the island and soon Mozambique Island assumed prominence in Portugal's campaign to take over trade with India and the East Indies. Nevertheless as the gold fields in the interior remained in Arab hands, the Portuguese decided to gain direct control over the inland trading posts. In 1511 António Fernandes undertook the first major journey inland and reached the Kingdom of Monomotapa (Mwene Mutapa, the title of the ruler) south west of present-day Tete, where trade in iron, copper, gold and ivory was extensive and prosperous. Several expeditions followed and by 1530 the Portuguese had established themselves in various inland trade settlements notably in the Zambezi Valley at Tete and Sena. Although the Portuguese increased their involvement in inland trade fairs over the following century, their influence in Mozambique remained weak and fragmented.

Mozambican Flag

Colonisation

During the 17th and 18th century, the Portuguese, in an effort to increase and strengthen their presence in the region, established privately owned agricultural estates (Prazos da Coroa) on land granted by the Portuguese Crown in exchange of a monthly rent and the provision of special services such as providing soldiers to the government and administrating the area under their jurisdiction. Nevertheless, because the owners of these agricultural estates (prazeiros) enjoyed considerable autonomy and had their own armies, the Portuguese Crown had little control over them. In 1752 the first governor was appointed for control over the Portuguese possessions of Mozambique, which remained concentrated in the district of Mozambique (present-day Nampula Province), Tete and Sena along the Rio Zambeze and a few coastal settlements. Later in 1782, the Portuguese established their first permanent settlement in the south of Mozambique in Baia de Lagoa. But with the break-up of the Portuguese South Atlantic Empire and the independence of Brazil in 1822, Portugal strongly increased its attention to Angola and Mozambique. In 1890s the Portuguese government, suffering of a lack of capital to administer and develop the country, started granting land concessions for the establishment of charter companies operated by private foreign firms. Through the Zambezia Company in present-day Tete and Zambézia provinces, the Mozambique Company (with 40% of its stock under British control) in present-day Manica and Sofala, and the Niassa Company in Cabo Delgado and Niassa provinces, the Portuguese government claimed effective occupation of these areas. Nevertheless these concessions, which operated independently, did little to consolidate Portuguese control, and the government of Portugal faced an increasing challenge: control the south of the country. Due to its strategic location, the south of Mozambique was increasingly attractive especially in terms of trade with the Zuid-Afrikaansche Republiek (ZAR), present-day South Africa. In fact a Treaty of Friendship and Commerce was signed in 1869 between the Zuid-Afrikaansche Republiek and Portugal, which recognized Portugal's sovereignty over Delagoa Bay. With the "Scramble for Africa" in the late 19th century, competition with Britain and other colonial powers for control over the area strongly increased. But Portugal's "right of occupation" of Mozambique was recognized at the Berlin conference of 1884-85, and further enforced by the Anglo-Portuguese conventions of 1891, which fixed on the map most of the present borders of Portuguese East Africa, as Mozambique was then known. Additionally in 1898 Portuguese East Africa's capital was transferred from Mozambique Island to Lourenço Marques (present-day Maputo) and subsequently the city grew to become an important port serving the South African goldfields, as well as an industrial centre.

Maputo city House

Colonial Times

Although Mozambique had become officially part of Portugal's Colonies, the country remained without cohesion. In fact the Portuguese authority mainly controlled the area South of the Save River and Mozambique Island, while the rest of the country was still administered by the chartered companies or prazeiros. Late 19th century and early 20th century were marked by large-scale labour migrations to South Africa and Rhodesia. Indeed the expansion of the gold mines in ZAR demanded a vast workforce and the Portuguese government, through labour agreements signed with the Zuid-Afrikaansche Republiek, rented human labour, which led to the forced migration of thousands of Mozambicans. Additionally in 1899 a citizenship law was past and divided the Mozambican population into non-indigenous (não indígenas or assimilados) and indigenous (indígenas). The non-indigenous population had full Portuguese citizenship rights, while the indigenous were considered as assets under the Portuguese Colonial Law and were forced to work, to pay tax and to adhere to colonial laws. In 1910 with the ousting of the monarchy in Portugal, it seemed that the faith of the Portuguese colonies was to change. The new Republican government introduced reforms in Portugal's overseas colonies, which gave them a greater degree of self-government although they remained provinces of Portugal, the mother country. But this relaxation of colonial laws was just temporary. Indeed in May 1926, the Republican government in Portugal was overthrown by a military coup and in 1932 António Salazar became Prime Minister. He then put in place the Estado Novo or New State which restricted the autonomy of the Portuguese territories, sealed them off from non-Portuguese investment, ended the leases of the chartered companies, abolished the prazos, and increased Portugal's control over Mozambique. To reduce Portugal's dependence on imports, Mozambique was used to provide agricultural products as well as raw materials. Despite a number of new economic policies, overall conditions in Mozambique worsened considerably. Additionally Salazar introduced cash crops such as cotton and rice and required all males over 15 to work on plantations for half the year, often in chains. Accompanying the rise in cash crops was a drastic drop in food production, leading to widespread famine in the 1940s and 1950s. Also the citizenship law that separated non-indigenous and indigenous was maintained and social investments in the native population were relatively inexistent. In 1960, at Mueda in the North of Mozambique, a peaceful and official meeting was held to protest against the strong tax regime. Portuguese soldiers opened fire and killed about 600 demonstrators. This was the spark that lid the fire. The independence movement was born.

The Liberation Struggle

Following the "massacre of Mueda" a nationalist movement slowly developed, backed by the country's educated elite, Mozambican exile groups and neighbouring countries, notably by the government of Tanganyika (present-day Tanzania). In 1962, the Frente pela Liberacão de Moçambique or Mozambique Liberation Front (Frelimo) was founded in Dar es Salaam (Tanzania) and Eduardo Chivambu Mondlane became its first president. Two year later, on the 25th of September 1964, the Luta Armada or armed struggle for national independence was launched with the attack of a Portuguese base in Chai, in the Province of Cabo Delgado. The first phase of the armed struggle took place in the Northern regions of Mozambique, but as Frelimo freed an increasing number of areas, it slowly progressed to the South. The first major setback for Frelimo came in 1969 when Eduardo Mondlane was assassinated by a letter bomb in his office of Dar es Salaam. He was succeeded by Samora Moises Machel, Frelimo's military commander. With Machel as President of the movement, operations to free the Southern regions of Mozambique intensified. Although the Portuguese government put in place a number of counter attack measures to stop Frelimo's advance, their lack of resources and the increasing international criticism meant they could do little. As Frelimo moved South, they infiltrated the Tete Province and disrupted the rail and road connection to Beira which were crucial to the Rhodesian government of Ian Smith. The Rhodesian government responded by sending its troops to guard the Tete Corridor and Beira Corridor. An important note to retain is that this infiltration by Rhodesian troops would lead, in the future, to the creation of the Renamo Rebel movement. The Carnation Revolution of April 1974, in which the Portuguese Prime Minister Marcello Caetano, was ousted by a military coup, brought a swift change of events in Mozambique. Although the socialist government of Spínola began negotiations with Frelimo, a ceasefire was not agreed until August 1974. At this point in time, many white settlers fled the country. On the 7th of September 1974 at a ceremony in Lusaka (Zambia), the Portuguese and the Frelimo movement agreed for a handing over of power and a transitional government was established. On the 25th of June 1975, the independent People's Republic of Mozambique was proclaimed with Samora Machel as President and Joaquim Chissano as Prime Minister.

Independence and The Civil War

As Mozambique became independent, the Portuguese and most white settlers left virtually overnight withdrawing their money from the banks, taking with them all their goods being afraid of the next communist regime. Mozambique suddenly found itself in a chaotic situation with very few skilled professionals to run the country. In 1977, Frelimo declared Mozambique a one-party state guided by the doctrine of Marxism-Leninism and consequently Mozambique became a planned economy. Private land ownership was replaced with state farms and cooperatives and private production facilities, banks and other businesses were nationalized. This socialist program did not have the results wished and Mozambique slowly went into crisis. In the meanwhile, the Resistência Nacional de Moçambique or Mozambique National Resistance (Renamo), which was created in 1977 by Rhodesia as part of its destabilization policy, stepped up its military campaign in Central Mozambique. This gave birth to Mozambique's 17-year civil war. Nevertheless because of the external links Renamo possessed, many consider the war was not a truly civil war but mostly a war between Frelimo's government and Renamo's external backers, which went from Rhodesia to South Africa's apartheid government passing by countries in the West. Although war continued, the mid-1980s saw many changes. In 1986 Samora Machel died in a plane crash and Joaquim Chissano with his more moderate point of view became president. The unsuccessful experiment in socialism and the near-total destruction of the country's infrastructure forced the government to open Mozambique to the West and abandon socialism for a free-market economy. In 1987 it agreed to a structural adjustment programme and in 1989 Frelimo became a social democratic party. Finally peace talks between the government and Renamo began in 1990 and an accord was signed on the 4th of October 1992 in Rome. A two year transition to democratic rule ensued and in October 1994, Mozambicans went to the polls for the first time ever and elected Joaquim Chissano with 53,3 per cent of the votes as their President.

Marechal Samora Machel

Peace and the Beginning of a New Era (the country today)

Since peace returned to Mozambique in 1992, the country has been successfully putting the past behind it and rebuilding itself. Indeed Mozambicans have been working together, putting the war behind them and building a new future for their country. The 1994 multiparty elections were acclaimed as a model for Africa in terms of fairness and transparency, and in 1999 were held the second national and presidential elections which resulted in a double victory for Frelimo with 133 deputies elected (48,5%) and Joaquim Chissano reconducted as President (52,3%). In terms of economic development, the government of Mozambique with the support of the World Bank and the IMF has been putting in place a wide range of economic reforms. Over the past years Mozambique has been one of the fastest growing emerging economies in the world and has managed to attract an increasing amount of foreign investors. Today Mozambique can be defined as a politically and economically stable country.

THE GOVERNMENT

Since 1992, when peace returned to Mozambique after almost 30 years of struggle and war, the country has enjoyed political stability. In fact many consider Mozambique as a success story in Africa and a model of successful transition many countries should follow.

The Republic of Mozambique's actual Constitution was adopted on the 30th of November 1990 and its political system is classified as a multiparty democracy. The executive branch consists of the President, elected by popular vote for a five-year term, the Prime Minister, named by the President, and a Cabinet. The legislative branch of the government is composed of representatives of political parties that are directly elected by popular vote using a system of proportional representation to the 250-member unicameral Assembly of the Republic or Assembleia da Republica to serve five-year terms. The judicial branch is composed of the Supreme Court, with judges appointed by the president and others elected by the Assembly. Mozambique's legal system is based on customary law and the Portuguese civil legal system. Although the constitution calls for a separation of powers among the executive, the legislative and the judicial branches of the government, in practice, as in many young democracies, the majority of power rests with the executive. Still, the national assembly is slowly gaining power and is playing an increasingly important role in the political ambit of Mozambique.

The two major political parties are Frelimo (Front for the Liberation of Mozambique) and Renamo (Mozambique National Resistance - Electoral Union), but there are also a dozen minor parties. Additionally as in many African countries, political allegiance still tends to be on a regional basis.

In terms of administrative division, Mozambique is divided in 10 provinces, each with a provincial capital. Nevertheless in many villages across the country, both local government administrators and chiefs or traditional leaders share authority.

All citizens of 18 years old and above are eligible to vote.

President Chissano talking with Kofi Annan

GEOGRAPHY

The Republic of Mozambique is situated on the East coast of Southern Africa, and covers an area of 799.380 square kilometres, three times the size of Great Britain, with a coastline more then 2500 kilometres long. It is a very stretched country, which is bordered in the North by Tanzania, in the South by Swaziland and in the West by South Africa and Zimbabwe. In the West of the northern Province of Niassa is located the Lake Niassa which is a natural border with Malawi. And in the Northwest, Tete Province shares its boundary with Zimbabwe, Zambia and Malawi. The Whole of the country's East coast is bordered by the Indian Ocean's Mozambique Channel. The country has an average altitude of 360 metres. Most of Mozambique's Northern provinces are characterized by mountains and plateaus and in fact Mozambique's highest peak, Mt Binga (2436m) in the Chimanimani mountains, is situated on the border with Zimbabwe.

Meanwhile Central and Southern Mozambique lay on broad plains. Some of Southern Africa's largest rivers run through Mozambique. These include the Zambezi River and the Limpopo River as well as other major rivers such as the Save and the Rovuma. Mozambique's coastline is characterized by numerous sweeping bays fringed with mangrove swamps, headlands and several islands off the coast. The vegetation of Mozambique is very varied as it is home to some 17 vegetation types. From evergreen forests in the mountains of the North to high dunes in the South, passing by savannah in the Centre, Mozambique is truly a unique country.

FLORA

Mozambique possesses a wide range of flora, including unique species, although much of this richness is still poorly known. The official number of plant species in the country lays at 5600, but the actual number is likely to be much higher. Mozambique hosts an estimated 250 endemic species. All of the country's diversified landscapes offer encounters with unique flora, but two areas are notable. The Chimanimani mountains in the North with at least 50 endemic species, and the Maputaland Centre of Plant Diversity, South of Maputo. Miombo woodland covers much of Northern Mozambique and is dominated by various types of Brachystegia. And in Southern parts of the country, Mopane woodland is predominant.

FAUNA

Mozambique's fauna is very diversified and is becoming, once again, one of the country's main attractions. Indeed during the war, most of the fauna was decimated but today an increasing effort is being put in place in order to recover the past wildlife glory. Currently the Mozambican territory hosts more than 200 mammal species and a wide range of reptiles, amphibians and insects. All the major African mammals can be seen roaming freely throughout the country. This includes elephants, lions, leopards, buffalos, hippos, wildebeests, zebras and other large mammals.

Recovery of wildlife population has become a major objective for the government and rehabilitation of their natural habitat is being reinforced. On the 9th of December 2002, the signing of an International Tripartite treaty between Mozambique, South Africa and Zimbabwe lead to the creation of the Great Limpopo Transfrontier Park (GLTP). Other major rehabilitation and conservation programmes are being implemented across Mozambique such as the rehabilitation of the Gorongoza National Park, in the Sofala Province, which once was one of the world's most important wildlife conservation areas.
In terms of marine life, notable species include spinner, bottlenose, humpback and striped dolphins and the endangered dugong. Loggerhead, leatherback, green, hawksbill and olive Ridley turtles are also found along the coast. Additionally, various whale species swim along the coast, which is used as a winter breeding ground.

Mozambique also possesses numerous bird species. Of the approximately 900 birds identified in the Southern Africa region, close to 600 have been recorded in Mozambique. Rare and endemic or near-endemic species include the dappled mountain robin, the chirinda apalis, Swynnerton's forest robin, the olive-headed weaver and the green-headed oriole. Other rare species include the Cape vulture, the east coast akalat and the long-billed apalis.

"Come to see me in Mozambique"

CLIMATE

Mozambique, which is situated largely within the tropics, enjoys a tropical or subtropical climate but still has significant regional variations. In fact there are three distinct climate zones. The coastal belt and the Northern Provinces of Zambezia, Nampula, Niassa and Cabo Delgado enjoy a humid tropical climate, while the interior of Maputo, Gaza, Inhambane and Southern Tete Provinces have a dry tropical climate. In the highlands to the West and the Northwest, altitude moderates the climate and temperatures tend to be more pleasant throughout the year.

Generally the dry season runs from April to November and this is when the temperatures are the lowest, ranging from 15 degrees to 25 degrees. In the rainy season from November to March, the temperatures can significantly increase and range from 27 degrees to 40 degrees.

Rainfall averages 750 millimetres (mm) annually in Maputo, and between 400 and 600 mm in Gaza and Western Inhambane Provinces (Mozambique's zone of lowest precipitation) to up to 1000 mm along the coast. The country's rainiest parts, which include the areas around Gurúè, the area South-West of Milange near the border with Malawi, and around the Zimbabwe border near Mt Binga, can have average annual rainfall as high as 1800 to 2000 mm.

Path to Mangrove paradise

CURRENCY

The Mozambican Currency is the METICAL (MZM, or MT), divided into 100 centavos. There are Bank notes of 100,000 MT, 50,000 MT, 20,000 MT, and 10,000 MT and coins of 5,000 MT, 1,000 MT and 500 MT. Also US$ and South African Rand are widely accepted. It is advisable to carry cash or travellers cheques as credit cards are not widely accepted and obtaining cash advances on credit cards in a bank is usually costly and time consuming. The Exchange rate in late 2003 with the US dollar was 24,300 MT per one dollar, and with the South African Rand was 3,480 MT per one Rand.

PEOPLE AND CULTURE

The total population of Mozambique is estimated at 18,4 Million and is mostly composed of a mosaic of ethnical groups mainly related to the Bantu speaking people. In fact Mozambique is a multicultural country and among its diverse peoples are Africans, Arabs, Indians and

Portuguese. Each ethnic group is defined by its dialect and its territory, but also by its habits, which are variations of traditional Bantu rites. These ethnical groups survived more or less to the influence of missionaries, the Arabs and the Portuguese and today the base of Mozambique's society rests on this cultural segmentation, conceived on the authority of traditional chiefs and the practice of ancestral rites. Indeed, these historical prints clearly mark and influence the country's economic, political and social life. Nevertheless throughout its history and up to now, Mozambique has remained free from tribal conflicts and disharmony. Most of its population consider itself Mozambican.

The country is composed of 16 main ethnic groups of which the Makua are the largest, followed by the Tsonga (Shangaan); the Ronga; the Sena; the Makonde; and various smaller groups.

Kids in Mozambique are now enjoying their youth

Makua

The Makua is the largest ethnic group in Mozambique and account for about 28 per cent of the total population. They inhabit the Northern Provinces of Nampula, Cabo Delgado, Niassa and parts of Zambézia. Little is known of their history and their traditions. The Makua society is divided into clans, which historically never made war among themselves, but would unit to defend themselves from external attacks. Their society is matrilineal. The Makua mythology says that Mukulu, their God, created the first man at the top of the mount Namuri. When the man came down the mountain, he slipped and fell, started bleeding and lost consciousness. When he woke up, he noticed a pond of blood that had the shape of a person. When the pond dried up, a woman came out of it. Cult to the ancestors is the most important aspect in the Makua beliefs, as well as the belief in the strength of the spirits. Overall, the Makua are known as a pleasant and peaceful society.

Tsonga (Shangaan; Ronga; Tswa)

The Tsonga are located in the Southern Provinces of Gaza and Maputo and represent the second largest ethnic group. They actually account for over 12 per cent of the population. The Tsongas, called Vatsonga in their traditional language, are composed of three principal ethnic groups: the Shangaan, Ronga and Tswa. According to early Portuguese accounts, the Tsonga people were already living in the central and southern areas of Mozambique, between the Indian Ocean and the Lebombo Mountains, during the early 16th century. Being fairly isolated, they lived a peaceful life in dispersed settlements, having some customs in common, but lacking a common political identity. However, the arrival of the Nguni refugees rudely shattered this peaceful way of life. These refugees had been displaced from their KwaZulu-Natal homeland by Shaka, the Zulu king. They subsequently entered the interior of the country and migrated as far as Mozambique where they subjected the local Tsonga people to their rule. Today the Tsongas, Shangaan, Tswa and Ronga ethnic tribes are also present in South Africa, Swaziland and Zimbabwe and represent the largest ethic group in the capital city of Maputo.

Shona

The Bantu speakers set up a network of kingdoms in southern Africa and the most powerful empire was made up by the Shona people. Their empire began in the 11th century and lasted until the 15th century. The Shona called their kingdom Zimbabwe and it was located between the Zambezi and Limpopo rivers and spread over parts of present day Mozambique and Zimbabwe. Shona wealth was previously based on cattle but with the arrival of the Arabs and Portuguese and the expansion of gold trade, they started mining for gold that they transported to the coastal cities, where it was exported to Asia. The Shona were also excellent builders and an example of their abilities could be seen in the construction of an oval shaped fort 30 feet high called the Great Zimbabwe. The Shona worshipped the God Mwari who was the creator and sustainer of life.

Sena

The Sena ethnic tribe is mostly found in the Province of Sofala, which has for Capital Beira, the second largest city in Mozambique. Most of their culture has remained intact as their homeland remains somewhat of hard access. The influence of modern society and western civilization has been limited over the decades and in fact much is to be learned about their culture.

Makonde

The Makonde are mostly settled in the Province of Cabo Delgado next to the Tanzania border. In fact The Makonde of Tanzania and Mozambique are separated by the Rovuma River and are culturally distinct as immigration from Mozambique to Tanzania has resulted in a blurring of ethnic identities and a sharing of certain ideas. Because of the relative isolation of their homeland, the first contacts with Europeans did not occur until 1910, and then they were very sporadic. The coastal location of the Makonde, however, indicates that they were involved with Swahili slave traders for centuries. The Makonde have retained their traditional religion despite centuries of influence by Islamic traders. Their practices centre on the celebration and remembrance of the ancestors but the Makonde are mostly known as master carvers throughout Eastern Africa. Their work can be seen in tourist markets and museums alike and their beliefs can be seen reflected in their carvings. The Makonde are matrilineal, meaning the heritage comes through the mother, and their carvings reflect the importance of the mother in their society.

Other Ethnic Groups

Other ethnic groups include the Twsa and the Chopi in the Inhambane Province; the Lomwe and Chuabo in the Zambézia Province; the Mwani in Cabo Delgado; the Nyungwe in Tete Province; and the Yao and Nynja located in the Province of Niassa.

As in many other African countries, Mozambique shares common languages and habits with bordering countries: South Africa with the Zulus and Shangaan; Swaziland with the Siswati; Zimbabwe with the Sena; Malawi with the Yao and Lomwe; and Tanzania with the Swahili and Makonde.

Wedding in Maputo

EDUCATION

Under Portuguese rule, local access to educational opportunities and health facilities was severely limited. The civil war also took its toll: by the end of the war 60 per cent of the primary school network had been destroyed or closed. Since 1992, substantial progress has been made in expanding the total number of schools and enrolment, reflecting increased spending on education as a share of the state budget over several years. It reached 22.6 per cent in 2001. As evidence of progress 96.7 per cent of the school network has been rebuilt, and literacy rates have grown from 22 per cent to 34 per cent. However, less progress has been made in higher education: there are only 23 secondary schools and graduation levels from the main university reach a low 20 per cent. Education policy is now focused on developing a strategic plan for higher education, extending primary education and raising the gross enrolment ratio.

Illiteracy (% of population age 15+)
54
Gross Primary Enrolment
(% of school-age population)
92
Male
104
Female
79

Source: World Bank, 2003

Following its Plan for the Reduction of Absolute Poverty (PARPA), Mozambique's government is giving priority to the improvement of the population's educational level. Its basic objectives are universal school enrolment and expansion of access to all levels of schooling with special emphasis on gender equity and improvement of the quality and relevance of schooling, in order to reduce the inefficiency indicated by student repetition and dropout rates.

The gross intake rate at EP1 level (Primary Grades 1-5) rose from 66,8 per cent in 1995 to 122,3 per cent in 2001. At the EP2 level (Primary Grades 6-7), while the gross intake rate remains below 40 per cent, it has risen from around 11,5 per cent in 1995 to 25,6 per cent in 2001.

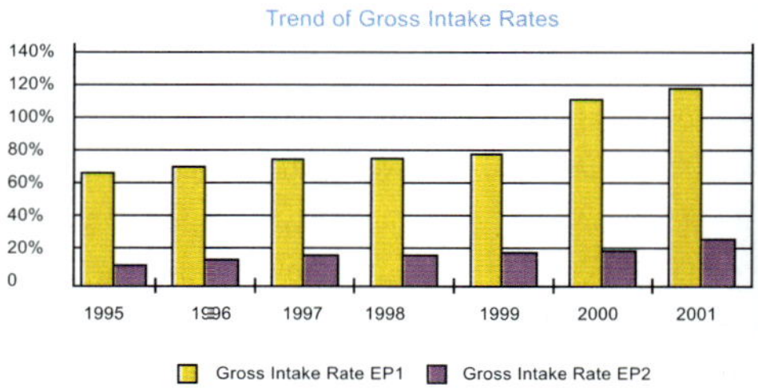

Source: MINED - National Planning Office, 2002

The basic difference in the performance of the intake indicator between EP1 and EP2 stems from the fact that some children enter the school system at the EP1 level older than the normal age, and there is also a high repetition rate. Another part of the problem is generated on the supply side at the EP2 level. The number of schools offering complete primary education (EP1 and EP2) has grown, but where this has not happened, students have to travel further to obtain EP2 schooling, and this acts as a disincentive to persevering with their studies.
Gross enrolment rates show a rising trend at the EP1 level.

This statistic is defined as the ratio between the total number of students enrolled in EP1 and the population in the official age group for that level. From a level of 56,9 per cent in 1995, the gross EP1 enrolment rate rose to 99,5 per cent in 2001. Gross enrolment rates in EP2 were around 27,9 per cent in 2001.

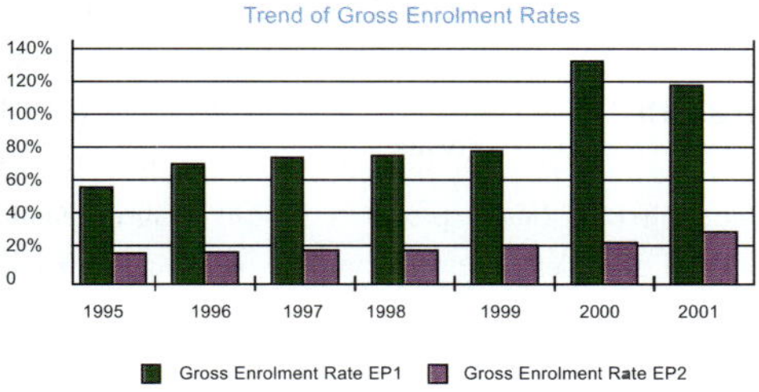

Source: MINED - National Planning Office, 2002

The analysis of intake and enrolment indicators points to a positive trend in access to education in the primary school subsystem. This is basically the outcome of efforts being made within the education sector, such as additional school building and initial teacher training. A total of 424 new schools were opened in 2001(an additional 6 per cent over the total number of schools in 2000). 956 teachers graduated from primary teacher training centres (CFPPs), 8 per cent more than in 2000. In 2001 another 1,546 teachers graduated from primary teacher training institutes (IMAPs).

In terms of education quality, dropout and repetition rates in the various school subsystems point to a series of constraints. In fact figures reveal a relative standstill in the recent trend of grade promotion rates at lower levels, which can be explained by several factors, pedagogic, administrative, socio-cultural and economic, among others.

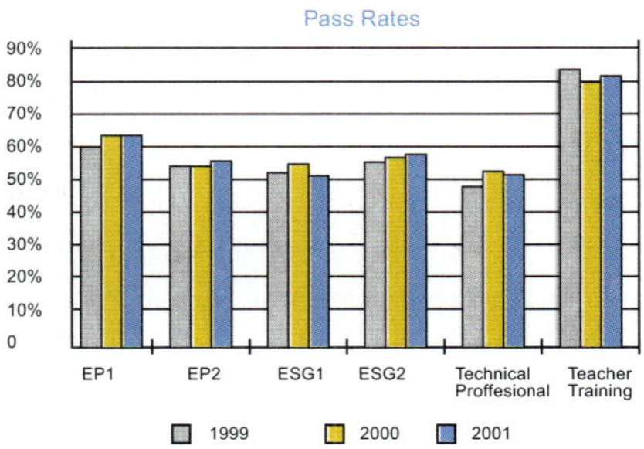

Source: MINED - National Planning Office, 2002

This relative standstill was also noticeable in the other educational levels such as ESG1 (Lower Secondary) and ESG2 (Upper Secondary), as well a technical-professional schooling (Elementary, Basic Commercial and Industrial) and teacher training. This situation shows that, without neglecting the quality, the sector has focused on expanding access, in order to satisfy the growing need at different educational levels.

Nevertheless through all the government's efforts as well as those of the international community and NGOs, Mozambique's literacy and educational levels are strongly improving over the years.

LANGUAGE

Portuguese is the official language and is widely spoken in the large Provincial Capital and less so in rural areas. In fact Portuguese is the home language of just over 1 per cent of the population and is spoken by less than a quarter of the population. Indeed the country's cultural diversity and rich history is reflected in the numerous African languages and dialects spoken. The exact number of languages and dialects spoken is still not established but there are three main groups: the Makua-Lomwe languages, spoken by more then 33 per cent of the population, mostly in the North; the Sena-Nyanja languages in the Centre and near Lake Niassa; and the Tsonga languages in the South. Knowledge of English is slowly spreading as an increasing number of tourists visit Mozambique, but nevertheless remains limited. It is mostly understood in the areas surrounding the Southern resorts and areas bordering Zimbabwe and Malawi. Near the Tanzanian border, Swahili can be heard from time to time and in some cases is more useful than Portuguese. In the capital city of Maputo, where most foreigners live, the use of English is widely spread. Also the main dialect spoken is Shangana.

RELIGION

It is estimated that about 35 per cent of Mozambique's population is Christian, about 25 per cent is Muslim, and the remainder practices traditional religions. Indeed traditional religions based on animist beliefs remain strong and widely practiced. The power of ancestors, forests, rivers and mountains play an important role in the lives of local communities. In the Southern part of Mozambique every family has to be reunited at least once per year on their land of origin to pray to their ancestors, and often these beliefs are incorporated into the practice of Christianity. The influence and practice of Christianity began with the arrival of the Portuguese in 1498 and today the major denomination is Roman Catholicism, although the influence of the evangelical Protestant church is rapidly growing. The Muslim practice is also strongly anchored in Mozambique's history as Mozambique was once home to various Arab traders settlements. Today Muslims are mostly found in the Northern Provinces of Nampula, Cabo Delgado and Niassa. The government tends to adopt a strictly secularist position on most issues.

A beautiful church to pray God

HEALTH AND SAFETY

Health

Mozambique's health profile is typical of sub-Saharan African countries. Amongst the local habitants the main causes of illness and death are the infectious and parasitic diseases associated with poor hygiene, limited water supply, low educational and economic levels, and high vulnerability to recurrent disasters (droughts, floods, epidemics). Medical infrastructures with western standards are only available in Maputo, in private clinics. Also in case of necessity, medical centres in South Africa offer high quality services. There are numerous and well-stocked pharmacies in Maputo.

Travellers will need vaccinations for Hepatitis A or immune globulin (IG), Hepatitis B, Meningococcal Meningitis, Rabies, Typhoid and Yellow fever. Recommended additional vaccinations include Diphteria & Tetanus, Polio, Cholera and Tuberculosis. Also it is compulsory to carry a health card with proof of vaccinations.

It is recommended to wear long-sleeved shirt, long pants, and a hat while outside whenever possible, to prevent illnesses carried by insects (e.g., malaria, dengue, filariasis, leishmaniasis, and onchocerciasis). Also have at home insect repellent containing DEET, flying-insect spray or mosquito coils to help clear rooms of mosquitoes. It is also recommended to carry anti-diarrhoeal medicine to take if you have diarrhoea. Finally take Iodine tablets and water filters to purify water if bottled water is not available. Make sure that you have adequate health insurance.

Safety

Mozambique is no longer the dangerous country it once was. Since the peace agreement was signed in 1992, Mozambique has become considerably safe although there are still cautions to be taken in order to minimize the chances of problems arising.

Driving at night is not recommendable especially in poorly lit areas where there is little traffic, as several risks exist including, drunken driving and hijacking.

During Mozambique's long war, an important number of land mines were placed all over the country. Today with an unknown number of unexploded land mines it is advisable to not go walking around in the bush. Sticking to well-used path is the safest option.

Theft in Mozambique is no worse than elsewhere. Petty theft is the main risk, although more violent crimes do occur notably in Maputo and Southern Mozambique. Most incidents can be avoided by taking the usual precautions: avoid driving at night; keep car doors locked; stick to busier areas of town; and other.

Most apartments and houses have personal security. Indeed various security forces operate in Mozambique and it is recommended to hire them.

On the road again, join the caravan

Driving Licence and Permits

There is some confusion as to what are the requirements in terms of driver's licence in Mozambique. Most foreigners present in the country drive with their national driver's licence. Nevertheless as the International Driving Permit is recognized by Mozambique, it is recommended to carry it along with your valid Driver's License. Also it is recommended to never hand your driver's licence. In fact if asked for, show it through the window, otherwise it may be kept.

VISA REQUIREMENTS & EXTENSION

Visa Requirements

All visitors to Mozambique must have a valid passport (minimum validity of six months) and a visa, which must be obtained in advance. At Mozambican embassies, the price of visas varies from US$20 for a one-month single-entry tourist visa to US$40 for a three-month multiple-entry visa. Within the region, a one-month single-entry visa will cost approximately US$10. One-month single-entry visas can also be obtained at Mozambique border posts. You will need a passport (minimum validity of six months) and it is advisable to have two passport size photos.

Visa Extensions

Normally Visas can be extended at the immigration office (Direcção Nacional de Migração) although these are not always operational and thus, it may be necessary to go to Mozambique border posts. Although multiple-entry six-month visas are extendible in theory, border posts will only issue one-month single-entry visas.

Important Note

NOTICE

It is important to constantly have a valid visa as fines tend to be significantly important and renewing an expired visa tends to be significantly complex.

MOZAMBIQUE EMBASSIES ABROAD

Angola

Mozambique Embassy
Rua Manuel Caldeira, n° 12
P.O.Box 12117
Luanda

Tel: + 244 - 2 - 331158

Fax: + 244 - 2 - 330811

Email: embamoc.lda@netangola.com

Belgium & European Union

Mozambique Embassy

Boulevard Saint Michel, n°97

10 40 Brussels

Tel: + 32 - 2 - 7360096 / 7362564

Fax: + 32 - 2 - 7356207

Email: embamoc.bru@skynet.be

Brazil

Mozambique Embassy

SHIS QL 12, Conjunto 07, Casa 09,

Lago sul, Brasilia, DF, CEP 71 63 0 - 275

Tel: + 55 - 61 - 2484222 / 2485319

Fax: + 55 - 61 - 2483917

Email: embamoc-bsb@uol.com.br

China

Mozambique Embassy

San Li Tun, entance n°1, 8th floor

Beijing

Tel: + 86 - 10 - 5325323

Fax: + 86 - 10 - 5325489

Email: embamoc@public.bta.net.cn

Cuba

Mozambique Embassy

7ma Av. n° 2203, entre 22 y 24 Miramar

Habana

Tel: + 53 - 7 - 332443 / 332445

Fax: N/A

Email: embamoc@ceniai.inf.cu

Ethiopia

Mozambique Embassy

Makamisa Road

H-23K-13-1804

P.O.Box 5671

Addis Abeba

Tel: + 251 - 1 - 722905

Fax: +251 - 1 - 710021

Email: embamoc-add@telecom.net.et

France

Mozambique Embassy

82, Rue Laugier

75017 Paris

Tel: + 33 - 1 - 47649132

Fax: + 33 - 1 - 44159013

Email: embamocparis@compuserve.com

Germany

Mozambique Embassy

Adenauerallee 46-A

5300 Bonn 1

Tel: + 49 - 228 - 224024 / 5

Fax: + 49 - 228 - 213920

Italy

Mozambique Embassy

Viale Nazionale, n° 5, 2 Piano, Intu

00184 Rome

Tel: + 39 - 6 - 4815688 / 4817419

Fax: + 39 - 6 - 4746595

Email: embmozambique.italia@excalhq.it

Malawi

Mozambique High Commission

Commercial Bank Building

Lilongue

Tel: + 265 - 784100 / 784696

Fax: + 265 - 781342

Email: mozambique@malawi.net

Portugal

Mozambique Embassy

Av. De Berna, n° 7

100 Lisbon
Tel: + 351 - 1 - 7971747 / 7971994 / 797353
Fax: + 351 - 1 - 7932720

Russia

Mozambique Embassy
Ul. Gilyarovskovo, n° 20
Moscow
Tel: + 7 - 095 - 2844007 / 28483215
Fax: + 7 - 095 - 2004235
Email: embamocru@hotmail.com

South Africa

Mozambique High Commission
199 Beeket Street
Arcadia 00 83
Pretoria 00 02
Tel: + 27 - 12 - 3437840
Fax: + 27 - 12 - 3436714

Mozambique possesses several representative cffices in South Africa:

Email Durban: mozalon@compuserve.com
Email Nelspruit: mozconns@mweb.co.za
Email Capetown: mozcpt@kingsley.co.za
Email Johannesburg: cgeral@interkom.co.za

Spain

Mozambique Embassy
Calle Goya, n°67, 1st Floor left
28001 MADRID
Tel: + 34 - 91 - 5773682
Email: embamocmadrid@worldonline.es

Swaziland

Mozambique High Commission
Highlands View
Princess Drive Road
P.O.Box 1212
Mbabane
Tel: + 268 - 43 - 700
Fax: + 268 - 43 - 692

Sweden

Mozambique Embassy
Sturegatan 46, IV Tr.
11436 Stockholm
Tel: + 46 - 8 - 6660350
Fax: + 46 - 8 - 6636729

Switzerland

Mozambique Embassy
Florissant 51
CH-1206 Geneva
Tel: + 41 - 22 - 3479046
Fax: + 41 - 22 - 3479045

Tanzania

Mozambique High Commission
Garden Avenue, n° 25 A
P.O.Box 9370
Dar-Es-Salam
Tel: + 255 - 51 - 33062 / 5
Fax: N/A
Email: embamoc@africaonline.co.tz

United Kingdom

Mozambique High Commission
21st Fitzroy Square
London W1P 5HJ
Tel: + 44 - 171 - 3833800
Fax: + 44 - 171 - 3833801

United Nations Organisation

Mozambique Embassy
70 East 79 Street New York
10021 New York
Tel: + 1 - 212 - 8616845
Fax: + 1 - 212 - 7343083

United States of America
Mozambique Embassy
1990 M Street, NW,
Suite 570,
Washington, D.C. 20036
Tel: + 1 - 202 - 2937146/9
Fax: + 1 - 202 - 8350245
Email: embamoc@aol.com

Zambia
Mozambique High Commission
Lufubo Road
Plot n° 5627
Lusaka
Tel: + 260 - 1 - 291251 / 290411
Fax: + 260 - 1 - 290411
Email: mozhclsk@zamnet.zm

Zimbabwe
Mozambique High Commission
152, Herbert Chitepo Avenue
P.O.Box 4608
Harare
Tel: + 263 - 4 - 790837 / 9
Fax: + 263 - 4 - 732898
Email: emba@embamoc.org.zw

FOREIGN EMBASSIES IN MOZAMBIQUE

Algeria
Embassy of Algeria
Av. Kenneth Kaunda, n° 305
P.O.Box 1709
Maputo
Tel: + 258 - 1 - 492070 / 492203
Fax: + 258 - 1 - 490582

Angola
Embassy of Angola
Av. Kenneth Kaunda, n° 783
P.O.Box 2954
Maputo
Tel: + 258 - 1 - 493139
Fax: + 258 - 1 - 493930
Email: embangol@virconn.com

Australia
Embassy of Australia
Rua de Tchamba, n°46
Maputo
Tel: + 258 - 1 - 493072 / 497328
Fax: + 258 - 1 - 493072
Email: ausaid@teledata.mz

Belgium
Embassy of Belgium
AV Kenneth Kaunda, n° 470
P.O.Box 1500
Maputo
Tel: + 258 - 1 - 490577
Fax: + 258 - 1 - 491641

Brasil
Embassy of Brasil
Av. Kenneth Kaunda, n° 294
P.O.Box 1164
Maputo
Tel: + 258 - 1 - 492387 / 292032
Fax: + 258 - 1 - 490986 / 492751
Email: abrasil@teledata.mz

Canada
Embassy of Canada
Av. Julius Nyerere, n° 1128
P.O.Box 1578
Maputo

Tel: + 258 - 1 - 492623 / 492624
Fax: + 258 - 1 - 492667

China
Embassy of China
Av. Julius Nyerere, n° 3142
P.O.Box 4668
Maputo
Tel: + 258 - 1 - 491560 / 491306 / 491321
Fax: + 258 - 1 - 491196

Cuba
Embassy of Cuba
Av. Kenneth Kaunda, n° 492
P.O.Box 387
Maputo
Tel: + 258 - 1 - 492700 / 491905 / 492444
Fax: + 258 - 1 - 491905

Denmark
Embassy of Denmark
Av. Julius Nyerere, n° 1162
P.O.Box 4588
Maputo
Tel: + 258 - 1 - 480000
Fax: + 258 - 1 - 480010

Egypt
Embassy of Egypt
Av. Mao Tsé Tung, n° 851
P.O.Box 4662
Maputo
Tel: + 258 - 1 - 491118 / 491287
Fax: + 258 - 1 - 491489

Finland
Embassy of Finland
Av. Julius Nyerere, n° 1128
P.O.Box 1663
Maputo

Tel: + 258 - 1 - 490578 / 491660
Fax: + 258 - 1 - 491661 / 2

France
Embassy of France
Av. Julius Nyerere, n° 1419
P.O.Box 4781
Maputo
Tel: + 258 - 1 - 491774 / 49511
Fax: + 258 - 1 - 491727
Website: http://www.ambafrance-mz.org

Germany
Rua Damiao de Gois, n° 506
P.O.Box 1595
Maputo
Tel: + 258 - 1 - 485033 / 492714
Fax: + 258 - 1 - 492888

India
India High commission
Av. Kenneth Kaunda, n° 167
P.O.Box 4751
Maputo
Tel: + 258 - 1 - 490584 / 492785
Fax: + 258 - 1 - 492364

Iran
Embassy of Iran
Av. Mártires da Machava, n° 1630
P.O.Box 1470
Maputo
Tel: + 258 - 1 - 490703 / 490229
Fax: + 258 - 1 - 492005

Ireland
Embassy of Ireland
Rua Don João IV, n° 213
P.O.Box 4654
Maputo

Tel: + 258 - 1 - 490970 / 491440
Fax: + 258 - 1 - 491440

Italy
Embassy of Italy
Av. Kenneth Kaunda, n° 387
P.O.Box 976
Maputo
Tel: + 258 - 1 - 492229 / 7
Fax: + 258 - 1 - 492046

Japan
Embassy of Japan
Av. Julius Nyerere,
P.O.Box 1380
Maputo
Tel: + 258 - 1 - 499819
Fax: + 258 - 1 - 727769

Libya
Embassy of Libya
Rua Pereira Marinho, n° 274
P.O.Box 4434
Maputo
Tel: + 258 - 49 - 0662
Fax: + 258 - 1 - 492450

Malawi
Malawi High Commission
Av. Kenneth Kaunda, n° 75
P.O.Box 4148
Maputo
Tel: + 258 - 1 - 491468 / 492676
Fax: + 258 - 1 - 490224

Mauritius
Mauritius High Commission
Rua D. Carlos B° Sommerschield, n° 42
Maputo
Tel: + 258 - 1 - 494182 / 494196
Fax: + 258 - 1 - 494729
Email: mhcmoz@virconn.com

Netherlands
Royal Netherlands Embassy
Rua Mukumbura, n° 285
P.O.Box 1163
Maputo
Tel: + 258 - 1 - 490031 / 490032
Fax: + 258 - 1 - 490429
Email: nlgovmap@virconn.com

Nigeria
Embassy of Nigeria
Av. Kenneth Kaunda, n° 821
P.O.Box 4693
Maputo
Tel: + 258 - 1 - 492457 / 490105
Fax: + 258 - 1 - 490991

Norway
Embassy of Norway
Av. Agostinho Neto, n° 620
P.O.Box 828
Maputo
Tel: + 258 - 1 - 429411
Fax: + 258 - 1 - 429410
Email: ambassade-maputo@mpm.norad.no

Portugal
Embassy of Portugal
Av. Julius Nyerere, n° 720
P.O.Box 1812
Maputo
Tel: + 258 - 1 - 490316 / 400319
Fax: + 258 - 1 - 491172 / 490203

Russia
Embassy of Russia
Av. Julius Nyerere, n° 360
P.O.Box 4676
Maputo
Tel: + 258 - 1 - 491134 / 419872
Fax: + 258 - 1 - 417515

Saudi Arabia
Embassy of Saudi Arabia
Av. D. Afonso Henriques, n° 81
P.O.Box 1634
Maputo
Tel: + 258 - 1 - 490760 / 490098
Fax: + 258 - 1 - 494705

South Africa
South Africa High Commission
Av. Eduardo Mondlane, n° 41
P.O.Box 1120
Maputo
Tel: + 258 - 1 - 490059 / 496250
Fax: + 258 - 1 - 492096 / 493029

Spain
Embassy of Spain
Rua Damião Góis, n° 347
P.O.Box 1331
Maputo
Tel: + 258 - 1 - 492025 / 492027
Fax: + 258 - 1 - 492055 / 494769

Swaziland
Swaziland High Commission
Rua R. Luís Pasteur, n° 1271
P.O.Box 4711
Maputo
Tel: + 258 - 1 - 491721 / 491746
Fax: + 258 - 1 - 492117

Sweden
Embassy of Sweden
Av. Julius Nyerere, n° 1128
P.O.Box 338
Maputo
Tel: + 258 - 1 - 490091 / 490092
Fax: + 258 - 1 - 490056 / 492374
Email: ambassaden.Maputo@sida.se

Switzerland
Embassy of Switzerland
Av. Julius Nyerere, n° 1213
P.O.Box 135
Maputo
Tel: + 258 - 1 - 492432 / 492744
Fax: + 258 - 1 - 402474

Tanzania
Tanzania High Commission
Av..Mártires da Machava, n° 852
P.O.Box 4515
Maputo
Tel: + 258 - 1 - 490110 / 490112
Fax: + 258 - 1 - 494782

United Kingdom
British High Commission
Av. Vladimir Lenine, n° 310
P.O.Box 55
Maputo
Tel: + 258 - 1 - 320111 / 321666
Fax: + 258 - 1 - 321666

USA
Embassy of the United States of America
Avenida Kenneth Kaunda, 193
P.O.Box 785
Maputo
Tel: + 258 - 1 - 492793
Fax: + 258 - 1 - 490114

Zambia

High Commission of the Republic of Zambia
Av. Kenneth Kaunda, n° 1286
P.O.Box 4655
Maputo
Tel: + 258 - 1 - 492452 / 491307
Fax: + 258 - 1 - 491893
Email: zhcmmap@zebra.uem.mz

Zimbabwe

Embassy of Zimbabwe
Av. Mártires da Machava, n° 1657
P.O.Box 743
Maputo
Tel: + 258 - 1 - 488877 / 486499
Fax: + 258 - 1 - 492237

GOVERNMENT MINISTRIES AND OFFICES

President's Office-State House

Gabinete da Presidência
Av. Julius Nyerere, n° 1780
Maputo
Tel: + 258 - 1 - 491121
Fax: + 258 - 1 - 492065

Prime Minister's Office

Praça da Marinha
P.O.Box 2604
Maputo
Tel: + 258 - 1 - 426861 / 426870
Fax: + 258 - 1 - 426881

Ministry of Planning and Finance

Praça Da Marinha
P.O.Box 272
Maputo
Tel: + 258 - 1 - 425071 / 5
Fax: + 258 - 1 - 424135 / 425235

Ministry of Foreign Affairs and Cooperation (MINEC)

Av. Julius Nyerere, n° 24
P.O.Box 4
Maputo
Tel: + 258 - 1 - 492258
Fax: + 258 - 1 - 491460
Email: minec@zebra.uem.mz
Website: http://www.minec.gov.mz

Ministry of Industry and Trade

Praça 25 de Junho, n° 37
P.O.Box 1831
Maputo
Tel: + 258 - 1 - 427204
Fax: + 258 - 1 - 321305

Ministry of Agriculture and Rural Development (MADER)

Praça dos Heróis Moçambicanos
P.O.Box 2290
Maputo
Tel: + 258 - 1 - 460011 / 7
Fax: + 258 - 1 - 460029
Website: http://www.map.gov.mz

Ministry of Tourism

AV. 25 de Setembro, n° 1018
P.O.Box 41011
Maputo
Tel: + 258 - 1 - 310755 / 420979
Fax: + 258 - 1 - 306212
Email: mitur@virconn.com
Website: http://www.moztourism.gov.mz/

Ministry of Transport and Communication

Av. Mártires de Inhaminga, n° 336
P.O.Box 276
Maputo
Tel: + 258 - 1 - 320223
Fax: + 258 - 1 - 431028
Website: http://www.mtc.gov.mz

Ministry of Environmental Coordination (MICOA)

Av. Acordos de Lusaka, n° 2115
P.O.Box 2020
Maputo
Tel: + 258 - 1 - 465843 / 466245
Fax: + 258 - 1 - 465849

Ministry of Fisheries

Rua Consiglieri Pedroso, n° 347
P.O.Box 1723
Maputo
Tel: + 258 - 1 - 324363
Fax: + 258 - 1 - 425087
Website: http://www.mozpesca.org/Default.asp

Ministry of Mineral Resources and Energy

Av. Fernão Magalhães, n°34
P.O.Box 2904
Maputo
Tel: + 258 - 1 - 320618
Fax: + 258 - 1 - 320618

Ministry of Public Works and Housing

Av. Karl Marx, n° 606
P.O.Box 268
Maputo
Tel: + 258 - 1 - 320543 / 430028
Fax: + 258 - 1 - 321369

Ministry of Work

Av. 24 de Julho, n° 2351
P.O.Box 258
Maputo
Tel: + 258 - 1 - 427051 / 424071 / 426219 / 428301 / 422273 / 424400
Fax: + 258 - 1 - 421881

Ministry of State Administration

Rua da Rádio Moçambique, n° 112
P.O.Box 4116
Maputo
Tel: + 258 - 1 - 426666 / 423335
Fax: + 258 - 1 - 428565

Ministry of Health (MISAU)

Av. Eduardo Mondlane, n° 1008
P.O.Box 264
Maputo
Tel: + 258 - 1 - 322159
Fax: + 258 - 1 - 322159 / 430970

Ministry of Education

Av. 24 de Julho, n° 167
P.O.Box 34
Maputo
Tel: + 258 - 1 - 492006 / 490830
Fax: + 258 - 1 - 492196
Website: http://www.mined.gov.mz

Ministry of Culture

Av. Patrice Lumumba, n° 1217
P.O.Box 1742
Maputo
Tel: + 258 - 1 - 420086 / 308532 / 493977
Fax: + 258 - 1 - 429700 / 493077

Information Cabinet

Av. Orlando Francisco Magumbwé, n° 780
Maputo

Tel: + 258 - 1 - 492614 / 491087 / 8
Fax: + 258 - 1 - 490209 / 492386
Email: gabinfo@teledata.mz

GETTING THERE

By Air

International flights to Maputo are operated by three airlines, namely LAM (Linhas Aéreas de Moçambique) the Mozambican national airline, TAP-Air Portugal and South African Airways also called SAA. Although main access from Europe and North America is via Johannesburg, LAM and TAP have direct services to Maputo from Lisbon. From Johannesburg, connecting flights to Maputo are operated by SAA and LAM. All three airlines have regular flights in and out of Maputo. Some regional flights are available.

By Land

Train

Years of war have destroyed Mozambique's rail system, and today there are few working lines within the country or into surrounding nations. A daily train from Johannesburg (South Africa) runs to the Mozambican border, namely at the Komatipoort / Ressano Garcia border (120 km from Maputo), where a bus connects to Maputo. There is also the occasional train service between Malawi and Beira. Nevertheless the government through public-private partnerships is re-establishing all of the country's rail system.

Road

Various roads connect Mozambique to its neighbouring countries. Maputo can be reached from South Africa via the Komatipoort / Ressano Garcia border (120 km from Maputo), or the Ponta d'Ouro border as well as via Swaziland crossing the Namaacha border (80 km from Maputo).

By Sea

Cargo vessels stop at the ports of Beira and Maputo, but no passenger lines have scheduled service.

GETTING AROUND

The best means of transport are taxis within cities, although one should be careful when choosing its taxi. The best place to takes taxis is in front of the main hotels. These are safe but tend to charge more. If you find a good taxi driver, do not hesitate to ask for their mobile number.

The bus is about the best means of getting around Mozambique. There are buses running between major towns usually once a day at least. There are three main private companies and each has express lines (which means less slow, not particularly quick). Where the roads are well maintained, this is a good way to go. Where the roads are in rough shape (and that includes nearly all rural areas), you'll probably have to use converted passenger trucks called chapa-cems (short for'tin one-hundreds' and usually just called chapas) to get around. These get very crowded and are not extremely safe. Also it is not recommended to take buses when dark.

LAM has flights within Mozambique, connecting Maputo, Beira, Tete and other cities. Flights are frequently delayed or cancelled; baggage is frequently lost or tampered with. There are also twice-weekly flights between the capital and the Bazaruto Archipelago. Private charter airlines can fly you just about anywhere you like, though it's more expensive than LAM.

If you're driving your own vehicle in Mozambique, the police has a reputation for finding 'trivial and imagined' problems with vehicles for which large 'fines' are imposed. If you're polite, have your vehicle and papers in strict order and obey all the road rules, you stand less chance of being hassled. Cars can be hired in Maputo and

Beira, where several major and a few local agencies have depots.

For a higher price, it is possible to rent a car with chauffeur services.

WHERE TO STAY - HOTELS

(See also Tourism section)

Pestana Rovuma Carlton Hotel
Arturo Esposito, Area Director of Operations
Pestana Rovuma Carlton Hotel, Rua da Sé, 114
Caixa Postal 4376, Maputo
Tel: + 258 - 1 - 305000
Fax: + 258 - 1 - 307288
E-mail: esposito@pestana.co.mz
Website: www.pestana.com
Strongly recommended by eBizguides' team.

Girassol Bahia Hotel
Paulo Varela, President of the Administration Council
Av. Patrice Lumumba, n° 737 / 739
Tel: + 258 - 1 - 360350
Fax: + 258 - 1 - 360330
Email: girassolbahiahotel@visabeiramoz.co.mz
Website: www.grupovisabeira.pt

Hotel Avenida
Manuel Pereira, General Manager
Av.Julius Nyerere, n° 627, Maputo
Tel: + 258 -1 - 492000
Fax: + 258 - 1 - 499600
Email: h.avenida@teledata.mz

Holiday Inn Maputo
Mr. Paul Norman, General Manager
Av. da Marginal, Caixa Postal 4354, Maputo
Tel: + 258 - 1 - 495050
Fax: + 258 - 1 - 497700
E-mail: Pauln@himaputo.co.mz
Website: www.southernsun.com

Hotel Cardoso - Maputo
John A. Elliott, General Manager
Avenida Martires De Mueda, n°707
P.O.Box 707, Maputo
Tel: + 258 - 1 - 491071 / 5
Fax: + 258 - 1 - 491804
E-mail: info@hotelcardoso.co.mz
Website: www.hotelcardoso.co.mz

Hotel Polana
David Ankers, General Manager
Av. Julius Nyerere, 1380
P.O.Box 1151, Maputo.
Tel: + 258 - 1 - 491001 / 7
Fax: + 258 - 1 - 491480
E-mail: gen@polana-hotel.co.mz
Website: www.serenahotels.com

Hotel Tivoli
Av. 25 de Setembro, n° 1321, Maputo
Tel: + 258 - 1 - 307600
Fax: + 258 - 1 - 307609
Email: Tivoli@teledata.mz

Hotel VIP Maputo
Abdul Agige Gulamhussen, Administrador
Av. 25 de Setembro 692, Maputo
Tel: + 258 - 1 - 351000 / 312920
Fax: + 258 - 1 - 351001 / 312921
E-mail: hotelmaputo@viphotels.com

Ibis Maputo Moçambique
Av. 25 de Setembro, n° 1743, Maputo
Tel: + 258 - 1 - 352200
Fax: + 258 - 1 - 352220
Website: www.ibishotel.com or www.accorhotels.com

WHERE TO EAT - RESTAURANTS

(See also Tourism section)

1908
Av. Edouardo Mondlane, n°560
Tel: + 258 - 1 - 424834
Upmarket Mozambican and Indian cuisine, and one of Maputo's most luxurious restaurants.

Clube Marítimo
Av. Marginal (next to the FACIM complex)
Standard Portuguese cuisine and excellent seafood.

Costa do Sol
Bairro Costa do Sol (20 mins drive from Maputo)
Tel: + 258 - 1 - 450115
Known as the best seafood restaurant in town. Particularly popular on Saturday evenings and Sunday afternoons.

Manjar dos Deuses
Av. Julius Nyerere, n° 162
Tel: + 258 - 1 - 496834
Try their 'carvoadas' of meat or shrimps, truly delicious and great for big meals with business partners or friends. Strongly recommended by Ebizguides team.

Miramar
Av. da Marginal (next to the Holiday Inn)
Standard Portuguese and Mozambican cuisine, and very good seafood.

Mi Casa
Av. julius Nyerere, n° 28
Tel: + 258 - 1 - 491130
Upmarket steakhouse, and great deserts.

Mimmo's
Corner of Av. 24 de Julho & Av. Salvador Aliende
Tel: + 258 - 1 - 309490 / 1
Standard, Italian and Portuguese Cuisine.

Mundos
Av. Julius Nyerere (in front of Cinema Xenon)
Tel: + 258 - 1 - 494080
One of the best places in town for a relaxed beer before a good standard meal. Try their pizzas, probably the best in Mozambique. Strongly recommended by Ebizguides team.

Restaurante o Escorpiao
Rua Belmiro Obadias Muianga (within the Feria Popular)
Economic Portuguese cuisine but probably one of the best restaurant in town.

Restaurante Sagres
Avenida da Marginal (next to the Holiday Inn).
Excellent Portuguese cuisine and delicious seafood. The service is very good. Strongly recommended by Ebizguides team.

Rodizio Real
Av. Julius Nyerere, n°794
Tel: + 258 - 1 - 497275
Upmarket Brazilian cuisine. The service is of very good quality.

Salsa Latina
Av. da Marginal (next to the Holiday Inn)
Standard cuisine and the possibility to eat with your feet in the sea.

Villa Italia
Av. Friedrich Engels, n°635
Tel: + 258 - 1 - 497298
Has a pleasant garden seating and serves upmarket Italian cuisine.

TRADE AND PROFESSIONAL ASSOCIATIONS

Confederation of Business Assoc. & Chambers of Commerce (CTA)

Av. 10 de Novembro
Maputo
Tel: + 258 - 1 - 311734 / 5
Fax: + 258 - 1 - 311732
Email: info@cta.org.mz

International Trade Fair Corporation (FACIM)

Av. 10 de Novembro
Maputo
Tel: + 258 - 1 - 423713 / 427151 / 52
Fax: + 258 - 1 - 427129
Email: sogex@sortmoz.com

Mozambique Chamber of Commerce

(see Investment Legal Framework section)
Rua Matteus Sansão Muthemba, n° 452
P.O.Box 1836
Maputo
Tel: + 258 - 1 - 492210
Fax: + 258 - 1 - 490428

Mozambique Information Agency

Rua da Rádio Moçambique, 5°Andar
P.O.Box 896
Maputo
Tel: + 258 - 1 - 430795 / 428603
Fax: + 258 - 1 - 421506
Email: aim@aimmpto.uem.mz

Mozambique Industrial Association (AIMO)

Av. 24 de Julho, n° 2023
P.O.Box 4379
Maputo
Tel: + 258 - 1 - 305302
Fax: + 258 - 1 - 305302

Mozambique and South Africa Chamber of Commerce and Industry

Rua Matteus Sansão Muthemba, n° 452
P.O.Box 4211
Maputo
Tel: + 258 - 1 - 495197
Fax: + 258 - 1 - 427129

Mozambique Trade Association

Av. 10 de Novembro, n° 30
Maputo
Tel: + 258 - 1 - 424387
Fax: + 258 - 424388

Portugal-Mozambique Chamber of Commerce

Hotel Rovuma Carlton Business Centre
Rua da Sé, n°114, 3°Andar
Maputo
Tel: + 258 - 1 - 300229
Fax: + 258 - 1 - 300232
Email: ccpm@mail.telepac.pt
Website: www.ccpm.pt

USA-Mozambique Chamber of Commerce

Rua Mateus S. Muthemba, n° 452
Maputo
Tel: + 258 - 1 - 492904
Fax: + 258 - 1 - 492779
Email: mail@mail.ccmusa.co.mz
Website: www.ccmusa.co.mz

AIRLINES & AIRPORTS

(see also Transport and Communications Section)

The following airlines all fly to and from Mozambique:

LAM - Linhas Aéreas de Moçambique

Aeroporto de Maputo
P.O.Box 2060
Maputo
Tel: + 258 - 1 - 465074 / 465075
Fax: + 258 - 1 - 465134
Email: jrviegas@lam.co.mz
Website: www.lam.co.mz

SAA - South African Airways

Rua Fernao Melo e Castro, n° 287
P.O.Box 323, Sommerschield
Maputo
Tel: + 258 - 1 - 498097 / 498223
Fax: + 258 - 1 - 499546
Email: femiesaa@teledata.mz
Website: www.flysaa.com

TAP - Air Portugal

Rua da Sé, n° 114, Centro Comercial do Hotel Rovuma, Loja n° 28
Maputo
Tel: + 258 - 1 - 303927 / 303928
Fax: + 258 - 1 - 303947
Website: www.tap.pt

Flights from Europe and North America are mostly via Johannesburg although TAP-Air Portugal and LAM Mozambique Airlines operate direct services to Maputo from Lisbon, Portugal. From Johannesburg connecting flights are operated by South African Airways (SAA) and LAM. These airlines and other operators serve various cities in Mozambique. Regional flights are also available from Durban (South Africa) and Harare (Zimbabwe).

A tax of US$20 is payable, at the airport, by passengers departing on international flights.

International Airports

International Airport of Maputo (MPM)

P.O.Box 2631
Maputo
Tel: + 258 - 1 - 465828 / 465352
Fax: + 258 - 1 - 466450

Beira International Airport (BEW)

P.O.Box 1213
Beira
Tel: + 258 - 3 - 301071 / 2
Fax: + 258 - 302331

Chimoio International Airport (VPY)

Chimoi
Tel: + 258 - 51 - 22242
Fax: N/A

Nampula International Airport (APL)

PO Box 419
Nampula
Tel: + 258 - 6 - 213100 / 214405
Fax: + 258 - 6 - 213164

Pemba International Airport (POL)

P.O.Box 119
Pemba
Tel: + 258 - 72 - 20312
Fax: + 258 - 72 - 20849

The following airlines fly within Mozambique:

STA - Sociedade de Transportes Aéreos

(see Transport and Communication section)
Rua de Tchamba, n° 405
P.O.Box 665
Maputo
Tel: + 258 - 1 - 491765 / 492022 / 495107
Fax: + 258 - 1 - 491763
Email: sta.tta@tvcabo.co.mz
Website: www.sta.co.mz

Metavia

Maputo Airport
Maputo
Tel: + 258 - 1 - 465487 / 465089

Transairways

Maputo Airport
P.O.Box 1599
Maputo
Tel: + 258 - 1 - 465108
Fax: + 258 - 1 - 465011
Email: transairways@virconn.com

BANKS

(see also Finance Section)

There are many banks spread out through Mozambique especially in the Capital City, Maputo, and the city of Beira. ATM services are widely spread and accessible on a 24-hour basis, and accept all major credit cards.

BM - Banco de Moçambique (Central Bank)

Av. 25 de Setembro, n° 1695
P.O.Box 423
Maputo
Tel: + 258 - 1 - 428151 / 59
Fax: + 258 - 1 - 428367
Email: daf.concurso@bancomoc.mz
Website: www.bancomoc.mz

ABC - African Banking Corporation SARL

Edificio 33 Andares
Rua da Imprensa, n° 256
Maputo
Tel: + 258 - 1 - 300451 / 300460
Fax: + 258 - 1 - 431290
Email: infor@africanbankingcorp.com
Website: www.africanbankingcorp.com/mz/index.html

BA - Banco Austral, SARL

Av. 25 de Setembro, n° 1184
P.O.Box 757
Maputo
Tel: + 258 - 1 - 300495 / 428125 / 7
Fax: + 258 - 1 - 424122
Email: buscentre@teledata.mz
Website: www.bancoaustral.com

BCI - Banco Comercial e de Investimentos, SARL

Av. 25 de Setembro, n° 1465
P.O.Box 4745
Maputo
Tel: + 258 - 1 - 307777
Fax: + 258 - 1 - 307152
Email: bci@bci.co.mz or apoioaocliente@bci.co.mz
Website: www.bci.co.mz

BCM - Banco Comercial de Moçambique, SARL

Av. 25 de Setembro, n° 1800
P.O.Box 865
Maputo
Tel: + 258 - 1 - 307490 / 4 / 307481 / 9
Fax: + 258 - 1 - 307554 / 307556 / 307545
Email: info@bcm.co.mz
Website: www.bcm.co.mz

BDC - Banco de Desenvolvimento e Comércio
Av. 25 de Setembro, n° 420
P.O.Box 4339
Maputo
Tel: + 258 - 1 - 313040
Fax: + 258 - 1 - 313047
Email: infor@bdc.co.mz
Website: www.bdc.co.mz

BF - Banco de Fomento, SARL
Av. Julius Nyerere, n° 210
P.O.Box 4233
Maputo
Tel: + 258 - 1 - 494010 / 1
Fax: + 258 - 1 - 494401
Website: N/A

BIM - Banco Internacional de Moçambique, SARL
Av. 25 de Setembro, n° 1800
P.O.Box 865
Maputo
Tel: + 258 - 1 - 307481 / 94
Fax: + 258 - 1 - 307554 / 307556
Email: mundobim@bim.co.mz
Website: www.mundobim.co.mz

BSTM - Banco Standard Totta de Moçambique SARL
Praça 25 de Junho
P.O.Box 2086
Maputo
Tel: + 258 - 1 - 420719 / 423041
Fax: + 258 - 1 - 426912
Email: administracao@bstm.co.mz
Website: www.bstm.co.mz

ICB - Banco Internacional de Comércio SARL
Edifício INSS - RC e 2° Andar,
Av. 24 de Julho n° 3549
Maputo
Tel: + 258 - 1 - 404080 / 3 / 406113 / 5
Fax: + 258 - 1 - 400475 / 6
Email: icbm@isl.co.mz

UCB - União Comercial de Bancos
Av. Friedrich Engels, n°400
P.O.Box 2063
Maputo
Tel: + 258 - 1 - 499900
Fax: + 258 - 1 - 498675
Email: banque_fc@teledata.mz
Website: www.bfcoi.com/pratique/mozambique.html

FOREIGN EXCHANGE

Banks in Mozambique offer good foreign currency exchange services and accept most international currencies although US dollars, Euros, and South African Rands are the best currency to carry around. Private exchange bureaus tend to give higher exchange rates then banks and offer easy access and rapid services. Additionally most hotels offer currency exchange services although these tend to be lower then bank rates. Traveller-cheques can be changed with not much difficulties in Maputo and provincial cities although it is necessary to show original purchase copies. It is necessary to show your passport or a photocopy in order to exchange foreign currencies.

Africambios
Av. 25 de Setembro, n° 1339 R/C
P.O.Box 1485
Maputo
Tel: + 258 - 1 - 430162 / 64 / 430208 / 11
Fax: + 258 - 1 - 430164

Afzal Cambios
Av. Ho Chi Min, n° 773
P.O.Box 10
Maputo
Tel: + 258 - 1 - 300965 / 67
Fax: + 258 - 1 - 300999

Express Cambios
Av. Olof Palme, n° 175
P.O.Box 267
Maputo
Tel: + 258 - 1 - 428758 / 64
Fax: + 258 - 1 - 428333

Executivo Cambios
Av. Samora Machel, n° 26
P.O.Box 267
Maputo
Tel: + 258 - 1 - 310432
Fax: + 258 - 1 - 310354

MPM Cambios
Av. Samora Machel, n°130
Maputo
Tel: + 258 - 1 - 314726 / 7
Fax: + 258 - 1 - 314725

CREDIT CARDS

For the past year, the situation has changed in Maputo and today International Credit Cards are widely accepted in most restaurants, hotels and upper market commerce. ATMs cash machines are available in most banks and five star hotels and are generally accessible 24 hours a day, 7 days a week.

Outside Maputo, payments by Credit Cards are limited and thus it is recommended to have MZM and a strong foreign currency in hand.

BUSINESS / WORKING HOURS

Banks
Monday - Friday: 7.30 - 15.30
Saturday & Sunday closed

Public Sector
Monday - Friday: 7.30 - 15.30

Private Sector
Monday - Friday: 8.00 - 12.00 and 14.00 - 17.30

Shops
Monday - Friday: 8.00 - 13.00 and 15.00 - 18.30
Saturday: 9.00 - 13.00

Official Public Holidays

1st January
New Year's Day
3rd February
Mozambican Heroes' Day (commemorating of the country's revolutionary heroes)
7th April
Women's Day
1st May

International Workers' Day
25 June
Independence Day (commemorating of independence from the Portuguese colonial government in 1975)
7th September
Lusaka Agreement/Victory Day (commemorating of the signing of the treaty granting Mozambique its independence)
25th September
Armed Forces Day (commemorating of the initiation of Mozambique's independence struggle in Xai Xai, Cabo Delgado province)
25th December
Christmas/Family Day

Near the ferry to Catembe, a place to relax

BUSINESS RESOURCES

INSURANCE COMPANIES

(see also Finance section)

CGSM - COMPANHIA GERAL DE SEGUROS DE MOÇAMBIQUE

Rua da Imprensa, n° 183 - R/C
P.O.Box 2659
Maputo
Tel: + 258 - 1 - 313280 / 9
Fax: + 258 - 1 - 313291
E-mail: info@cgsm.co.za

EMOSE - EMPRESA MOÇAMBICANA DE SEGUROS SARL

Av. 25 de Setembro, n° 1383
P.O.Box 1165
Maputo
Tel: + 258 - 1 - 322095 / 96 / 97
Fax: + 258 - 1 - 324526 / 326869

HOLLARD - MOÇAMBIQUE COMPANHIA DE SEGUROS, SARL

Av. 25 de Setembro, n° 420 R/C, Edificio JAT
P.O.Box 428
Maputo
Tel: + 258 - 1 - 313114
Fax: + 258 - 1 - 313115
E-mail: info@hollard.co.za

IMPAR - COMPANHIA DE SEGUROS DE MOÇAMBIQUE SARL

Av. 25 de Setembro, n° 1800
P.O.Box 616
Maputo
Tel: + 258 - 1 - 307736 / 306080
Fax: + 258 - 1 - 305894

MOÇAMBIQUE COMPANHIA DE SEGUROS SARL

Av. 25 de Setembro, 420 - 1° Andar, Edificio JAT
Maputo
Tel: + 258 - 1 - 312600 / 313120
Fax: + 258 - 1 - 313140
E-mail: mcsegurcs@teledata.mz

SIM - SEGURADORA INTERNACIONAL DE MOÇAMBIQUE, SARL

Av. 25 de Setembro, n° 1800, 18th floor
P.O.Box 616
Maputo
Tel: + 258 - 1 - 306199
Fax: + 258 - 1 - 305896
E-mail: info@bim co.mz

SECURITY SERVICES

In Mozambique most houses, companies, warehouses and other private installations are watched by private security guards. These tend to be well trained and equipped. Although security is good in Maputo and the other major cities, it is advisable to contract one of the many security services companies in Mozambique.

ALERTA - EMPRESA DE SEGURANÇA SARL

Av. Angola, n° 2671
P.O.Box 2351
Maputo
Tel: + 258 - 1 - 465532 / 465356
Fax: + 258 - 1 - 455601

ALFA - SEGURANÇA DE PESSOAS E INSTALAÇÕES SARL

Av. Ahmed Sekou Touré, n° 3458
P.O.Box 4153
Maputo
Tel: + 258 - 1 - 402211 / 12

Fax: + 258 - 1 - 402215
E-mail: alfasegurança@virconn.net

BURGLAR ALERT SARL

Av. Karl Marx, n° 749 - R/C
P.O.Box 1098
Maputo
Tel: + 258 - 1 - 430911 / 323509 / 323520
Fax: + 258 - 1 - 427042
E-mail: burglar@emilmoz.com

DELTA FORCE DE SEGURANÇA SARL

Rua do Alba, n° 13 - Br. Malhangalene
Maputo
Tel: + 258 - 1 - 417417 / 419347
Fax: + 258 - 1 - 419349
E-mail: deltaseg@pcimoz.co

MOSEG - SEGURANÇA DE MOÇAMBIQUE SARL

Av. Emília Daússe, n° 148
Maputo
Tel: + 258 - 1 - 313964
Fax: + 258 - 1 - 313964
E-mail: moseg1@teledata.mz

MEETING AND SPECIAL EVENT LOCATIONS

Maputo and the other major cities in Mozambique offer many conference facilities. In fact Maputo has just inaugurated its new conference centre, which held the second African Union Summit from the 4th to the 12th of July 2003. It is extremely well equipped with up-to-date conference technologies. Additionally most upper class hotels, namely the 4 and 5 stars hotels listed in the Tourism Section, also offer good conference and business facilities.

International Conference Centre "Joaquim Chissano"

Armando Pedro Muiuane, Jr., Deputy Director
Av. Marginal, n° 51
Maputo
Tel: + 258 - 1
Fax: + 258 - 1 - 487025
E-mail: muiuane@hotmail.com
Website: www.ccm.org.mz

Mozambique and its government have been working hard over the years to create a modern and beautiful confe-

Hon. M. Gaddafi at the African summit in Maputo

rence centre. With the help of China, the Government of Mozambique built the new "International Conference Centre-Joaquim Chissano" which was inaugurated on the 25th of June 2003. It notably held the African Union Summit from the 4th to the 12th of July. It was created with the objective of being a place where people can come to discuss different issues, a place of understanding and dialogue. Through its conference centre, Mozambique strives to be part of the shaping of the world, participating in historical events. Thanks to it, Mozambique will become an increasingly important political, social and economic player in the international scene. The International Conference Centre-Joaquim Chissano is geared to fulfil the needs of the businessmen, politicians and other personalities. Indeed it can host a wide range of events from political conferences to product launching. The conference centre is modern and equipped with the latest communications systems. Additionally, the conference centre is extremely well located in a beautiful area of the Capital City, Maputo and is easily accessible. The centre offers packages, which include transportation, accommodation and meals. Through all of its influence, the conference centre strives to participate in Mozambique's economic and social development. The International Conference Center-Joaquim Chissano will continue growing in size and influence. In fact it remains significantly young and a number of investments are still to be carried out in order for it to become a major pole of attraction in Mozambique and the region.

Committed to the businessman or woman, the Rovuma Carlton pulls out all the stops to ensure that your business trip is successful. Its meeting and banqueting facilities cater for up to 450 delegates, and business facilities are of an international standard. A comprehensive range of modern conference equipment is available and includes simultaneous translation services.

WEB AND IT SPECIALISTS

The Telecommunication sector in Mozambique is going through a strong development phase. In fact it is being liberalized and thus IT companies are increasing in numbers and quality. Today high quality Internet connections are available in all of the major cities.

Computers, Hardware, Software

Bytes & Pieces

Henrik Arentsen, Director
Rua Comte Baeta Neves, n° 53, 1st Floor
P.O.Box 85
Maputo
Tel: + 258 - 1 - 400446
Fax: + 258 - 1 - 402329
E-mail: info@bytespieces.com
Website: www.bytespieces.com

Bytes & Pieces began operations in Maputo in 1997. The company began with two employees and grew rapidly with a reputation for technical capacity, reliable service and punctual delivery of equipment. In April 2000, Bytes & Pieces was appointed as the official, exclusive authorized distributor of Dell Computers in Mozambique. In fact Bytes & Pieces is an IT company involved in the sale of computers, servers, printers, computer components, monitors, networking products, network cabling products, uninterruptible power supplies (UPS) and a wide range of other accessories. The company has direct relationships with a number of manufacturers, including Dell Computers, CTX monitors, Legrand networking products, Acorp computer components and MGE UPS. In addition, products from other first tier manufacturers such as HP, Epson, CISCO, APC and Microsoft are distributed through Bytes & Pieces. One of the key strengths of the company is the provision of complete turnkey network solutions that utilize the products from this extensive product range. Bytes & Pieces has gained a reputation in Mozambique as a leading supplier of IT equipment and networking solutions. It actively works with the some of the largest and most respected companies and organizations in Mozambique, including Ernst & Young, M-Cel and Banco Austral, to name a few.

Dataserv

Av. 24 de Julho, n° 1580
P.O.Box 4490
Maputo
Tel: + 258 - 1 - 300600
Fax: + 258 - 1 - 326959
E-mail: adm@dataserv-mz.com
Website: www.dataserv-mz.com

EMIL - Computer Business Centre

Av. 25 de Setembro, n° 1131 R/C
P.O.Box 684
Maputo
Tel: + 258 - 1 - 428741 / 320351
Fax: + 258 - 1 - 428772
E-mail: emil@emilmoz.com
Website: www.emilmoz.com

Internet Providers

(see also Transport and Communication sector)

Teledata de Moçambique

Av. 24 de Julho, n° 1895 R/C
P.O.Box 4170
Maputo
Tel: + 258 - 1 - 302580
Fax: + 258 - 1 - 321604
E-mail: teledata@teledata.mz
Website: www.teledata.mz

TropicalWeb

Av. Emilia Dausse, n° 857 R/C
P.O.Box 2016
Maputo
Tel: + 258 - 1 - 304358 / 308354
Fax: + 258 - 1 - 306837
E-mail: admin@tropical.co.mz
Website: www.tropical.co.mz

TV Cabo Comunicações Multimedia

Av. Presidentes, n° 68
P.O.Box 4268
Maputo
Tel: + 258 - 1 - 480500
Fax: + 258 - 1 - 480501
E-mail: tvcabo@tvcabo.co.mz
Website: www.tvcabo.co.mz

Virtual Connection (Internet Providers)

Av. da Base N'Tchinga, n° 457
P.O.Box 2895
Maputo
Tel: + 258 - 1 - 417022
Fax: + 258 - 1 - 417047
E-mail: susadmin@virconn.com
Website: www.virconn.com

IT Consultants and Systems

Syscom - Sistemas, Computadores, Redes

Av. Guerra Popular, n° 20, 6th Floor
P.O.Box 2967
Maputo
Tel: + 258 - 1 - 302494
Fax: + 258 - 1 - 3025 06
E-mail: syscompt@teledata.mz
Website: www.syscom.com

TELEConsultores - Consultores de Telecomunicações

Av. Julius Nyerere, n° 1187
P.O.Box 474
Maputo
Tel: + 258 - 1 - 492376
Fax: + 258 - 1 - 492377
E-mail: bnilsson@teledata.mz

Teleserve

Av. Romao Fernandes Farinha, n° 378 / 6
P.O.Box 2866
Maputo
Tel: + 258 - 1 - 360274 / 429070
Fax: + 258 - 1 - 429070
E-mail: teleserve@visabeiramoz.co.mz
Website: www.visabeira.co.mz

Televisa - Sociedade Técnica de Obras e Projectos

Av. Presidentes / Campus Universitarios
P.O.Box 1750
Maputo
Tel: + 258 - 1 - 480600
Fax: + 258 - 1 - 417772
E-mail: televisa@visabeiramoz.co.mz
Website: www.visabeira.co.mz

ACCOUNTANTS AND CONSULTANTS

(see also Finance Section)

Austral - Consultoria e Projectos Lda

Av. Zedequias Manganhela, n° 95, 1st Floor
P.O.Box 2242
Maputo
Tel: + 258 - 1 - 322780 / 430143
Fax: + 258 - 1 - 307369
E-mail: austral@austral.co.mz
Website: www.austral.co.mz

Consultec - Consultores Associados Lda

Rua Dr. Antonio J. Almeida
P.O.Box 75
Maputo
Tel: + 258 - 1 - 491555 / 491832
Fax: + 258 - 1 - 491578
E-mail: consultec@tvcabo.co.mz

Deloitte Touche Tohmatsu

Av. Zedequiase Manganhela, n°95, 4th Floor
P.O.Box 4318
Maputo
Tel: + 258 - 1 - 320955 / 430594
Fax: + 258 - 1 - 429163
E-mail: dt2@virconn.com

Ernst & Young

Rua Belmiro Obadias Muianga, n° 179
P.O.Box 366
Maputo
Tel: + 258 - 1 - 353000 / 324043
Fax: + 258 - 1 - 321984
E-mail: ern.young@teledata.mz
Website: www.ey.com

KPMG

Av. 24 de Julho, n° 2096, 3rd Floor
P.O.Box 2451
Maputo
Tel: + 258 - 1 - 313351 / 7
Fax: + 258 - 1 - 313358
E-mail: mail@kpmg.co.mz
Website: www.kpmg.co.mz

PriceWaterhouseCoopers

Rua da Sé, n° 114, Hotel Rovuma Carlton
P.O.Box 76
Maputo
Tel: + 258 - 1 - 307620
Fax: + 258 - 1 - 307621 / 320299
E-mail: Jose.azevedo@mz.pwcglobal.com
Website: www.pwcglobal.com

LEGAL REFERENCES

José Caldeira & Associados Lda

Attorneys and Consultants
Rua General Pereira D'Eça, n° 90
P.O.Box 1839
Maputo
Tel: + 258 - 1 - 496900
Fax: + 258 - 1 - 496802
E-mail: info@caldeiraadvogados.com
Website: www.caldeiraadvogados.com

José Caldeira e Associados LDA was established in 2002, following the merger of José Caldeira LLP, a legal practice established in 1983, and Suimo LDA, a Swiss-managed business consultancy firm. The firm's partners and directors are José Caldeira and Adrian Frey. The firm has a strong commercial focus. Areas of specialisation include investment and tax law, labour law, administrative law, land law and intellectual property law, in which the firm is the market leader. The firm's litigation team is one of the most experienced and successful in Mozambique.

MGA - Advogados e Consultores

Av. 25 de Setembro, n° 420, Edificio JAT
P.O.Box 2322
Maputo
Tel: + 258 - 1 - 306230
Fax: + 258 - 1 - 302341
E-mail: mga@mga-law-mz.com

Vasconcelos Porto e Asociados Sociedade de advogados

Av. Martiros de Inhamiga, n° 170, 4th Floor
Maputo
Tel: + 258 - 1 - 312070 / 80
Fax: + 258 - 1 - 312060
E-mail: avp@vasconcelosporto.co.mz

H. Gamito, Couto, Goncalves Pereira, Castelo Braveo e Associados

Av. Kim IL Sung, n° 961
Maputo
Tel: + 258 - 1 - 486438 / 45
Fax: + 258 - 1 - 486441
E-mail: hgegpeb@tvcabo.co.mz

OFFICE SUPPORT

L. Duarte Santos Lda (LDS)

Amina H. Camal, General Director
Av. de Angola, n° 2416
P.O.Box 1819
Maputo
Tel: + 258 - 1 - 465232 / 48
Fax: + 258 - 1 - 465245
E-mail: julaia@lds.co.mz
Website: www.lds.co.mz

L Duarte Santos Lda. (LDS) is present in Mozambique since 1959. The company started with Portuguese shareholders but after the independence it was nationalized. In 1994 it was privatized and Mrs. Camal became its major shareholders. Today with more then 40 years of experience in Mozambique, LDS is a successful furniture company. LDS is specialized in the design, the production and the distribution of Metallic Desks, Office Furniture, Prefabricated Houses, Metallic Structures, Kitchens, laminated furniture amongst others. It has its own design teams, production facilities and a showroom situated in Maputo. They also have an office in Beira. The company offers high quality and comfortable products. LDS's competitive advantages lie in its optimum prices, the high quality of its products, an efficient delivery system, a personalized service, and a guaranteed technical assistance. LDS has several major clients in Mozambique such as the Bank of Mozambique, the BIM group, the Ministry of Health and various ONGs. Its strategy is based on establishing long-term relationships with its customers.

Mabuko

Rua Valentim Viti, n° 333
P.O.Box 3673
Maputo
Tel: + 258 - 1 - 415865
Fax: + 258 - 1 - 415879
E-mail: info@mabuko.co.mz

Office Centre

Av. Eduardo Mondlane, n° 3016/24
P.O.Box
Maputo
Tel: + 258 - 1 - 401922 / 3 / 4
Fax: + 258 - 1 - 401366
E-mail: office.center@emilmoz.com

Papeleria Rex

Av. 24 de Julho, n° 881/7
P.O.Box 50
Maputo
Tel: + 258 - 1 - 426933
Fax: + 258 - 1 - 321286
E-mail: agraficas@teledata.mz

RENT A CAR

(see also Tourism section)

Today there are various car hire companies in Maputo, Beira and other major cities. They offer competitive prices and a wide range of models, from a two-door car to a four-by-four. Cars can be hired with or without drivers.

AVIS RENT-A-CAR

Av. Angola, n° 22
P.O.Box 1816
Maputo
Tel: + 258 - 1 - 467007 / 15
Fax: + 258 - 1 - 466512
E-mail: avismoz@avis.co.za

Avis is also present at the Maputo International Airport as well as the Beira International Airport.

EUROPCAR

Av. Julius Nyerere, n° 1418
P.O.Box 4233
Maputo
Tel: + 258 - 1 - 497337 / 8
Fax: + 258 - 1 - 497334
E-mail: europcar@virconn.com

Europcar is also present at the Maputo International Airport.

HERTZ CAR HIRE

Av. 24 de Julho, n° 2006
P.O.Box 905
Maputo
Tel: + 258 - 1 - 494982
Fax: + 258 - 1 - 326077
E-mail: hertz.reservations@tropical.co.mz

Hertz is also present at the Maputo International Airport and the Polana Hotel.

IMPERIAL - CAR RENTAL

Av. Mao Tsé Tung, n° 591 R/C
Maputo
Tel: + 258 - 1 - 493545
Fax: + 258 - 1 - 493543
E-mail: imperial.mpm@virconn.com

Imperial is also present in the cities of Beira and Nampula.

REAL ESTATE AGENCIES

DOMUS - Sociedade de Gestão Imobiliária

Av. 25 de Setembro, n° 1230, 6th Floor
P.O.Box 4072
Maputo
Tel: + 258 - 1 - 428136 / 37
Fax: + 258 - 1 - 428140
E-mail: domus@mail.tropical.co.mz

IMOVISA - Imobiliária de Moçambique Lda

Av. 25 de Setembro, n° 1113
P.O.Box 1750
Maputo
Tel: + 258 - 1 - 310788
Fax: + 258 - 1 - 321674
E-mail: imovisa@visabeira.co.mz
Website: www.grupovisabeira.pt

ADVERTISING AGENCIES AND GRAPHIC ARTISTS

DDB Moçambique

Vasco Rocha, General Manager
Rua "B" Bairro da Coop, n° 121
Maputo
Tel: + 258 - 1 - 414986 / 7
Fax: + 258 - 1 - 414988
E-mail: vasco.rocha@ddb.co.mz
Website: www.ddb.co.mz

The company was first created as M-Promotion and Marketing in 1998. Ever since it has now a fast and strong growth in the Mozambican market due to its recognition as a modern, creative, calm, innovative, dynamic, capable and compromised agency in presenting solutions that continuously exceed their customers' expectations. In 2000, the company became affiliated to the DDB Worldwide Communication Group. Today the company offers a wide range of services such as communication, consulting, editing, strategic marketing, graphic designs, and event management amongst others. DDB Moçambique is currently centering its efforts in the consolidation of its structure through its skilled and creative people in order to make DDB even more competitive. DDB Mozambique will shortly start offering its services in Angola, and will open a dynamic office in the capital city of Luanda. DDB is developing its business into the new era by investing in digital areas for TV and Internet purposes. Recently, it has also integrated the International Marketing Company RAPP Collens specialized in Direct Marketing & Promotion.

Golo - Agencia de Publicidade

Av.Mao Tsé Tung, n° 488
P.O.Box 2192
Maputo
Tel: + 258 - 1 - 492542 / 493419
Fax: + 258 - 1 - 492560

E-mail: golo@golo.co.mz
Website: www.golo.mz

Publicita
Rua Almeida Garret, n° 28 R/C
P.O.Box 1682
Maputo
Tel: + 258 - 1 - 416329
Fax: + 258 - 1 - 416327
E-mail: publicit@virconn.com
Website: www.fcb.com

MEDIA

Newspaper

Noticias
Rua Joaquim Lapa, n° 55
P.O.Box 327
Maputo
Tel: + 258 - 1 - 32019 / 320120
Fax: + 258 - 1 - 34531

Savana
Av. Amilcar Cabral n° 1049
P.O.Box 73
Maputo
Tel: + 258 - 1 - 304265 / 302406 / 301737
Fax: + 258 - 1 - 302402
E-mail: savana@medcop.uem.mz

On-line News

All Africa - Mozambique
www.allafrica.com / mozambique

Maputo News
www.maputo.com

Mozambique News
www.mozambicuenews.com

Moçambique on-line
www.mol.co.mz

Radio and Television

(see also Transport and Communication section)

Rádio Moçambique
Rua da Rádio, n° 2
P.O.Box 2000
Maputo
Tel: + 258 - 1 - 321814 / 329836
Fax: + 258 - 1 - 321816
Website: www.teledata.mz/radiomoçambique

R.T.P - África
Rua Peru da Naia, n° 246
Maputo
Tel: + 258 - 1 - 497344 / 48
Fax: + 258 - 1 - 497347
E-mail: rtpafrica@rtp.pt
Website: www.rtp.pt

TV Cabo Comunicações Multimedia
Av. Presidentes, n° 68
P.O.Box 4268
Maputo
Tel: + 258 - 1 - 480500
Fax: + 258 - 1 - 480501
E-mail: tvcabo@tvcabo.co.mz
Website: www.tvcabo.co.mz

TVM - Televisão de Moçambique
Av. 25 de Setembro, n° 154
P.O.Box 2675
Maputo

Tel: + 258 - 1 - 308123 / 4
Fax: + 258 - 1 - 308122
E-mail: administração@tvm.co.mz
Website: www.tvm.co.mz

SHIPPING, CLEARING AND FORWARDING SERVICES

(see Transport and Communication Section)

ADENA - Agencia Nacional de Despacho E.E.

Rua Mesquita, n°33
P.O.Box 722
Maputo
Tel: + 258 - 1 - 326252 / 429839
Fax: + 258 - 1 - 323412
E-mail: adena@tvcabo.co.mz

GARP - C.F. Gama Afonso Despachante Oficial, Lda.

C.F. Gama Afonso, Associate
Av. de Maguiguana, n° 1880
P.O.Box 1347
Maputo
Tel: + 258 - 1 - 225200
Fax: + 258 - 1 - 400260
E-mail: despachos@mail.garp.co.mz
Website: www.garp.co.mz

King & Sons (Moçambique) Lda

Liam McKenzie, General Manager
Praça dos Trabalhoras, n°51 - 4th Floor
P.O.Box 2902
Maputo
Tel: + 258 - 1 - 430021 / 2 / 3
Fax: + 258 - 1 - 322262

E-mail: mckenzie@virconn.com
Website: www.kingandsonsmoz.co.za

Manica Freight Services (Moç) SARL

Fernando Amado Couto, C.E.O
Praça dos Trabahadores, n°51
P.O.Box 292 or 557
Maputo
Tel: + 258 - 1 - 324023
Fax: + 258 - 1 - 430674
E-mail: fcouto@manica.co.mz
Website: www.manico.co.mz

MOCARGO - Empresa Moçambicana de Cargas, S.A.R.L

Manuel Amaral, Managing Director
Rua Consiglieri Pedroso, n° 430
P.O.Box 888
Maputo
Tel: + 258 - 1 - 428318 / 321440
Fax: + 258 - 1 - 302067 / 305263
E-mail: msamaral@teledata.mz
Website: www.mocargo.co.mz

MOZLINE, Empresa de Transp.Marítimos e Rodoviários de Moç., S.A.R.L

Liam McKenzie, General Manager
Av. Karl Marx, n°478, 2nd Floor,
P.O.Box 2902,
Maputo
Tel: + 258 - 1 - 303076 / 8 / 9
Fax: + 258 - 1 - 303073
E-mail: mozline2@virconn.com
Website: www.mozline.com

MEDICAL SERVICES

Medical infrastructures with western standards are only available in Maputo, in private clinics. Also in case of necessity, medical centres in South Africa offer high quality services.

Hospital Central de Maputo

Av. Eduardo Mondlane
Maputo
Tel: + 258 - 1 - 320014
Fax: + 258 - 1 - 320828

Clinica Especial - Hospital Central

Av. Eduardo Mondlane
Maputo
Tel: + 258 - 1 - 429522
Fax: + 258 - 1 - 308540

Clinica Cruz Azul

Av. Karl Marx, n° 414
Maputo
Tel: + 258 - 1 - 305146 / 7
Fax: + 258 - 1 - 305151

Clinica Sommerschield

Rua Pereira do Lago, n° 52
P.O.Box 2500
Maputo
Tel: + 258 - 1 - 493924
Fax: + 258 - 1 - 493927

Clínica 222

Av. 24 de Julho, n° 821, R/C
Maputo
Tel: + 258 - 1 - 313054 / 7
Fax: + 258 - 1 - 313054

DENTAL CLINICS

Clinica Dentaria - Dentamed Lda
Av. Francisco Orlando Magumbwe, n° 954
Maputo
Tel: + 258 - 1 - 493370
Fax: + 258 - 1 - 493368
Email: dentamed@tropical.co.mz

Clinica Dentaria - Dente Feliz
Av. Julius Nyerere, n° 657, 1st Floor
Maputo
Tel: + 258 - 1 - 491426
Fax: N/A
E-mail: demiro@hotmail.com

Clinica Elim
Av. Patrice Lumumba, n° 290
P.O.Box 3267
Maputo
Tel: + 258 - 1 - 308882
Fax: + 258 - 1 - 301900
Cell: + 258 - 82- 311066

PACKERS AND MOVERS

CCC Transportes Urbanos
Luis Brazuna, General Manager
Av. Organizaçao de Unidade Africana n° 500, Maputo
Tel: + 258 - 1 - 407588 / 9 / 407590
Fax: + 258 - 1 - 405060
E-mail: lbrazuna@tu.mz
Website: www.ccc.pt

(see Transport and Communication Section)

EXPRESS COURIER

DHL Moçambique Lda

Joao Pereira, Country Manager
Av. 25 de Setembro, n° 1622.
P.O.Box 4384
Maputo
Tel: + 258 - 1 - 307290
Fax: + 258 - 1 - 301943
E-mail: joao.pereira@dhl.com
Website: www.dhl.co.mz

As a worldwide company, DHL is present in every country of the globe. In 1986 DHL came to Mozambique and was at that time, the first express company to do so. DHL's primary service is the "inbound - outbound transport on an international level" but today it is increasingly focusing on domestic market offering express transport services between the country's provinces especially in terms of imports. In fact they offer solutions for fast and easy importing to Mozambique. DHL Mozambique operates through its headquarter in Maputo, an office in Beira and agents present all over the country. DHL functions on a philosophy that simple is better, and thus it strives to maintain the different work processes as simple as possible nevertheless offering high quality services to the client. It differentiates itself from its competitors through its availability, as they work 24 hours, 7 days a week, and through the development of new adapted services, such as domestic cargo services. DHL Mozambique is mostly proud of the opening in September 2003 of its Gateway System present at Maputo International Airport, which makes it the only express transport company operating a bonded warehouse in the country.

EMS - Express Mail Service

Av. Zedequias Manganhela, n° 308
P.O.Box 111
Maputo
Tel: + 258 - 1 - 321784 / 5
Fax: + 258 - 1 - 321786
E-mail: emsmaputo@teledata.mz

SKYNET Worldwide Express Lda

Av. Karl Marx, n° 219
P.O.Box 219
Maputo
Tel: + 258 - 1 - 305353 / 46
Fax: + 258 - 1 - 305352
E-mail: skympm@virconn.com
Website: www.skynet.com.lb/xpress.asp

INVESTMENT & LEGAL FRAMEWORK

DOMESTIC LAWS

The Constitution of the Republic of Mozambique, approved and enacted in November 1990, is the basis to all laws in the country. It is strongly focused on the affirmation of the Mozambican character, its traditions and other social and cultural values as well as its independence and sovereignty. In terms of economic and social organization, the Constitution states that the ownership of natural resources located in the soil and the subsoil, in interior and territorial waters, on the continental shelf, and in the exclusive economic zone is vested in the State. In fact the economic order of the Republic of Mozambique shall be based on the value of labour, on market forces, on the initiatives of economic agents, on the participation of all types of ownership, and on the role of the State in regulating and promoting economic and social growth and development in order to satisfy the basic needs of the people and to promote social well-being. Thus the State shall ensure that economic activities are conforming to the Constitution and the law.

INVESTMENT LEGISLATION

The investment legislation regulating investment activity in Mozambique is as follows:

Law of Investment in Mozambique (3/93 of 24.6.93) establishes the legal framework for both national and foreign investment.

The regulations of the investment law, approved by decree 14/93 of 21.7.93 and updated by decree 36/95 of 8.8.95.

The code of fiscal benefits of investments in Mozambique (approved by the decree 12/93 of 21.7.93), defines the fiscal incentives offered to investors and updated by the decree 37/95 of 8.8.95, decree 45/96 of 22.10.96.

Regulation on the Industrial Free Zones approved by decree n° 18/93 of 14.9.93, with amendments as stated in decree n°38/95 of 8.8.95 and the Regulation introduced by decree 75/99 of 12.10.99.

Decree 16/98 of 16.4.98 created a Special Tax Regime for the Zambeze River Valley Region.

Decree 73/99 of 12.10.99 created a Special Tax Regime for the Hotel and Tourism Industry.

Under the legislation, the investment project must be submitted to the Investment Promotion Centre's approval through the Project Application Form (Formulário de Apresentação do Projecto).

The Investment Promotion Centre (Centro de Promocão de Investimentos or CPI) was established in order to attract investment into Mozambique. Investment programmes that have been approved by the CPI qualify for a number of fiscal and customs incentives, which will be discussed below. A minimum investment of US$5,000 is required for national investors and US$50,000 for foreign investors.

Investment guarantees

The Government of Mozambique offers certain guarantees to investment projects that have been approved by the CPI:

- It guarantees the security and legal protection of property, both goods and rights, including industrial property rights, in connection with the investment project.

Foreign investors in Maputo

- It guarantees the remittance of funds abroad in connection with:
- Exportable profits resulting from investments eligible for export of profits under the law.
- Payment of royalties associated with the granting and transfer of technology.
- Loan repayments due abroad where the loan was used for the investment project.
- Invested and re-exportable foreign capital.

It guarantees the repatriation of invested capital upon the liquidation or sale of an investment.

Investment incentives

Investments in new or paralysed undertakings

New undertakings are those that involve the constitution of a new company and investment in new plant and buildings. Paralysed undertakings are those that have become obsolete and are being injected with new capital. This usually involves the erection of new buildings and new infrastructure.

Customs duties

Investments in new undertakings are exempt from the payment of customs duties in respect of Class K products imported exclusively for carrying out investment project feasibility studies or for implementing investment projects. Class K goods are capital goods, mainly equipment and heavy plant and machinery.

Tax relief

Both new and paralysed undertakings are granted a reduction in Industrial Contribution Tax and Supplementary Tax rates during the period of recovery of investment expenditure, provided that this period does not exceed ten years. The amount of the reduction depends on the location of the investment.

When the ten-year period for recovery of investment capital has expired, investments can continue to benefit from reduced Industrial Contribution Tax rates for a certain period of time. The amount of the reduction and the length of time depend on the location of the investment.

Location of investment	Reduction in tax rate
Niassa, Tete and Cabo Delgado Provinces	80 per cent
Other provinces as long as outside the provincial capitals	65 per cent
Other provinces, within provincial capitals	50 per cent

Location of investment	Reduction	Extension period
Niassa, Tete and Cabo Delgado Provinces	50 per cent	Six years
Sofala, Manica, Zambezia and Nampula Provinces, excluding the provincial capitals	40 per cent	Three years
Inhambane, Gaza and Maputo Provinces, excluding the provincial capitals	25 per cent	Three years

Investments in existing undertakings

Investments made in the rehabilitation or expansion of operating projects benefit from deduction from taxable income for a period of up to five years on the following items:

- Up to 100 per cent of the sums invested in new equipment for the operation of the undertaking.

- Up to 100 per cent of the sums invested in civil construction of plant and infrastructure for operational use by the undertaking.

- Up to 100 per cent of the sums invested in the construction of agricultural infrastructures for the undertaking's operational use.

All investments

All undertakings may consider the following as losses for the purpose of determining taxable income for Industrial Contribution Tax:

- Up to 120 per cent of expenses incurred in the construction and renovation of public infrastructures such as roads, railways, schools, hospitals and the supply of water and electrical energy.

- Up to 100 per cent of expenses incurred either in the purchase, for private ownership, of works of art, or in other actions contributing to cultural development.

- Up to five per cent of expenses incurred by the company in training Mozambican workers.

Moreover, own equity capital, loans and accrued interest, which is used for an approved investment, are tax-exempt.

Special regime for the hotel and tourism industry

Projects involving the construction, renovation, expansion or modernisation of hotels or the development of national reserves and parks benefit from the deferral of payment of customs duties and VAT relating to goods imported for the benefit of the project. The duties and VAT will be extended during the period of execution of the project, up to a maximum of two years.

Special regime for the sugar industry

Investment in an existing sugar factory or related agricultural industry will be exempt from import duties for goods classified as capital goods (Class K), raw materials (Class M) and intermediary goods (Class I). Consumer goods (Class C) are also exempt provided that the value of such goods does not exceed one per cent of the total investment value of the project.

This regime will only be in place until 2004.

Industrial Free Zones

Industrial Free Zones (IFZs) enable certain investment projects to benefit from generous tax and customs incentives. The project must have a minimum investment of US$5million. The goods produced or processed in an IFZ must be destined for export, only 15 per cent of the goods may be sold on the domestic market. Moreover, the following activities are excluded from IFZs:

- The exploration and extraction of natural resources.
- The processing of cashew nuts, prawns and fish of national origin.
- Any activity which is reserved by law for the State.
- The authorisation for the establishment of an IFZ is subject to the creation of at least 500 permanent jobs for Mozambican nationals and at least 20 jobs in each enterprise established within the IFZ.

Investors can participate in an IFZ in one of two ways:
- As a developer, i.e. in the development and operation of the IFZ infrastructure or estate.
- Or as an enterprise, i.e. in the operation of a manufacturing, processing or services enterprise within an IFZ.

Customs incentives

IFZ developers are exempt from customs duties, VAT and Specific Consumption Tax on the importation of construction materials, machinery, equipment, accessories, accompanying spare parts and other goods necessary for the establishment and operation of the IFZ.

IFZ enterprises are exempt from customs duties, VAT and Specific Consumption Tax on the importation of goods and merchandise destined for the implementation of an approved project

Tax incentives

Neither IFZ enterprises nor developers pay Corporate Tax on profits derived from the approved activity. They are also exempt from Real Property Tax and Real Property Transfer Tax ("Sisa") payments.

From the seventh year onwards, developers pay an annual royalty fee in lieu of Corporate Tax. This fee is based on one per cent of invoiced gross quarterly revenue.

Special Economic Zones: the Zambezi River Valley

Special Economic Zones enjoy certain tax reductions and exemptions. The only Special Economic Zone approved to date is the one for the Zambezi River Valley, which covers all the districts in Tete Province, the northern districts of Sofala and Manica Provinces and the central and southern districts of Zambezi Province. Activities eligible for the customs and tax benefits are agriculture, forestry, hydroponics, wildlife management, water supply, electricity generation, transmission and distribution, telecommunications, civil construction and public works, manufacturing and industry, banking and insurance.

Customs incentives

Goods in Classes K, I and M (equipment, intermediary goods and raw materials) are exempt from import duties when destined for new undertakings or the rehabilitation or expansion of existing undertakings.

Tax incentives

- Undertakings in agriculture, livestock, forestry and hydroponics are exempt from Corporate Tax until 2025.
- All other undertakings are exempt from Corporate Tax for five years from the start of operations and benefit from an 80 per cent reduction from the sixth year onwards.
- Income generated from undertakings in the Zambezi Valley is exempt from Complementary Tax.
- All undertakings are exempt from Real Property Transfer Tax ("Sisa").

Procedure for obtaining CPI's approval

In order to qualify for CPI's approval, an investor must provide the following to the CPI:

- A completed application form. The application form requires investors to give details of the investment value, the proposed sources of funding and technical details, including raw material inputs and sources, the destination of the final goods, the anticipated environmental impact of the project and labour requirements. These forms can be found on the CPI website (www.cpi.co.mz) or at the CPI offices, Rua de Imprensa, No. 332, Maputo.

- A copy of the passport or identification card of each investor or, if it is a company that will be providing the investment capital, a copy of the company's Articles of Association and Certificate of Registration.

- A list of the equipment that will be imported into the country in order to realise the project.

- Bank references and evidence that the investor has the necessary financial capacity to undertake the project. If the investor is a company or group of companies, this will take the form of financial accounts and the most recent annual report for each investing company.

- Details of the land concession where the project will be implemented.

If the investor is foreign, the following must be provided to the Banco de Moçambique in order to register the investment:

- In cases where the investment will take the form of freely transferable currency.

- Copy of the investment authorisation from CPI.

- Proof of the deposit of the capital from the Commercial Bank.

In cases where the investment will take the form of equipment, machinery and other imported materials:

- Copy of the Bulletin of Import Registration (BRI).

- Three copies of a list of equipment exempted from customs duties.

- Invoices for the equipment.

- Certificate of inspection of the embarkation of the equipment.

Please note that the value of the investment shall be taken to be the FOB value of the equipment and other materials unless the transport and insurance have been carried out by Mozambican companies and the payments have been made in foreign currencies.

INTERNATIONAL LAWS AND AGREEMENTS

Access to Markets

With the implementation of the SADC (Southern African Development Community) Trade Protocol, AGOA (African Growth ad Opportunity Act), the Cotonou Accord (ACP/EU) and EBA (Everything But Arms) new opportunities for market access are opening - to the SADC market, the American market and the European market respectively. Economic agents may produce the eligible products in Mozambique and export them to those markets.

SADC Trade Protocol

Mozambique is a joint member of the Trade Protocol, the main objective of which are to encourage the liberalisation of intra-regional trade in goods and services, on the basis of just, balanced and mutually beneficial commercial agreements, to guarantee efficient and effective production within SADC, to contribute towards improving an environment favourable to national, cross-border and foreign investment, to increase economic development, and to establish a Free Trade Area in the SADC region. In fact the SADC Trade Protocol is an instrument that creates advantages in both trade and industry. Economic agents have great opportunities to develop their commercial activities and make investments in the country since they have the privilege of counting on the regional development corridors and the ports for supplying the countries of the hinterland.

African Growth and Opportunity Act (AGOA)

Mozambique is also eligible under the African Growth and Opportunity Act (AGOA), which is the unilateral granting of preferential treatment by the government of the United States of America, allowing eligible African countries to export goods to that country, mainly textiles and clothing. The purpose of this law is to promote the growth and economic development of the countries of sub-Saharan Africa.

Cotonou (ACP/EU) and EBA (Everything But Arms)

Under these agreements, economic agents may export products originating in Mozambique to the European market. The Cotonou Accord is a new commercial agreement between 77 countries of the ACP (Africa, Caribbean and Pacific) group and the EU (European Union). This agreement is an extension of the Lome Conventions, the central goal of which is to establish an economic partnership in order to reduce poverty, thus contributing to sustainable development and promoting the gradual integration of the ACP countries into the World Economy. EBA is an extension of the General System of Preferences, and is an additional opportunity for least developed countries and Mozambique to enjoy access to the European market free of taxes and quotas.

International Guarantee Agreements

Mozambique has been a member of the World Trade Organization (WTO) since 26 August 1995. Also in 1994, it became a member of the Multilateral Investment Guarantee Agency (MIGA) and since then Mozambique has become MIGA's largest host country in Africa and its guarantees have facilitated FDI worth $2.8 billion into the country. Today, MIGA is guaranteeing projects in an array of sectors including the agribusiness, financial, infrastructure, manufacturing, oil and gas and tourism sectors. Additionally Mozambique is member of OFIC (the American Overseas Private Investment Corporation) and offers recourse to arbitration through the International Convention and Centre for Settlement of Investment Disputes (ICSID) and the Paris based International Chamber of Commerce. It has also adhered to the New York Convention on the Recognition and Enforcement of Foreign Arbitrage Awards of 1959 and has Investment Protection Conventions with Algeria, Egypt, Italy, Indonesia, Mauritius, Portugal, South Africa and Zimbabwe.

IMPORT AND EXPORT RULES AND REGULATIONS

As part of the effort to liberalize trade in Mozambique, exchange controls have been relaxed. The exchange market has been opened to market forces based on supply and demand, which has made redundant the control of exchange operations in terms of documentation and approval. At the same time, UTRA (Technical Unit for the Restructuring of Customs) was bearing its responsabilities to carry out the minimum supervision necessary, in order to control and register fiscal revenues collected in places of customs jurisdiction. As for imports and exports, a Single Document (DU) has been established to serve as the support for all foreign trade operations undertaken in the country. This is part of the reforms carried out in several spheres of the economy which aim, among other objectives, to simplify administrative procedures so as to promote a good climate for economic activity, without damaging the functions of control, establishing norms and collecting revenues which should be undertaken by the state.

The DU revokes legislation on the licensing system for foreign trade operations, model customs dispatch forms, guides and other documents concerning customs clearance that were previously used by the customs service. Apart from the Single Document, other documents were created in order to control foreign trade operators and their transactions.

The Main Legal Provisions that Regulate Commercial Activity in Mozambique

- Decree n°56/98, of the 11.11.98 which creates the Single Document.
- Ministerial Diploma n°202/98, of the 12.11.98 which approves the Regulations on the Registration of Foreign Trade Operators.
- Ministerial Diploma n°203/98, of the 12.11.98 which defines the single annual fee applicable to importers.
- Decree n°43/98, of the 9.9.98, which approves the Commercial Activity Licensing Regulations. The objective of this is the licensing of the wholesale and retail trade, cumulative trade, general trade, imports, exports, the provision of services and other commercial activities not regulated by specific legislation.
- Resolution n°25/98, of the 25.11.98, which approves the Commercial Policy and Strategy, approved by the

Council of Ministers.

- Ministerial Diploma n°206/98, of the 25.11.98, which approves the Merchandise Dispatch Regulations and the respective annexes.
- Ministerial Diploma n°207/98, of the 25.11.98, which approves the Pre-Shipment Inspection Regulations.
- Ministerial Diploma n°20/98, of the 25.11.98, which lays down the regime for the temporary import of vehicles.
- The 1999 Law on Customs Procedures, which regulates important procedures, namely the computerisation of customs duties, exemption from and reimbursement of customs duties, and also the recently introduced customs timetable (Harmonised Eight Digit System).

LIVING AND WORKING IN MOZAMBIQUE

This information sheet aims to assist foreigners who are either living or wanting to live in Mozambique. The information below is general and is not intended to cover every aspect of work and residence authorisation in Mozambique.

General Information

How can a foreigner work in Mozambique?

Any foreign person wishing to work in Mozambique has to obtain a work permit and a residence permit. The residence permit is called a DIRE (Documento de Identificade Residência para Estrangeiros). An application for a DIRE can only be made once the person has been granted a work permit or has been authorised to work in Mozambique.

What is the difference between a work permit and authorisation of a work contract?

A work permit is granted to people who are shareholders in a company and who therefore do not need to submit an employment contract. Work permits are issued for a period of two years, which may be renewed. Authorisation of a work contract is for those foreigners who are employed in Mozambique. The authorisation of a work contract can be granted for a period equal to the contract period provided that this does not exceed two years.

What are the requirements for a work permit?

In the event of a person being a shareholder in a company, that person may request a work permit by virtue of the fact that he or she is the company's representative and is mandated as such by the other shareholders. The company representative will require the following in order to obtain permission to work:

- A Power of Attorney stating that the applicant has the power to represent the company and its shareholders. This power of attorney has to be signed by all the shareholders.
- The company's Articles of Association.
- The business licence (alvará).
- The company's VAT certificate if already registered.
- The company's Commercial Registration certificate.
- A notarised copy of his or her passport.

For each work permit that is granted, a fee is payable of twice the national minimum wage, which is currently set at 812,165 MZM.

Authorisation of contract

All employment contracts (including tenders awarded) with foreign employees have to be authorised by the Ministry of Labour. However, as a result of decentralisation, the provincial labour departments have the authority to process the applications. The application has to be made in the province where the employee will be physically working for the majority of the time.

The following is required for an authorisation of contract to be granted:

- Three copies of the employment contract, which the employee has entered into with the relevant Mozambican entity. If the contract is in English, it will need to be officially translated into Portuguese. Any subsequent variation in the terms of the contract, unless concerned with the duration of the contract, must be submitted to the Ministry of Labour.
- Identification of the foreign worker, a description of the position that he or she will be taking up, the remuneration agreed on and the duration of the contract.
- Justification for the request of authorisation of the work contract.
- Certificates of educational and technical or professional qualifications of the employee as well as a documentary proof of professional experience (a CV with references should suffice).
- A programme and schedule for professional training, conversion or improvement regarding foreigners in positions of management. During the first two years after its incorporation a company may have 60 per cent of its positions of leadership and management filled by foreign workers. From the second to the fifth year this must be reduced to 40 per cent; from the sixth to the tenth year, to 20 per cent; and thereafter to 10 per cent.
- A declaration from the relevant Employment Centre confirming that the employer attempted to employ a Mozambican national in the position and advertisements for the position published in one of the major national newspapers.
- The opinion of both the Union Committee of the company and the state office that supervises the area of activity of the applicant that the job the applicant will be taking up is a necessary one.

For each work authorisation application that is granted, a fee is payable of seven per cent of the employee's monthly remuneration as stipulated in the contract.

Can foreigners do short-term work in Mozambique?

Yes, but the time spent working in the country cannot exceed 30 days. In cases such as these the contract does not need to be submitted to the Ministry of Labour. However, the employer must inform the Ministry of Labour that it has a foreigner that is providing a service to them and submit proof that the foreigner has a visa to enter and stay in the country for the required period.

Do you need to pay tax on money earned in Mozambique during a short-term contract?

A foreigner who is doing short-term work in Mozambique is considered to be a non-resident employee and therefore a withholding tax of 20 per cent is payable.

Getting residency in Mozambique

NOTICE

A DIRE (residency permit) will only be granted to those people who have a work permit or who have their employment contracts authorised.

A formal application has to be made on a form available from the Ministry of Immigration. The following has to be attached to the application:

- The applicant's residence visa. This can be obtained at any of the Mozambican consulates abroad.
- A police clearance form which is obtained from the country of origin and cannot be more than three months old.
- Work authorisation or work permission.
- A notarised copy of the applicant's passport.
- If the applicant is the shareholder of a company then the company's business license, Articles of Association, Commercial Registration certificate and registration with the Ministry of Finance.
- Three passport sized photographs.

The costs involved:
- Stamps to the value of 1,220 MZM.
- Payment of 432,000 MZM. If the application needs to be processed urgently then the payment is 756,000 MZM.

What about spouses and children?

Spouses and children can obtain residency if the person who has permission to work or whose contract is authorised makes a declaration stating that the spouse and children are financially dependent on him or her.

What are the tax implications of working in Mozambique?

All people working in Mozambique have to pay the following taxes:

- Income tax (IRPS)

IRPS is an individual income tax for residents and non-residents based on the civil status of the worker and on the number of their dependants as well as on their earnings. There are five tax brackets with rates varying from 10 per cent for annual incomes up to 28 million meticais to 32 per cent for annual incomes of over 1,008 million meticais.

- Imposto de Reconstrução Nacional (IRN)

This tax is for national reconstruction and is payable at each city or town council each year before the end of February. The Council of Ministers decrees the amount each year and it varies from town to town. For 2002 the amount was 30,000 MZM per employee in Maputo.

The BIM Building on the Avenida 25 de septiembre

- INSS -Social Security

Employers are required to pay a Social Security tax to the Instituto Nacional Segurança Social. This tax is assessed at seven per cent of the employee's wages. Of this, three per cent is deductible from the employee's wages whilst the employer must contribute to the remaining four per cent. Foreign resident workers may be exempt if they can prove that they are contributing to an equivalent tax in their country of origin.

(see Taxation and Bookkeeping Section too).

Employees

Foreign Employees

- Foreign employees need both a work and a residence permit before they can start working. A foreigner working without these permits will be fined US$50 per day.
- The Ministry of Labour usually grants one work permit for the foreign representative of a company quite easily. Additional foreign staff can only be employed when the company proves that there are no national professionals available for the position in question. This must be proved by advertising the position in the newspapers.
- The work permit is usually granted for a period of two years.
- Every year until the end of January a company must submit to the Ministry of Labour a list indicating every foreign employees of the company, failing which the company will be fined 300 USD per employee.
- As soon as the work permit is issued one can apply for the residence permit at the Immigration Office. The residence permit is called "DIRE" and must be renewed every year.
- All alterations of company details, such as address of company, civil status of employee, profession etc. must be immediately communicated to the Immigration office and the DIRE has to be amended accordingly.

Employees in general

Contract of employment

- All employees must have a contract of employment, a copy of which must be registered with the Ministry of Labour.
- Employment contracts may have a fixed or indefinite term. Fixed term contracts may be signed for a period of up to two years. This period may be renewed only once.
- Employment contracts may include probationary periods. The duration of the probationary period shall not exceed 30 days for fixed term contracts and 90 days for permanent contracts

Working hours

- The normal working period should not exceed 48 hours per week and eight hours per day. This can be extended to nine hours per day if the employee is given an additional half-day off per week.
- In the case of shift work, each shift cannot exceed the maximum period of a normal working day.
- Work that is undertaken on a Sunday or on a public holiday should be remunerated at twice the standard hourly rate.
- A form with the opening hours of the business has to be submitted to the Ministry of Labour. A stamped copy has to be displayed on the company premises.

Annual leave

- For every year of service the employee is entitled to 21 days' leave after having completed 12 months of effective work, to be taken during the second year, and 30 days' leave during each subsequent year. Public holidays and sick leave will not be counted as part of an employee's annual leave.
- Each January, the company must send a company holiday plan to the Ministry of Labour, containing an indication of leave in respect of every employee.

Minimum wage

- The minimum wage is currently 583,000 MZM for employees in the agricultural sector and 812,165 MZM for employees in other sectors.

Termination of employment

- An employer may rescind a contract of employment with at least 90 days' prior notice. If the contract is terminated without just cause, the employer must compensate the employee concerned.
- In the case of a fixed contract, the employee has the right to be paid all salaries due until the end of the fixed term.
- In the case of a permanent contract, the employee has the right to compensation to the value of 45 days' salary when the contract lasted for a period between three and six months; three months' salary when the contract lasted more than six months but less than three years, and then three months' salary for every two years of service where the contract was for more than three years.

The Central Market in Maputo

Miscellaneous

- The company must keep a separate file for each worker containing all relevant documents. This file must be kept for a period of two years after the contract has finished.
- A form called Relação Nominal, including data on all employees, must be submitted to the Ministry of Labour every May. A stamped copy of this document must be displayed on the company premises.
- The Ministry of Labour can provide you with an English translation of the Labour Law on request.

SETTING UP COMMERCIAL COMPANIES IN MOZAMBIQUE

The following summary intends to set out the steps required to establish a business in Mozambique. The summary is based on the general law and is not intended to cover special regimes that may be in place for particular areas of activity or particular investment projects.

Formation and Registration of a Company

The first step is to incorporate a company in Mozambique. Mozambican commercial law provides for different types of companies, the most common being the Limitada type company, a closely held limited liability company.

For a Limitada type company, two shareholders (corporate or individual, foreigners or nationals) are required. The company's articles of association must be recorded at the Notary and at the Commercial Registry and must also be published in the Official Gazette. A company can be duly incorporated within three weeks.

Applying for a business license

No company may commence business in Mozambique before the relevant business licence has been obtained. The licence sought and the body to whom the application is made will depend upon the nature of the company's business (various industrial and trading licenses exist). Construction licenses must also be applied for, where applicable. According to experience, it will take between one and three months to get licensed, depending on the licensing body.

Registration for taxes, employment purposes and social security

At the latest two weeks before the company commences business, it must register with the Ministry of Planning and Finance for tax purposes (VAT, Income Tax). Thereafter, tax returns must be filed on a monthly basis.

At the same time, commencement of activity must be communicated to the Ministry of Labour, including information on the national and foreign employees. Please note that before foreign employees (including shareholders) may work in Mozambique, they must apply for a work permit from the Ministry of Labour and thereafter for a residence permit from the Immigration Office (this process will take approximately two months).

Finally, the employees must be registered at the Institute of Social Security. The company contributions must be submitted on a monthly basis.

To complete these registrations (excluding the permits for foreign employees) it will take approximately one week.

Once all the above-mentioned steps have been completed, the company is legally established and operational in Mozambique

TAXATION IN MOZAMBIQUE

The economic sustainability of a country depends to a large extent on the fiscal contribution of its citizens and on taxing activities that generate income. Thus several legal instruments have been established these last few years in Mozambique to improve fiscal management.

Registration of the company with the Ministry of Planning and Finance

As soon as the company has been incorporated in the

Public Notary, it can be registered with the Ministry of Planning and Finance. We usually recommend registering with the Ministry of Planning and Finance after the business has been licensed, as you are obliged to submit monthly tax returns after registration. However, if the company is incurring costs and paying VAT prior to having obtained the business license, registration with the Ministry of Planning and Finance may be advisable. The Ministry of Finance will allocate a VAT number (NUIT) to the business.

Taxation

The Mozambican Tax System incorporates direct and indirect taxes, used at various levels.

Value Added Tax (VAT)

This tax is charged on transactions involving the transmission of goods and provision of services, undertaken in the Mozambican territory, as well as the import of goods.

- VAT is charged at a rate of 17 per cent on the supply of goods and services within Mozambique, including the importation of goods. VAT is chargeable whether or not the supply of goods and services is for profit.
- As soon as the VAT number has been attributed, the company can prepare its invoices. These invoices must always indicate the VAT number. A company can either have the invoices printed at an especially licensed printing company or can produce its own invoices on the computer. In the case of the latter, a special request has to be submitted to the Ministry of Finance to obtain approval.
- The VAT declaration has to be submitted on a monthly basis by the last day of the following month. The VAT return for January, for example, must be submitted by the end of February.
- The VAT declarations must be submitted on a special form. This is available for free at the VAT offices.
- VAT is not chargeable when a national company renders services to a client resident abroad or when goods are exported. Agriculture, forestry, livestock and farming activities are also exempt.

Corporation Tax

This is a tax on the results of the financial year, even if accidental, of any commercial or industrial activity on Mozambican soil and, additionally, in the case of companies with their headquarters or effective management in the country, as well as public or state companies, on a third of the profits net of tax earned abroad. Corporate Tax is charged at 10 per cent for agriculture and livestock for the tax years 1998 to 2007 and thereafter at 35 per cent. For all other activities, Corporate Tax is charged at 35 per cent. The amortisation rate for each category of asset varies, generically between 2 and 33 per cent. Depreciation is regarded as an admissible expense for purposes of calculating the tax owing. Losses in any financial year may be set off against profits, if there are any, in the following three financial years. Companies in the same economic group are taxed as separate entities, and no form of compensation for the profits and losses verified amongst them is permitted.

Personal Income Tax (IRPS)

IRPS is an individual income tax for residents and non-residents based on the civil status of the worker and on the number of their dependants as well as on their earnings. In fact this tax is levied on all remunerations derived from professional activity on Mozambican soil. There are five tax brackets with rates varying from 10 per cent for annual incomes up to 28 million meticais to 32 per cent for annual incomes of over 1,008 million meticais.

Withholding tax

A non-resident who is not registered with the tax authorities but who renders services in Mozambique is liable to pay a withholding tax of 17 per cent on any payment received.

Complementary Tax

This is only a surtax applied in the case of an owner and concerns income resulting from economic activities in his or her own name, or the rent of properties.

Income (in US Dollars)	Rates %
Up to $420	8%
$420 to $1600	15%
$1600 to $3300	27%
Over $3300	40%

Consumption Tax

This has the characteristics of selective taxation, for the fact that it is applied only to a list of products, and is paid once, by the producer or the importer. The current consumption tax rates are between 20 and 75 per cent, depending on how "essential" the taxed merchandise is. The payment and collection of the taxes on beer, alcohol and tobacco are regulated by special legislation.

Social security

Employers are obliged to pay a Social Security tax to the Instituto Nacional de Segurança Social charged at seven per cent of the employee's wages. Of this, three per cent is deductible from the employee's wages and the remaining four per cent must be made up by the employer. Foreign resident workers may be exempt if they can prove that they are contributing to an equivalent tax scheme in their country of origin.

Immovable Property Tax

The Immovable Property Tax is assessed on income from urban real estate property at the rate of 10 per cent.

Immovable Property Transfer Tax (SISA)

This is paid on the transfer of real estate property or property rights, including the particular case of the transfer of quotas in a private limited company, the assets of which include any real estate. The tax is on the value determined or the value of the transaction. For state-owned real estate, the rate is fixed at 7.5 per cent while for private property it is equivalent to 5 per cent or 10 per cent, depending on whether this is the first transfer or subsequent transfers of the building. An additional amount of about 2 per cent of the transfer value must be paid out.

Tourism Tax

The Tourism Tax rate is 3 per cent for the hotel industry and similar and 2 per cent for services provided by travel agents, tourism agents and tour operators.

Tax on Petroleum Products

This tax is payable by the petrol producer and is based on the petrol production. The rate is defined by the Ministry of Planning and Finance for each contracted producer within the following parameters:

Rates applied on production on land
Between 8 and 12,5% for crude
Between 5 and 7,5% for natural gas
Rates of production originating at sea
For crude:
8% up to 250 meters
6% between 250 and 500 meters
4% between 500 and 1000 meters
2% when over 1000 meters
For natural gas the rate applicable is 5%

Tax on mining production

The following royalties are payable in relation to production under mining concessions:

Diamonds	10% of production
Precious and semi-precious stones	6% of production
Precious metals	5% of production
Other mineral products	3% of production

The following royalties are payable in relation to production under mining certificates or permits:

Precious and semi-precious stones	8% of production
Ornamental rocks	6% of production
Precious metals	5% of production
Mineral resources for construction	4% of production
Other mineral products	3% of production

National Reconstruction Tax

Nationals and resident foreigners are subject to this tax. These rates are fixed annually by the Ministry of Planning and Finance. It becomes due in the year following that in which residence within the national territory was established. This tax is paid once only debiting the salary of the month of February of each year. In areas where there are local authorities, this tax is replaced by the Personal Municipal Tax and the rates are fixed annually by the Municipal Assembly.

Tax on Gifts and Inheritance

The rates vary from 1 per cent to 30 per cent according to the value of the inheritance and the relationship between the donor and the beneficiary.

Municipal Taxes

The municipal Immovable Property Tax is assessed on the property vale of all buildings situated in the municipality. The rates, ranging from 0.2 per cent to 1 per cent of the property value, are fixed by the Municipal Assembly.

The Economic Activity Levy is due for any activity of a commercial or industrial nature, including the provision of services, within the area of the respective municipality, where the activity is carried out in an establishment. The rate is fixed annually by the Municipal Assemblies.

Remuneration for Technical Service Fees and Royalties on Non-resident Entities

Payments effected within the ambit of technical services agreements are considered to be expenses for tax purposes. In order to pay such expenses abroad there needs to be a contract specifying the amount and nature of these expenses. The contract needs approval of the Ministry of Planning and Finance.

Royalties are also subject to the approval of the Ministry of Planning and Finance, and may be approved, but are normally restrictive in terms of percentage and definition of revenues on which royalties may be paid. (Refer Corporate Tax).

Tax Treaties

Mozambique has signed and ratified a double-taxation agreement with Portugal and Mauritius.

Bookkeeping

- All companies must maintain accounting records in Portuguese and in accordance with the national plan of accounts. According to this plan, the accounts must be divided into the following eight classes: current assets; stock; fixed assets; creditors; capital; expenses; income; and other income, expenses and appropriations.
- Companies are legally obliged to maintain the following books in addition to normal accounting records: a balance sheet book (inventário e balanço), a journal (diário), a ledger (razão) and a minute book. The pages of these books must be stamped and numbered by the court.
- The original accounting records must be kept in Mozambique at the registered office of the company. Copies are not acceptable. Records must be kept for at least 10 years.
- As a general rule, the accounting year ends on 31 December. Tax returns must be submitted to the Ministry of Planning and Finance by 31 July for foreign-owned companies and by 31 May for nationally owned companies. The documents that must be submitted are a balance sheet, profit and loss account, depreciation schedule, list of employees and details of salaries paid.
- All financial statements that are to be presented for tax purposes have to be signed off by a registered accountant (téchnico de contas). An accountant can only have ten clients registered and so it is important to verify that the accountant can sign your books.
- A Limitada, or limited liability company, does not have to have its accounts audited. The law only requires an audit for SARL companies.

CUSTOM DUTIES

Duties are applied to the CIF (cost, insurance and freight) value of imported goods:

Essential Goods	0%
Raw Materials	2.5%
Capital Goods (equipment and machinery)	5%
Intermediate Goods	7.5%
Consumer Goods	35%

These customs duties are for imports only as exports are exempt from the payment of duties, and thus the rate fixed is 0 per cent.

The law requires the pre-shipment inspection of all imported goods valued at over $2,500. The Customs Services Levy is 1 per cent of the value of the goods, regardless of whether or not the goods to be imported are exempt from customs duty.

Ship in Maputo Port

TRANSFER OF CAPITAL AND PROFITS

Capital Outflow Policy - Investment laws guarantee foreign investors the right to remit loan repayments, dividends, profits and invested capital abroad. Investment registration and repatriation procedures must be followed for amounts greater than US$ 5000. These include the presentation of audited accounts and registration through the Investment Promotion Center. A repatriation certificate is then issued from the Central Bank. Debt servicing also requires a letter from the Central Bank indicating bank approval at the time of the loan. Recent changes in regulations allow for 100 per cent repatriation of profits and the full retention of earned foreign exchange in local accounts.

INVESTMENT DIRECTORY

CFM - Portos e Caminhos de Ferro de Moçambique (Ports and Railways of Mozambique)

Praça dos Trabalhadores
Maputo
Tel: + 258 - 1 - 431706
Fax: + 258 - 1 - 431703
E-mail: ruifonseca@cfmnet.co.mz
Website: www.cfmnet.co.mz

Confederation of Business Assoc. & Chambers of Commerce (CTA)

Egas Mussanhane, President
Av. 10 de Novembro, Recinto de Facim
Maputo
Tel: + 258 - 1 - 311734 / 5
Fax: + 258 - 1 - 311732
E-mail: egamalda@teledata.mz

CTA - the Confederation of Business Associations & Chambers of Commerces of Mozambique called in Portuguese the "Confederação das Associações Económicas de Moçambique", was created on the 5th of April of 1999. It is a non-governmental economic organization which mission is to contribute to the economic and social development of Mozambique through the growth of the Private Sector, notably promoting investment opportunities and cooperation amongst different associations. CTA was created to represent the private sector. Indeed it is the main voice for above 50 associations from a wide range of sectors. Together they have set up a common agenda for the creation of a better business environment, the establishment of positive relationships with labour unions, the promotion of potential opportunities and the mobilization of financial resources for the strengthening of the private sector's institutional representations. With the collaboration of the Mozambican government and international partners, CTA has put in place a strategy based on the overall improvement of the business environment in the country through the participation of its different member associations. In fact action plans are allocated to each association for an increased effectiveness. Additionally CTA strategy is based on the promotion of Mozambican private companies with the programs for the improvement of employee skills, business information, and financial resources. Since its creation, CTA has managed to put in place a real momentum of collaboration between the different economic players in Mozambique, notably with the Mozambican government and international organizations. Today not only does CTA show the problems in the actual situation, but it also participates in the solution finding. It has become a necessary passage for investors interested in Mozambique. CTA is promoting the creation of a Joint Committee composed of representatives from the private and public sectors.

CPI - Centro de Promoção de Investimentos (The Investment Promotion Centre)

Rafique Jusob, Director
Rua de Imprensa, n°332 - R/C
Maputo
Tel: + 258 - 1 - 313310 / 70
Fax: + 258 - 1 - 313325
E-mail: rafique@cpi.co.mz
Website: www.cpi.co.mz

CPI is the national investment promotion agency, which was created in 1984, but in its current form, has only been in existence since the new law on investments was passed in 1993. The three-year plan of 1997 saw sweeping changes being implemented which ushered in a complete restructuring of CPI, towards creating a world-class investment promotion agency. A number of new divisions were created, and this framework has allowed CPI to really come into its own over the past three to four years although it is continuously improving it services. CPI has the mandate to promote and facilitate national and foreign investments in Mozambique. CPI offers a comprehensive range of services in support of foreign investors wishing to invest anywhere in the country. The main divisions of the organization are: the Facilitation division - which provides technical assistance and support to the investor to the investor throughout the period of application. The Research division - which produces investment and country information. Free Zone division - which provides special support to major projects in the country, and examines the linkages to the local economy. Linkage division - which help local businesses, to participate in the current and future industrial development in the country and maximize the number and amount of materials, and services supplied locally by Mozambican businesses. CPI is the entry door to foreign investors in Mozambique, and investors truly benefit from CPI's services. These include: Information about the investment law; Registering investment project proposals; Assistance in registering new companies related to investment projects; Facilitating the approval of submitted projects; Identification of investment opportunities; Lending advice and support to investors. In fact CPI aims to become a "one-stop-shop" for investors. Over the past years, CPI has managed to change its image and modernize its organization, and today it has become a world- class investment promotion agency. Additionally it has managed to attract an important number of investments to the county, which have had strong economic and social impacts. CPI strives to continuously fulfill its mandate and continuously improve the services they offer.

FUTUR - Fundo do Turismo Nacional

Zacarias B. Sumbana, Chief Executive Officer
Av. 25 do Setembro 1203
Maputo
Tel: + 258 - 1 - 307320 / 2
Fax: + 258 - 1 - 307324
E-mail: futur@futur.imoz.com

The creation of FUTUR arose from the need to direct the investments in the tourist areas in Mozambique and to assist the development of this sector. FUTUR's objective is to make Mozambique become a renowned tourist destination through promotion actions at an international level and infrastructure developments at a national level. The institute's activities include: Production and distribution of promotional material; Presence at tourism fairs around the world (Germany, Portugal, Spain, UK, South Africa, Italy, etc...); Training Programs; Financial Support to small businesses through specialized support programs; and Closely collaborate with tourism related activities such as shows, festivals amongst others. In Mozambique the Tourism destinations are divided into three areas: the North, the Centre and the South. Today FUTUR's growth strategy is highly focused on developing the northern regions as a tourist destination. They also wish to promote Eco-Tourism in the central regions where there are many cultural activities and natural parks available. Finally

FUTUR is actively promoting tourism at the southern tip of Mozambique especially around Ponta d'Ouro known for its water sports activities. In its effort to make Mozambique a major tourist destination known throughout the world, FUTUR has to increase its levels of investments in marketing and promotion. Therefore it is necessary for them to increase their production of promotional materials and have it distributed through specialized distribution channels. These necessary actions are being actively examined and will soon become reality. FUTUR also strives to offer higher support to small businesses at local level in order to promote the country's various provinces. In fact FUTUR has realized that there is a need to provide financial services to build tourism infrastructure at all the level of the country, including the community level.

GPZ - Zambezi Valley Development Authority

Eugènia Mapanzene, Executive Secretary
Tete
Tel: + 258 - 1 - 5222222
Fax: + 258 - 1 - 5229002
E-mail: emapanzene@teledata.mz

The Zambezi Valley Development Authority called the "Gabinete do Plano de Desenvolvimento da Região do Zambeze" (GPZ) was created on the 22 of August 1995 by the Council of Ministers Decree 40/95. GPZ is a governmental institution, which is by law responsible for planning, promoting, managing, coordinating and supervising the development of the Zambezi region. It is also involved in various companies in different sectors that contribute to the development of the region. GPZ is also considered as the investors contact point for those who are interested in installing their activity in the Zambezi region. Additionally GPZ actively works with international donors such as the European Union, the World Bank and NEPAD. The Zambezi Valley in Mozambique covers an area of 225,000 Km and contains over 4 million inhabitants. It is one of the richest areas in terms of natural resources but remains one of the poorest in economic terms. It is has a strategic location as it is at the cross roads between various neighbouring countries. It also possesses the largest water and energy resources in the subcontinent. It has excellent conditions for cultivation of cereals, vegetables and for cattle raising. Finally it has large deposits of ferrous and non-ferrous minerals. Therefore the Zambezi Valley is a key element in the sustainable development of Mozambique, the SADC member countries and even Eastern Africa. Through bilateral and multilateral cooperation, and private investments, the Zambezi Valley can become an engine for regional development and GPZ is the Mozambican institution working towards this goal. Over the past years, GPZ has managed to re-launch the agricultural sector in the Zambezi Valley as well as to put in place a sustainable momentum for the economic and social development of the region. The Zambezi Valley possesses a wide range of opportunities in various sectors and GPZ strives to successfully expose these to the world in order to obtain a sustainable development.

IGEPE - Instituto de Gestão das Participações do Estado

(Institute for the Management of the Government's Participation)

Madalena Ernestina Atanasio, Economista
Rua de Kassuende, n° 118 - 1° Andar
Maputo
Tel: + 258 - 1 - 485643 / 4 - 485640
Fax: + 258 - 1 - 485641
E-mail: igepe.zebra@tvcabo.co.mz

The "Instituto de Gestão das Participações do Estado - IGEPE" was created in order to manage the government's participation and interests in various companies in different sectors of the economy. In fact IGEPE is a Government Institution, which falls under the control of the Ministry of Planning and Finance. As the government has put in place a policy to reduce its direct involvement in the economy, IGEPE is also in charge of managing these progressive disinvestments from non-strategic companies. With a portfolio of about 200 companies in which the government has shares, IGEPE's activities involve: the management of the government's participation within these companies; the progressive reduction of government participation; the promotion and rehabilitation of companies to attract investors; and the catalytic role of creating new partnerships with investors. The government's policy is to reduce the number of companies in which it has participation from around 200 to around 20. The objective is to maintain participation in companies which are of strategic importance to the country. Thus IGEPE has the role of promoting these disinvestments to potential investors with which they create partnerships. IGEPE is actually carrying out several negotiations on the possible entry of foreign investors in Mozambican companies. If these negotiations give positive results then IGEPE would have obtained its first major achievements. In fact the year 2004 will demonstrates IGEPE's performance. The major challenge facing IGEPE is getting investors to effectively rehabilitate Mozambican companies in order to give them a major role in the country's economic development.

INA - Instituto Nacional do Açucar

(National Sugar Institute)
Arnaldo Ribeiro, Director
Liria Nhaquila, Agronomist
Anna Locke, Economist
Rua de Gávea, n° 33 - 1° Andar
C.P. 1772, Maputo
Tel: + 258 - 1 - 326550 / 307957 / 300626
Fax: + 258 - 1 - 427436
E-mail: dir.gpsca.ina@tvcabo.co.mz
or gpsca.ina@tvcabo.co.mz

The National Sugar Institute (INA) is a Government Institution. It was created in 1977 and falls under the auspices of the Ministry of Agriculture and Rural Development (MADER). In the early 1970s, sugar was Mozambique's largest agro-industrial sector and its third main export product. Unfortunately with the independence in 1975, came a mass exodus of skilled workers and management staff working for the sugar companies, which led the government to intervene. This led to the creation of INA that had the role to manage and coordinate these companies as well as the whole industry. Today as five of the six companies have been privatized, INA's role has changed. Its activities include monitoring developments in the sugar sector, promoting investment in sugar and related activities, and advising the government in all sector-specific matters. INA maintains a close dialogue with the sugar companies and investors, and plays an important role in the design of sectoral policies and interventions. INA is actively working for the development of the sugar industry in Mozambique and strives to actively participate in the increase of sugar production. In fact the aim today is to completely rehabilitate the sugar mills and reach and surpass production levels of pre-independence times. Since 1996, they have successfully attracted more than $300,000 Million of investments. It collaborates with several national and international institutions. INA is proud to have successfully re-launched sugar production in Mozambique which has now become a net surplus producer and thus has started to export its product. INA strives to increase Mozambique's competitiveness in the global market, diversify the industry and create in the future a complementary processing industry as well as generate entrepreneurship for the cultivation of sugar cane.

IPEX - Instituto para a Promoçao de Exportações

(Export Promotion Institute)
José Fernando Jossias, General Director
Av. 25 de Setembro N°1008, 2° Andar
Caixa Postal 4487, Maputo
Tel: + 258 - 1 - 307257 / 8
Fax: + 258 - 1 - 307256

E-mail: ipex@teledata.mz
Website: www.ipex.gov.mz

The Mozambique Institute of Export Promotion (IPEX) is a non-profit government organization established in 1990 with the purpose of boosting and coordinating the execution of policy measures towards the development of national exports. The Institute's activities include: Identification and development of export markets; Organization of trade missions; Organization of trade fairs and exhibitions; Organization of training for export operators and other related businesses; and Linkages and collaboration with foreign trade promotion organizations. For its trade dissemination strategy the IPEX has a Trade and Market Information Center (TMIC); an extensive and comprehensive website; and regular publications, among which the Mozambique Export Directory and Exporters' manual. A wide range of products and market development activities and services are available also, such as a National Export Audit, an Identification of Export Markets review, Buyers and Sellers Meetings, and Trade Fairs. Since its creation IPEX has had a strong contribution in the economic development of Mozambique and the development of national exports. It continuously participates in trade fairs all around the world and the number of links with foreign organizations is on the rise. IPEX strives to increase its activities and services and constantly improving them. In fact they are increasingly considered as the External Trade Organization of Mozambique.

Nakosso - Niassa Business Centre

Orlando Conceiçao, Director & Head of Legal Team
Rua General Pereira D'Eça, n° 90
P.O.Box 1839, Maputo
Tel: + 258 - 1 - 496900
Fax: + 258 - 1 - 496802
E-mail: nakosso@niassa.info
Website: www.niassa.info

The Nakosso - Niassa Business Centre was launched in September 2002 as a joint effort between the Government of Mozambique and the Swedish International Development Agency (Sida). In fact it results from a private sector support programme in the Niassa Province and its aim is to contribute towards the improvement of the business environment and to the promotion of the Province in order to attract an increasing number of investors. To this end, the Niassa Business Centre provides legal services (middle man services when dealing with government department or other), and business information services. The Niassa Business Centre is here to assist all business ventures and some say it is the Investment Promotion Centre of the Province of Niassa. The Province of Niassa is the biggest in Mozambique and it offers a great number of opportunities to businessmen. It has been described as the last true wilderness in Africa, and thus offers great potential in farming and tourism. Additionally it is a rich province in terms of mineral resources and cultivable land. It is considered as one of the Provinces with most potential. Nevertheless it is also one of the poorest and economic and social development remains little. Therefore the Niassa Business Centre strives to promote all of the Province's potential. The Niassa Business Centre is still in a set up phase but it is a long-term project, which actively works to achieve long-term sustainable development for the Province and the region. Niassa possesses all the resources necessary for a strong economic and social development. All is needed now is for investors to realize this. Through the Niassa Business Centre, expectations are high.

Mozambique Chamber of Commerce (Camara de Comércio de Moçambique)

Manuel Notiço, General Secretary
Rua Mateus Sansão Muthemba, n°452
P.O.Box 1836, Maputo
Tel: + 258 - 1 - 492210
Fax: + 258 - 1 - 490428

After independence, the Mozambique Chamber of Commerce was the first economic association to be created. In fact it was created in 1980 in order to assist pri vate companies in their effort to successfully grow. Today Mozambique possesses a wide number of economic associations but the Mozambican Chamber of Commerce remains essential as it represents companies from all sectors and of all size. The Mozambique Chamber of Commerce has branches in Maputo and Beira. Today it has members from a wide range of economic sectors and of different sizes to whom it offers them business services including market studies, legal services, and certification of origin services amongst others. Additionally, it also acts as arbitrary when conflicts arise between member compa nies. It is also a strong promoter of investment opportunities available in Mozambique. In this perspective it can be said that it acts as a middleman putting in contact foreign investors with local companies. The Chamber's priority today is to restore Mozambique's industrial sector, which was badly damaged after independence and during the civil war. Thus it is actively working with the Confederation of Business Association and Chambers of Commerce (CTA) to improve the business environment in order to make Mozambique an increasingly attractive destination for foreign direct investments as well as national investments. The Mozambique Chamber of Commerce strives to successfully grow with the Mozambican economy in order to continuously meet the needs of its members. Thus it is also planning to open other branches in the rest of the country.

TVM

THE COUNTRY ECONOMY

OVERVIEW

These last few years, Mozambique's economy has known strong growth rates. Excluding the year 2000, where massive floods abated the country, Mozambique has been growing with an average of two digits: 13.9 per cent in 2001 and 10 per cent in 2002. However the devaluation of the Metical, the national currency, has been a major constraint to the real growth of the Mozambican economy.

During the year 2002, the Central Bank and the Ministry of Planning and Finance put in place several monetary policies in order to contain and improve some macroeconomic Indexes. Consequently the inflation Index fell between 2001 and 2002 from 21.9 per cent to 12.8 per cent.

Actually the government's aim for 2003 is an economic growth of 12% and to maintain the inflation at 17.7 per cent. Despite the continuous fall in international prices for agricultural exports, upon which Mozambique heavily

KEY ECONOMIC RATIOS AND LONG TERM TRENDS		**1982**	**1992**	**2001**	**2002**
GDP (US$ Billions)		3.6	1.9	3.4	3.6
Gross domestic investment/GDP		6.0	15.6	26.5	23.7
Exports of goods and services/GDP		8.3	13.9	21.8	23.5
Gross domestic savings/GDP		-11.9	-17.2	12.8	8.9
Gross national savings/GDP		-	-	5.4	3.6
Current account balance/GDP		-13.7	-19.0	-46.7	-
Interest payments/GDP		0.0	2.3	0.2	0.8
Total debt/GDP		3.5	276.8	129.5	128.1
Total debt service/exports		0.2	19.7	7.6	8.4
Present value of debt/GDP		-	-	26.7	-
Present value of dept/GDP		-	-	78.9	-
(Average annual growth)	**1982-92**	**1992-02**	**2001**	**2002**	**2002-06**
GDP	2.4	8.1	13.0	8.3	-
GDP per capita	1.1	5.7	10.6	6.1	-
Exports of goods and services	1.8	15.3	50.1	12.3	-

Source: World Bank, 2003

relies, the government's objectives have been reached thanks to the strengthening the peace environment and the fostering of economic reforms, which started in 1987 with the Programme for Economic and Social Rehabilitation (PRE).

Indeed, after independence in 1975, Mozambique's economy was extensively nationalized and the country experienced around a decade of socialist rule with a centrally planned economy. In 1987, the government, with the collaboration of the IMF introduced the PRE (Programme for Economic Rehabilitation) programme in order to revert the deficit tendencies of the Mozambican economy. The most important policies included the liberalization and privatisation of the economy with the main objective of attracting more foreign direct investments. In 1991, the government added a social component the ongoing rehabilitation programme. This gave birth to the PRES (Program for Economic and Social Rehabilitation) programme with the goal of creating an equilibrium and bring stability to the overall economic system.

At an International level, Mozambique is actually member of the Multilateral Investment Guarantee Agency (MIGA) and of the World Trade Organization (WTO). Its main objectives are to strengthen and improve its capacities to take advantage of the opportunities brought up by the implementation of the Commercial protocols of Southern African Development Community (SADC), the Cotonou Accord (ACP/EU) as well as the African Growth and Opportunity Act (AGOA) and Everything But Arms (EBA's) initiatives.

Today Mozambique's economy is strongly growing and perspectives for the future are bright. The Plan for the Reduction of Absolute Poverty (PARPA) has been effectively increasing standards of living for the Mozambican population and effective restructuring has brought an increasing number of opportunities for private investments.

Economic ratios*

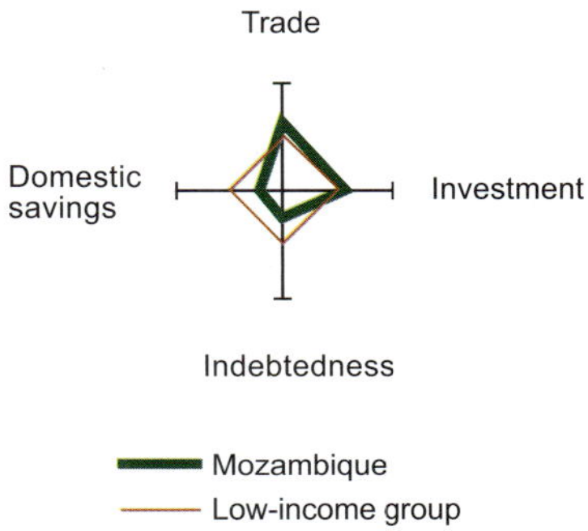

Source: World Bank, 2003

GDP AND FDI

Mozambique's GDP stands at about US$ 3,880 Million. Agriculture has always been significantly important for the Mozambican economy. In 1982 it accounted for around 33 per cent of the GDP. Today it accounts for 26,8 per cent of the GDP and for 7.3 per cent of the country's export earnings. Although production and revenues have strongly increased, the sector has been badly hit by the fall in international prices for agricultural exports. To revert that situation the government is trying to improve productivity and competitively through private investment, especially in agro-industry, as well as to improve irrigation systems and the commercial network. In fact by developing a national agro-industry, the government strives to protect the sector from international price fluctuations. Nevertheless the sector is going through a strong recovery in food crops from the effects of the 2000 floods, and important increases in some cash crops, particularly sugar. Important to note is that the relative fall of agriculture's contribution to GDP and export earnings is also due to the growth of industrial production and export, especially with the arrival of the aluminium smelter Mozal. Indeed, with the entrance of Mozal, industry's contribution to the GDP has grown to around 30 per cent and now accounts for about 50 per cent of total export revenues.

Mining and tourism still have little contribution to GDP and export earnings, but with major investments taking place, their contribution will most certainly increase. In fact it is most probable that these two sectors will become Mozambique's future engines for economic growth.

Foreign aid to Mozambique continues to be significant. In 2002, foreign direct aid for governmental budget was about 13 per cent of the GDP. It is mainly directed to the restructuring of the public sectors and the improvement of infrastructures.

Mozambique's tax performance has strongly improved

STRUCTURE OF THE ECONOMY (% of GDP)	**1982**	**1992**	**2001**	**2002**
Agriculture	33.8	32.0	26.7	26.8
Industry	32.6	16.3	27.6	27.7
Manufacturing	-	7.6	15.3	15.4
Services	33.6	51.7	45.7	45.5
Private consumption	97.7	104.6	76.4	80.1
General government consumption	14.1	12.6	10.8	11.0
Imports of goods and services	26.2	46.7	35.4	38.2

Source: World Bank, 2003

since reforms have been implemented. Tax revenues represented in 2002, 13 per cent of the GDP.

Growth of investment and GDP (%)

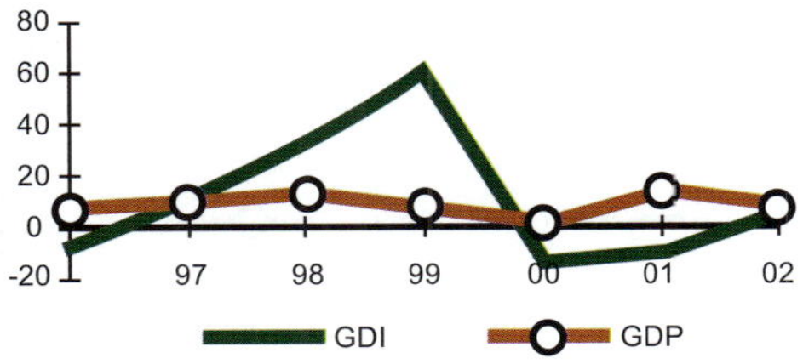

Source: World Bank, 2003

Mozambique's economy is undergoing important changes as an increasing number of investments are taking place in a wide range of sectors. In 2002, the Investment Promotion Centre (CPI) approved 128 projects, with a total value of US$ 1,5 billion. Of this value, US$ 1,2 billion correspond to investments carried out in the Limpopo Corridor Sands project (mining). Apart from this project, it is the service industry that has attracted the major number of initiatives (27), with a total value of US$ 130 million. Agriculture and agro-industry attracted more then US$ 60 million, while US$ 50 million were invested in industry. Although it concentrated almost 80 per cent of total foreign direct investment, the mining sector only contributed to the creation of 48 new employments. On the contrary, investments in agriculture created more then 2,500 new jobs.

Foreign Direct Investments in 2002

Sector	**Projects**	**Job Creation**	**Investment (US$)**
Agriculture and Agro-industry	21	2.550	61.931.498
Aquaculture and Fisheries	4	110	1.286.666
Construction	15	974	24.955.410
Industry	38	2.455	48.211.987
Mineral Resources	2	48	1.200.498.220
Transport	7	115	4.093.153
Tourism and Hotels	14	573	24.743.538
Services	27	2.671	130.681.671
Total	128	9.496	1.496.402.148

Source: Investment Promotion Centre (CPI)

COST OF LIVING

Mr. Chissano's government has successfully put in place tight monetary policies to stabilize Mozambique's financial situation and improve its macroeconomic indexes. Indeed the Minister of Planning and Finance, Mrs. Diogo, has strongly collaborated over the past years with the World Bank and IMF to bring down inflation. From an above 40 per cent yearly increase before 1997, inflation as decreased to around 13 per cent in 2003. In fact the 12-month rate of inflation declined from 21.9 per cent at end-2001 to 9.1 per cent at end-2002. Following a sharp decline in inflation through October 2002, prices have risen at a faster pace in recent months largely because of the effects of drought and floods on some agricultural products, the increase in oil import prices in the last quarter of 2002 and early 2003, and the recent strengthening of the South African Rand. As a result, the 12-month rate of inflation rose to 14.7 per cent in April 2003.

PRICES AND GOVERNMENT FINANCE	1982	1992	2001	2002
Domestic prices (% changes)				
Consumer prices	17.7	45.1	9.0	16.8
Implicit GDP deflator	17.5	44.6	10.6	10.6
Government finance (% of GDP, includes current grants)				
Current revenue	19.2	20.3	18.2	18.0
Current budget balance	3.2	4.4	3.7	2.2
Overall surplus/deficit	-5.0	-10.0	-16.5	-15.8

Source: World Bank, 2003

Inflation (%)

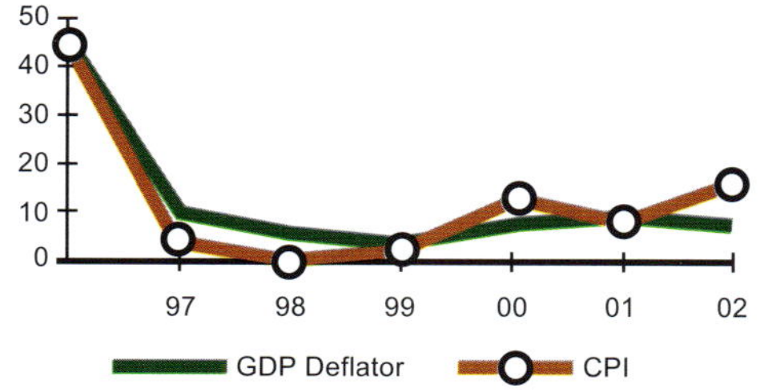

Source: World Bank, 2003

The exchange rate (December 2003): US$1 = MZM 23,300

Water

In terms of water expenses, Mozambique remains significantly cheap. The water authority operating in all the country's provinces is "Aguas de Moçambique, SARL".

The general tariffs for Maputo and Matola are the following (Minimal Consumption):

Up to 25m = MZM 286,700/Month for public and commercial uses.

Up to 50 m = MZM 573,400/Month for industrial use MZM 11,500/Month for excess consumption Tariffs for Rent and Maintenance of Counter Meter:

Counter Diameter	Counter Rent (MZM
1/2"	10,200
3/4	14,300
1"	31,800
1.1/4"	38,100
1.1/2"	63,600
2	127,100
3"	190,500
4"	222,300
6	254,100
8	281,100

Commercial Consumption (MZM)

m_/Month	Up to 25 m_	Value	Excess	Value	Counter	Subtotal	VAT**	Total
20	25	286,700			10,200	296,900	37,855	334,755
80	25	286,700	55	561,000	10,200	847,700	108,082	955,787

Industrial Consumption (MZM)

m_/Month	Up to 25 m_	Value	Excess	Value	Counter	Subtotal	VAT**	Total
20	50	573,400			10,200	583,600	74,409	658,009
80	50	573,400	30	306,000	10,200	879,400	112,123.5	991,523.5

*) Tariff for Counter 1/2"

**) VAT on 75% of the Subtotal

Electricity

The company operating in the generation and distribution of electricity throughout the country is "Electricidade de Moçambique E.P - EDM". Distribution of electricity is significantly reliable in Mozambique.

Social Domestic, Agricultural and General Tariffs (Low Voltage)

	Sale Price				
Registered Consumption (kWh)	**Social Tariff (MZM/kWh)Social Tariff (MZM/kWh)**	**Domestic Tariff (MZM/kWh)**	**Agricultural Tariff (MZM/kWh)**	**General Tariff (MZM/kWh)**	**Fixed Tax (MZM)**
From 0 to 100	856				
From 0 to 200		1,863	1,877	2,086	60,000
From 201 to 500		2,483	2,682	2,980	60,000
Up to 500		2,608	2,934	3,260	60,000
Pre-payment		2,546	2,808	3,120	

For consumers under the social tariff (1.1 KVA and consumption not exceeding 100 kVh/month) whose installations use pre-paid (CREDELEC), a limited volume power of 5 Amperes will be fixed.

Great Consumers of Low, Medium and High Voltage

Voltage Unity		**Low Utilization**	**Medium Utilization**	**High Utilization**
High Voltage (AT)	MZM/KW	80,065	97,523	115,348
	MZM/kWh	1,013	648	528
Medium Voltage (BT)	MZM/KW	91,503	111,44	131,837
	MZM/kWh	1,180	809	594
	MZM/KW	95,309	116,080	137,327
G.Cons. (BT) > 19,8 KVA	MZM/kWh	1,187	827	620

Telecommunications

The national company operating in telecommunications is "Telecomunicações de Moçambique E.P - TDM". Telecommunications in Mozambique are well developed and tariffs tend to be competitive.

Fixed Telephone Calls

Tariffs (MZM)					
Description	Installation Fees	Rental of equipment /month	Single Customers (MZM /impulse)	Public Cabines ((MZM /impulse)	Penalty for late payment
Telef./Fax	415,000	192,000	2,430	2,950	83,000

Petroleum Products

Product	Unity	A	B
Gas (GPL)	Kg	14,641.30	12,040.10
Gasol. RON 93	Litre	13,790.00	12,618.80
Jet A1	Litre	7,950.20	6,943.40
Petrol	Litre	7,250.00	6,243.10
Diesel	Litre	11,400.00	10,222.00
Fuel Oil	Litre	7,019.40	6,907.20

- Public Price of sell from the distributor companies in Maputo and Matola for GPL and in Maputo, Matola, Beira and Nacala for other products.

- Price of sell from the oil import and distributor companies in the oceanic terminals in Maputo, Matola (Lingamo) for GPL and in Maputo, Matola (Lingamo), Beira and Nacala for other products.

Labour and Salaries

Since April 2003, the government has set new minimum monthly wages.

MZM 982,717.00/month	Commercial, industrial workers and in other sectors of activity
MZM 700,386.00/month	Agro-Industry
	Other minimum salaries are defined in accordance with categories specified in the professional collective agreements. These salaries also depend on the profitability, economic and financial situation of each company.

EMPLOYMENT

Of the estimated labour force of 8.8 million, 80 per cent work in the agricultural sector, as most of the Mozambique's population lives in rural areas and mainly work in subsistence activities, 3 per cent in the industrial sector and 1.2 per cent in transport and communications and other services. There are no reliable figures on unemployment or underemployment, but estimates of unemployment range from 50 to 80 per cent. Up to one million Mozambicans are estimated to be working legally and illegally as migrant workers in South Africa - mainly from the three southern provinces of Inhambane, Gaza and Maputo. Most work in the South African mining industry, but also in the agricultural, construction and industrial sectors.

The government is putting emphasis on the creation and improvement of technical formations so as to encourage foreign investors to employ an increasing number of Mozambicans on their projects. Self-employment, micro-finance and small entrepreneur are other issues stressed by the government to increase the number of formal employees and employment in general. However, despite all these efforts the informal sector still plays a major role in terms of total employment in Mozambique.

Company	Position TOP 100 listing	Number of employees 2001	Number of employees 2002	Variation % 01/00
CFM-Ports and Railways of Mozambique	5	12.480	15.835	-21,19%
Alfa-Segurança de Pessoas e Instalaçoes	41	3.852	4.060	-5,12%
EDM-Electricidade de Moçambique	8	3.311	3.271	-1,22%
TDM-Telecommunicaçoes de Moçambique	3	2.308	2.287	0,92%
C.M.C Di Ravenna	14	1.860	1.500	24,00%
BIM-Banco Internacional de Moçambique	6	1.550	528	193,56%
CETA-Construçoes e Serviços	28	1.463	1.401	4,43%
UGC-Uniao Geral Coop. Agro-Pecuarias Maputo	64	1.300	1.313	-0,99%
Banco Austral	45	1.272	1.236	2,91%
Ergogeste	36	1.003	461	117,57%

Ref. KPMG, 'the top 100 companies' 2001

PRIVATISATION PROCESS

As part of the ongoing economic reforms introduced in Mozambique since the start of the Economic Rehabilitation Program (PRE) in 1987, legislation has been passed since 1989 to enable the privatisation and sale of state owned enterprises, establishments, installations, or financial holdings of the Government. This legislation includes Decree no. 21/89, which regulates the sale of state owned assets through a public tender and establishes the administrative procedures for these sales. Law 15/91, regulated by Decree no. 28/91, establishes norms for the restructuring, transformation, and reshaping of the State enterprise sector, including its privatisation, and Law 27/91 of 21st November, created the Inter-Ministerial Commission for Enterprise Restructuring (CIRE). Ministerial Diploma no. 87/92 of June 1992 attributes UTRE - the Technical Unit for Enterprise Restructuring, within the Ministry of Planning and Finance, with the function of co-ordinating body for the restructuring of large enterprises. Further decrees were passed up to April 1994, including Decree no. 30/91, Decree no. 3/93 and Decree no. 4/94, whereby the Council of Ministers identified enterprises to be restructured under Article 14 of Law 15/91. Also of interest to investors, is Decree n° 24/88, with the alterations of Decree n° 13/93, relating to the conversion of Mozambican external debt, either into direct foreign investment or other applications, as mentioned in the Decree. Assets of companies to be privatised can also be acquired through recourse to debt conversion, so long as this intention is referred to in the investor's bid proposal.

"After the change from a central planned economy to a market oriented economy in 1987, we had a set of first generation reforms designed to restore basic equilibrium and to re-kindle growth through pricing, exchange rate and interest rate reforms, tax and expenditure reforms and the establishment of rudimentary market institutions accompanied by a stabilization program as well as through the privatisation of a significant number of state-owed companies".

Honourable L.D. Diogo,
Minister of Planning and Finance

Since the privatisation legislation was passed in 1989, the Government has successfully restructured a significant number of companies through the sector ministry CNAAs (National Valuation and Sale Commissions), CPAAs (Provincial Valuation and Sale Commissions) and the CEPs (Executive Privatisation Commissions). There have been continued efforts to involve more Mozambicans investors into the privatisation of companies, as a result of the policy to ensure that nationals have more opportunities to participate and benefit from the transfer of State enterprises to the private sector. Recently, the Council of Ministers approved alterations to Decree n°21/89 of 23rd May, and Decree n° 28/91 of November, relative to the privatisation process. The alterations to the Decrees have been made, in order to promote national entrepreneurs, namely by extending the terms of payment, application of a more favourable interest rate, and the possibility for the owner to mortgage the acquired asset, even before all payments have been made. As well, the "Fund to Support Economic Rehabilitation" (FARE) was launched in August 1996. With initial funds of 15 billion MTC, using some of the net proceeds from privatisation, FARE will concede loans to micro-enterprises in the first instance in selected provinces, namely Sofala, Manica, Tete and Niassa. A Management Council of the Fund was created, with the Institute for the Development of Local Industry (IDIL) being designated as the Executing Agency.

In 2001, the "Instituto de Gestão das Participações do Estado - IGEPE" was created in order to manage the government's participation and interests in various companies in different sectors of the economy. In fact IGEPE is a Government Institution, which falls under the control of the Ministry of Planning and Finance has the objective of maintaining government participation only in companies of strategic importance to the country. Thus IGEPE has the role of promoting these disinvestments to potential investors with which they create partnerships.

The privatisation of State-owned enterprises has played a pivotal role in the structural adjustment process taking place in Mozambique and restructuring is now reaching those sectors of the economy formerly considered "strategic".

Honourable T.A. Salomão, Minister of Transport and Communication

More than 1,000 companies have been sold since the privatisation process began in the early 1990s under the structural adjustment programme backed by the World Bank and the International Monetary Fund (IMF). Indeed Mozambique's government has privatised and restructured an important number of the state-owned companies, small and big, including EMOSE, EDM (Electricidade de Moçambique), ADM (Aeroportos de Moçambique) and all of its banks. Since 1998, several tenders for the operating concession of the railways and port terminals have been launched and successfully carried out. Today the government is seeking a buyer for a 51 per cent stake in the national airline Linhas Aereas de Moçambique (LAM) in which it currently holds an 80 per cent stake, with the remaining shares belonging to employees and management. Indeed after a first privatisation attempt failed in 1996, LAM was transformed from a state company into a limited liability company.

"The model for port and rail development is private sector concessions"

Honourable T.A. Salomão, Minister of Transport and Communication

Although several major companies remain state-owned, the privatisation program is on track and additional privatisations are scheduled for the years to come.

Over 90 per cent of all enterprises privatised in Mozambique were acquired by Mozambican individuals and enterprises, approximately 50 per cent of the equity amount represented in the sales completed to date is foreign, namely from Portugal, South Africa, USA, Great Britain, Holland, Denmark, Norway, Cyprus, Zimbabwe, Swaziland, Mauritius, India and China.

BALANCE OF TRADE

The Mozambican structural deficit economy is a heritage of the colonial era as Mozambique was conceived as a raw material resource and preferential market for the Portuguese Industry. Consequently Mozambique's industry was turned into a pre-manufacturer of raw material, which would be exported to Europe. As a consequence, Mozambique has continuously imported most of its necessary products.

BALANCE OF PAYMENTS (US$ Millions)	1982	1992	2001	2001
Exports of goods and services	337	304	1008	1187
Imports of goods and services	893	860	1578	1837
Resource balance	-556	-556	-570	-650
Net income	-20	-183	-254	-190
Net current transfers	-	-	0	0
Current account balance	-497	-352	-1604	-
Financing items (net)	356	392	1607	-
Changes in net reserves	141	-40	-3	-192
MEMO				
Reserves including gold	-	-	-	-
Conversion rate (DEC, local/US$)	37.8	2566.5	20703.6	23678.0

Source: World Bank, 2003

The deficit status of Mozambique increased with the floods of the year 2000. Additionally, although foreign investments are positive for the growth of the economy, the fact that Mozambique lacks of a strong developed industrial sector causes the country to import most of the technical components and material necessary for the successful completion of these investments projects.

Export and import levels (US$ mill.)

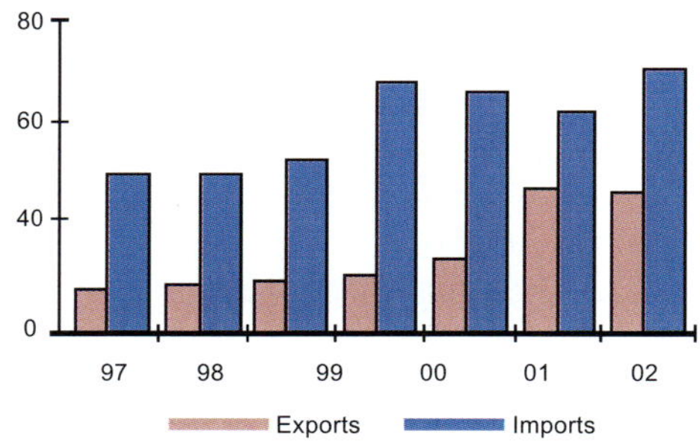

Source: World Bank, 2003

Also, compliance with the WTO agreements meant significant reductions on tariffs, which led to the opening of Mozambique's economy and consequently to increased pressure on the trade balance. Thus the government is striving to increase local production through the establishment of export promotion zones as well as significant tax incentives.

Growth of exports and imports (%)

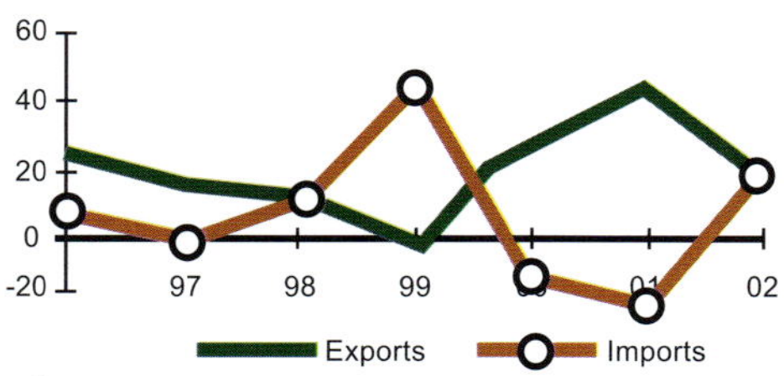

Source : World Bank, 2003

Current account balance to GDP (%)

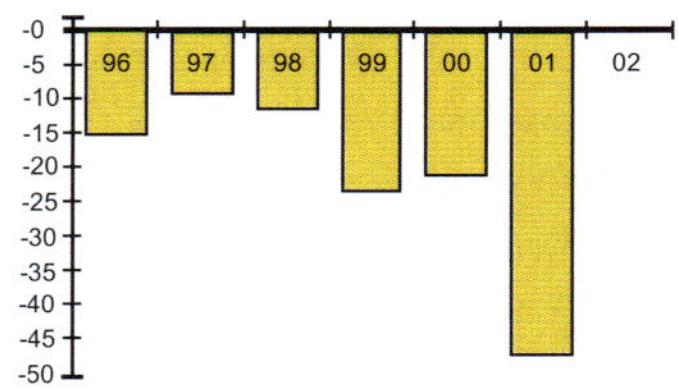

Source: World Bank, 2003

FOREIGN TRADE

Mozambique's current foreign trade is a reflection of the investments efforts made these last few years. Exports were traditionally dominated by agricultural and fishing commodities such as prawns, cotton, cashew, sugar, wood and copra but today they are dominated by aluminium, which accounts for 36.4 per cent of total exports. This tendency to shift to high value added exports is expected to increase as major investments projects are taking place in the transformation industry as well as manufacturing. Nevertheless, prawns, cotton, sugar and cashew exports will remain significant. Mozambique's main export destination is South Africa with more then 15 per cent of total exports. Spain, Japan and Portugal are the other major export destinations. Mozambique's imports are mainly dominated by mineral products such as petrol derivatives (9%), machinery and equipment (7.7%), transport equipment (7.7%), various alimentation products (14%) and chemical products (3.4%). South Africa accounts for more then 40 per cent of Mozambique's imports.

Mozambique has preferential trade with the EU through the Cotonou Agreement and the EBA (everything but arms), the USA with the AGOA (African Growth and Opportunity Act) and all of Southern Africa through the SADC trade protocol. Thus Mozambique's government is encouraging investors to take advantage of these new opportunities, but remains conscious that major efforts are to be done in order to fully grasp this existing potential.

AGRICULTURE & FISHERIES

ebiZ guides

OVERVIEW

Agriculture is the most important sector in the Mozambican economy. It contributes with $963 million to 27 percent of the total GDP which amounts to $3 569 million (2002). This sector also employs about 80 percent of the country's 18 million habitants and contributes with important amounts in foreign earnings on exports to the State. The sector represents around 10 per cent of the total exports.

Agricultural outputs (Million US$)

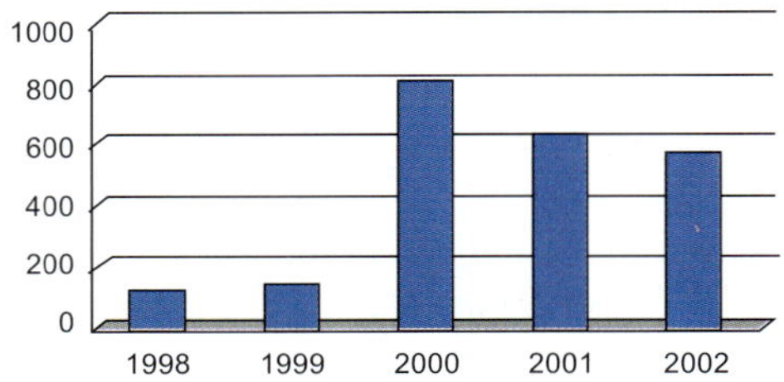

National Institute of Statistics, annual rapport 2002

Mozambique offers very good natural conditions for the practice of agriculture activities. These natural conditions include the localization, its soils and the climate. In fact Mozambique is a very large country with a low population. The country has an area of 799 380 Sq Km, like two times Italy, and an average of 23 inhabitants per Sq. Km with regions reaching an average of 7 inhabitants per Sq. Km. Therefore Mozambique offers large areas for agriculture.

Of the country's total land area, 360 000 Sq Km are available for the practice of agriculture. Of these 360 000 Sq Km only 90 000 Sq Km, 25% of the total available agriculture area, is currently being used for agricultural purposes.

Land Use	Area in ha	Percentage (%)
Total land	799 380	100
Total agricultural land	360 000	45
Actual land cultivated	90 000	11.3
Potential irrigated land	33 333	4.1
Actual irrigated land	--	--

Mozambique is located on the South-East African coastal zone where most of the inland rivers drain their water, and therefore land irrigation is relatively easy. Additionally, thanks to this geographical location and the access to communication infrastructures such as roads, railways and ports, transport cost tend to be low and access to international markets efficient.

The country has rich and varied soils. Indeed Mozambique has red and brown clay soils that are good for the production of cotton, and cashew. It has dark soils, good for the production of tea, tobacco, maize, fruit trees, sun flower, flowers and others crops. And finally it has fertile fluvial soils on the low lands, which are good for the production of sugar cane, rice and horticultures.

In terms of climate Mozambique has also a variety of tropical climate. This provides the country with the necessary conditions to produce almost all the different species of tropical crops.

Main Tropical Crops (tons)

Main Products	Out put 2000 (tons)	Output2001 (tons)	Out put 2002 (tons)
Maize	1 019 000	1 143 000	1 236 000
Beans	146 000	154 000	177 000
Peanut	114 000	109 000	110 000
Rice	151 000	167 000	168 000
Cashew	52 578	53 613	50 177
Cotton	35 000	71 000	83 000
Tobacco	9 470	11 170	25 611
Cane sugar	397 276	675 623	1 586 260
Coconut	44 001	29 631	45 740
Tea	10 466	9 029	12 579

Source: National Institute of Statistics, annual rapport 2002

Main Tropical Crops (US dollars)

Main Products	Out put 2000	Output 2001	Out put 2002
Maize	100 951 660.10	73 963 380.25	79 981 363
Beans	31 821 072.84	25 029 777.32	25 198 012
Peanut	33 881 715.16	21 160 127.15	17 471 657
Rice	24 932 451.21	18 010 913.53	18 118 755
Cashew	15 279 332.61	10 176 575.97	9 254 497
Cotton	7 397 177.58	9 801 388.15	11 133 280
Tobacco	9 424 202.37	6 344 802.65	14 135 410
Cane sugar	3 857 099.73	4 284 526.70	9 774 316
Coconut	4 940 389.97	2 173 086.82	3 259 418
Tea	691 239.82	389 510.27	527 279

Source: National Institute of Statistics, annual rapport 2002

The family farm system with smallholder's agriculture is the dominant system in the Mozambican agriculture sector. Family labour force and low mechanization grade characterize it. Agricultural inputs such as tractors, ploughs, fertilizers, pesticides and others are low. Additionally the number of irrigated areas, in spite of the abundance of irrigable areas, is mainly limited to bigger farms in lowland areas and mainly directed to vegetable production. Also productivity per hectare is low. Hence, the potential for agricultural growth is significant.

In order to increase the sector's productivity the government has engaged various programs, the following two being of major importance: the SG2000 program and the MOZAGRIUS program, both sponsored by the European Union International partners and the Mozambican government. Both programs aim to improve productivity as well as the revenues of small farmers through the introduction of ameliorated seeds, fertilizers, improved technology and better access to major markets. These two programs are coordinated by the DNER, Direcção Nacional de Extensão Rural (National Directorate of Extension services) and INIA, Instituto Nacional de Investigação Agrária (National Institute of Agricultural research).

The government and the World Bank are also creating and helping financial institutions for the provision of agricultural credits as a way to improve the financial capacity of the farmers.

Main staple crops produced in the family agriculture sector are maize, sorghum, rice, millet, potatoes, sweet potatoes, cassava and beans. Grown vegetables (horticultural production) are most frequently tomatoes, cabbage, pumpkin, garlic, piri-piri, pepper, okra, cucumber and onions. However, Mozambique's main cash crops are: cashew nut, cotton, tobacco, sugar cane, copra, and tea.

MAIN CROPS

Cashew Nuts

Production of cashew nuts has long historical roots in Mozambique. The crop was brought into the Northern provinces of Mozambique by the English Concessionary Companhia de Moçambique. Today cashew nut trees are cultivated across the whole country. Cashew nuts have become one of the country's major exports and in fact in 1972, Mozambique produced about half of total world production.

Because of the civil war, the lack of resources and unfortunate natural disasters, cashew production has strongly decreased. With an estimated 40 million cashew trees, which can produce over 200 thousand tons per year, Mozambique's cashew sector is actually producing one third of its potentialities. In order to re-activate the sector, the Government and the European Union are putting in place important measures aiming at enhancing the sector's production capacity, reconstruct processing facilities and attract foreign investors through various incentives.

Nevertheless, cashew nut production represents Mozambique's third most important export product after Cahora Bassa Electricity and prawns (2002). Currently Mozambique mostly exports raw cashew to India, which represents the main destination. A small amount of processed cashew is sold in the European market.

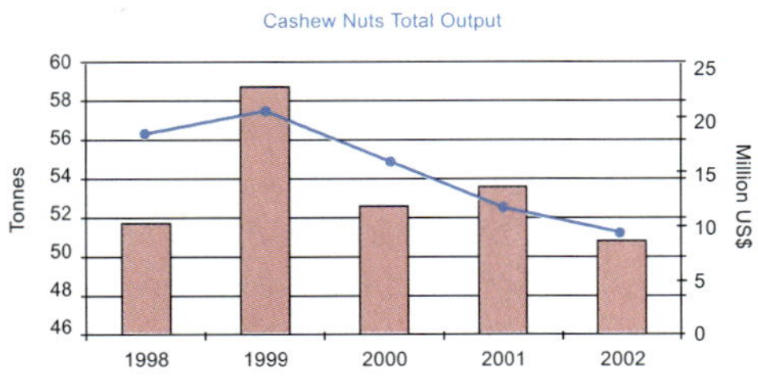

National Institute of Statistics, annual rapport 2001

Recently there have been clear signs that the sector is slowly recuperating notably thanks to the efforts made by INCAJU, the Cashew Institute of Mozambique. The government and INCAJU have plans to invest around $2 millions in the sector with the objective of reaching a production of 100,000 tons in 2005 and 200,000 tons in 2008.

Cotton

Cotton production gained a vital economic role in the early 1920 with the emergence of economic Nationalism in Portugal and the plan to use the Portuguese colonial empire as a boost to the Portuguese Textile Industry. In the 1960s, the cotton industry went through a modernization process and production gradually increased to pick in 1972 with a production of 144,000 tonnes. Nevertheless after independence, production strongly decreased.

As a result, all the processing factories successively closed their operations and today the national textile industry has totally disappeared. Mozambican cotton is therefore mainly produced for export markets. The raw cotton is sold from the peasants to the factories, which pre-elaborated it and then sell it abroad on the world market.

There are 12 companies involved in cotton production in Mozambique but the bulk of the sector is composed by family businesses. Cotton production employs about 300,000 peasants and 10,000 employees.

Currently the cotton industry is going through difficult times because of low International Prices and therefore the government is actively working for the re-development of the textile industry, which will then protect Mozambique's cotton industry from the fluctuation of international prices.

Cotton Total Output

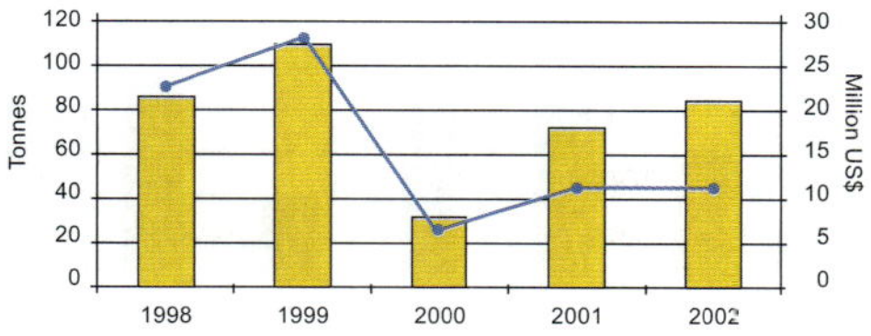

National Institute of Cotton, report 1998 - 2002

Tobacco Total Output

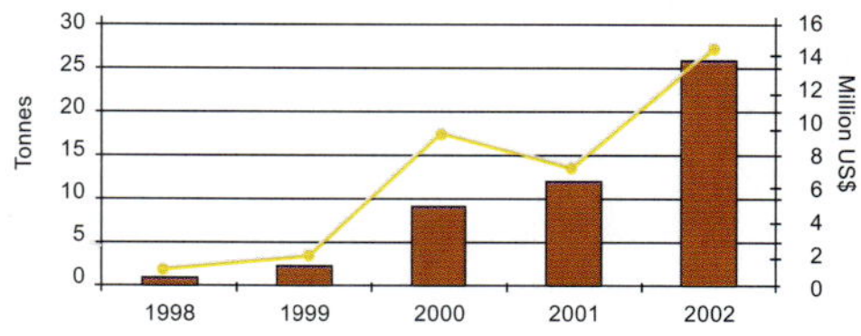

National Institute of Cotton, report 1998 - 2002

Mozambique is a privileged place for cotton cultivation and this is seen through the high quality of its cotton characterized by 1,3 cm to 3,3cm fibres. Therefore there are many investment opportunities available in the cotton industry. On one side, there are opportunities to develop the textile industry with existing installations only needing to be renovated, and on the other, opportunities exist in the mechanization of cotton production.

Tobacco

Tobacco has a long history in Mozambique but it is only recently, with the intention of the government to improve peasantry revenues by fomenting commercial crops, that it has become a new force as an export crop.

Tobacco is cultivated in the high land of the Manica, Tete, Zambezia and Niassa provinces, regions neighbouring Zimbabwe and Malawi, where the soil is volcanic and well drained, and the temperatures are fresh with abundant rainfall 1600 ml per year. The quality of Mozambican tobacco is regionally and internationally recognized for its consistent natural quality. The most produced tobacco is the Virginia varieties but many varieties of Burley and Turkish tobacco can be found.

Production of tobacco strongly increased these last years notably through the government's program to diversify the production of commercial crops and the increasing price of tobacco in the international market. Nevertheless production levels of tobacco are still relatively weak in comparison to the potentials. Therefore there are various opportunities in tobacco production.

On the other hand, processing capacities have not followed the increase in production and this situation has caused a lot of constraints on national producers because Malawi, the main processor of Mozambican tobacco, does not have enough capacity to process all of Mozambique's production. Thus there exists a huge necessity in tobacco processing and the government is currently looking for potential investors in a new factory in Tete province to process the tobacco produced in the central regions of Mozambique.

Sugar

Mozambique is endowed by favourable natural conditions for the cultivation of sugar cane. The Southern and Central provinces of Mozambique and a little portion of the North, are composed by fluvial low lands on the mouth of rivers, with high-grade humidity and fertility with large deposits of organic elements and have rainfalls of 800 to 1400 ml per year and an average temperature of 25 degrees Celsius.

Sugar cane was introduced in Mozambique during colonial times by the British Concessionaries Sena Sugar States. The highest sugar production in the country was reported in 1972, when over 325,000 000 tonnes were produced from six mills. With the independence, production has declined sharply, due largely to the sabotage and destruction of several mills during the war, the lack of specialised human and financial resources.

Nevertheless sugar production has regained a certain momentum as new foreign investors have entered the sector and have successfully rehabilitated the country's sugar mills. The government, in an attempt to re-launch the sector, has also put in place protectionism measures which limit the importation of sugar and export opportunities have increased through the AGOA initiatives (Africa Gross Opportunity Act) which has opened the American market to the Mozambican sugar. Today Mozambique is a net surplus sugar producer and sugar production is planned to double in the years to come.

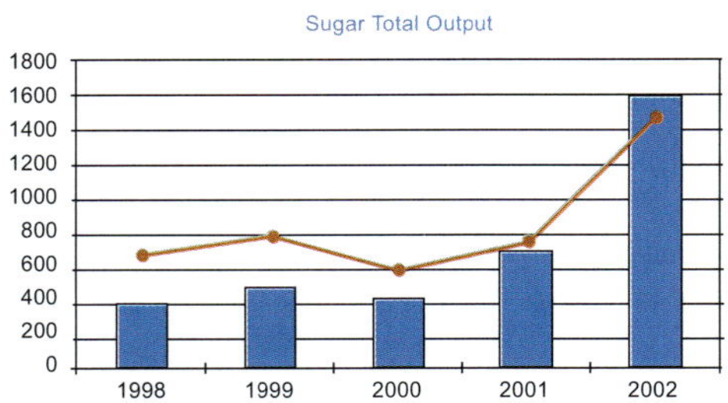

National Institute of Cotton, report 1998 - 2002

Coconut

As far as our collective memory goes, coconut has always been present in Mozambique and is an important element of the population's day to day life. In fact coconut trees are one of the main characteristics of Mozambique's 2500 Km coastline.

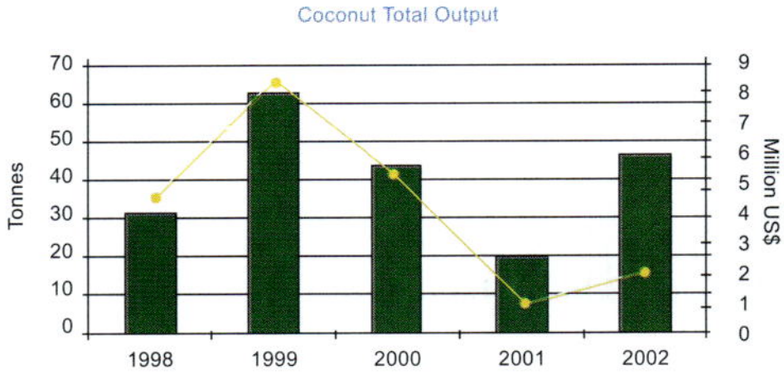

National Institute of Cotton, report 1998 - 2002

Coconut production has being prejudiced these last years by a disease in its trees. The government is taking actions to induce small producers to use pesticides to combat the problem as well as to introduce new, more productive, species. In 2002 the country produced 45 740 tonnes of coconut but natural capacity can withstand a doubling of that figure.

Tea

Mozambican tea is known throughout the world for its rich taste and high quality. In fact Mozambique's Northern regions allow all year cultivation of tea. Only available in powder, but with plans of introducing tea bags in the local market, Mozambican tea is commercialised internally but the bulk of it is exported to Asia and the Middle East where it has an assured market.

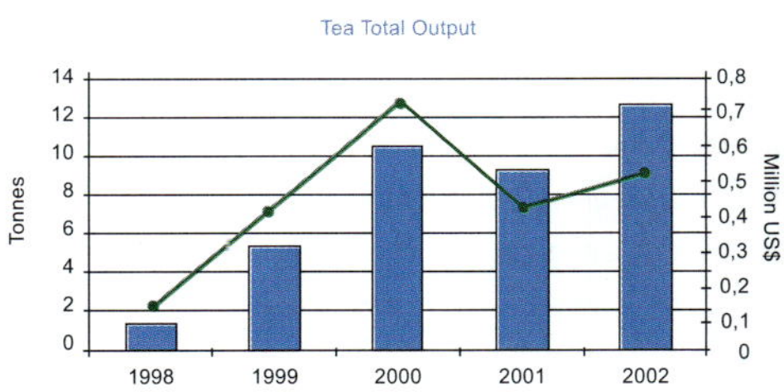

National Institute of Cotton, report 1998 - 2002

MAIN COMPANIES

AgriFocus

Fernando Ricardo Segueira, General Manager
Av. Mao Tse Tung 997
CP 3678, Maputo
Tel: + 258 - 1 - 303433
Fax + 258 - 1 - 303665
E-mail: agrifocus@mail.tropical.co.mz

They distribute agroquimical products and they promote public and social activities. They are going to do product diversification and are expanding into other regions.

Açucareira de Xinavane SARL / Açucareira de Moçambique SARL

Daniel Robert, Executive Director
Av. Samora Machel n° 285, 2nd floor, Flat A-F
P.O.box 583, Maputo
Tel: + 258 - 1 - 303106
Fax: + 258 - 1 - 427316
E-mail: danrob@teledata.mz

Both factories, Açucareira de Xinavane and Açucareira de Moçambique were created during colonial times. In fact they were respectively created in the early 1900s and 1960s. After independence, as most Portuguese investors left the country and especially with the war, the whole of the sugar industry came close to a shut down and in an attempt to save the industry, the government nationalized the factories. In 1994, as Mozambique gained political stability, a privatization process was put in place and in

1996, Tongaat-Hulett Sugar from South Africa signed a management agreement for Açucareira de Moçambique. In 1998, Tongaat-Hulett Sugar acquired 49% of Açucareira de Xinavane and in December 2000, it acquired 75% of Açucareira de Moçambique. Today Tongaat-Hulett Açucar Lda, a subsidiary management company of Tongaat-Hulett Sugar, manages both factories. Both factories have had their mills and estate completely rehabilitated and today they are totally operational. They carry out the following activities: on an agricultural aspect, they plant sugar cane and manage an irrigation system; on a processing aspect, they harvest and manufacture the sugar cane to produce sugar. This activity takes place during a 30-week crushing season. Açucareira de Xinavane and Açucareira de Moçambique market 60% of their product to the local market, 15% to preferential markets such as the USA, E.U, and Southern African countries, and the remaining 25% compete on the international market.

Plans are in progress to expand the Xinavane factory capacity but the timing is not yet set as future market prospective is still undetermined, and to bring Açucareira de Moçambique to its full capacity level.

British American Tobacco (BAT)

Luiz Ribeiro, General Manager
Avenida Angola 2298
Maputo
Tel: + 258 - 1 - 466538 / 41
Fax: + 258 - 1 - 465292
E-mail: luiz_ribeiro@bat.com
Website: www.bat.com

BAT Mozambique integrates three companies that were traditional Mozambican tobacco companies: SAT, SIT, SUT. In fact former Rothmans Company first made the acquisition of these three companies years before. Then through the BAT - Rothmans global merger in 1999, all the Rothmans assets were incorporated into BAT. Consequently BAT gained ownership and control of SAT, SIT and SUT activities in Mozambique. Since then BAT has grown to become the leader in Mozambique's tobacco industry. BAT carries out several activities in Mozambique: Manufacturing of cigarettes; Importing of International BAT brands from other countries into Mozambique; and Distribution of cigarettes to the whole country. At the moment BAT is focusing its growth strategy on becoming a "World Class Company with a Mozambican Flavour". There are four pillars that BAT Mozambique considers necessary in order to reach its target: the quality of its products, the satisfaction of its shareholders, the satisfaction and commitment of its employees and the development of the surrounding society. Therefore BAT's growth strategy is centred on continuously improving these four pillars. BAT Mozambique is proud of its consumers. In fact it is proud to have maintained and strengthened its relationship with its customer over the years. The tobacco sector involves high controversy. It is therefore a necessity for BAT to ensure that its business acts responsible, working in collaboration with all key stakeholders.

INCAJU - the National Cashew Institute (Instituto de Fomento do Caju)

Clementina Machungo, General Director
Rua da Resistência n°1746, 4° Andar
Maputo
Tel: + 258 - 1 - 417723 / 416898
Fax: + 258 - 1 - 418552
E-mail: rafaela@incaju.co.mz

Main Sectors Of The Economy: Agriculture & Fisheries

Cashew production has historical roots in Mozambique and in 1972 Mozambique cashew production accounted for about half of total world production. Due to pests and disease, aging of the trees, bushfires, abandonment of orchards due to civil war cashew production strongly decreased. In 1998, in an attempt to re-launch the production and marketing of cashew nuts in Mozambique, the government decided to change the status of the Secretary of State and create a national body responsible for the development of cashew orchard: the National Cashew Institute. INCAJU is the National Cashew Institute in charge of developing the cashew extension programs, the trade and processing of cashew. In fact it has the following objectives: Promote development programs for cashew; Promote cashew processing giving emphasis on low costs technologies and the used of intensive labour; Promote the use of false fruit and CNSL; Encourage the existent industry to plant cashew orchards; Promote educational programs for prevention of bushfire, disease and pest. Apply research results in coordination with research and extension institutions; Control soil management and environmental issues related to cashew; propose to government authority the prices to producers and trade license, export tax. INCAJU plans to increase cashew production to 100,000 tons by the year 2005. To achieve this goal, INCAJU is actively putting in place development programs with the collaboration of the private sector, NGOs, farmers associations and traders to increase its involvement in cashew production, commercialisation, and processing. As a public institution, INCAJU also give technical support to the previous organizations. INCAJU has successfully managed to re-launch Mozambique's production and commercialisation of cashew. Indeed for the period 2002-2003 the commercialisation of Mozambican cashews amounted to 64,000 tons compared to 50,000 tons the year before. INCAJU is actively working to give

Mozambique its previous production rate back. For the campaign 2005-2006, target commercialisation is of 100,000 tons and INCAJU is putting in place all the means to effectively meet it.

Instituto de Algodão de Moçambique (IAM) Mozambique Institute for Cotton Development

Erasmo Cardoso Muhate, Director
Av. Eduardo mondlane, N°2221, 1° Andar
Caixa Postal 806, Maputo
Tel: + 258 - 1 - 424264 / 413015
Fax: + 258 - 1 - 430679
E-mail: iampab@zebra.uem.mz

Cotton was introduced in Mozambique in the early 1900s under colonial rule. In the 1960s, Mozambique's cotton industry went through a modernization process and production gradually increased to pick in 1972 with a production of 144,000 tons. Nevertheless with the independence in 1975 production strongly decreased due to the departure of the Portuguese settlers. The Mozambican government nationalized all the cotton companies in order to maintain production and employment levels. In 1987, with the structural adjustment program, these companies were privatized and the "Instituto de Algodão de Moçambique"(IAM) was created to lead the cotton subsector under the new market oriented economical reality. IAM is in charge of the general promotion of cotton development through policies, strategies, legislation and practical interventions. The Institute exercises monitoring, arbitration of production and trade conflicts, classing of cotton lint and technical assistance activities. In fact today IAM is the executive arm of the Ministry of Agriculture and Rural Development in cotton related issues, hence actively participate in the development of investment projects advising investors and smallholders in their decision-making process. IAM strives to make Mozambique a major raw cotton producer in Africa by increasing production, productivity and quality. In fact IAM is proactively working for the reactivation of the textile industry in Mozambique which would then permit a more effective development of the cotton industry. In cooperation with the Ministry of Industry and Trade, the Institute is working for the development of an internal textile industry that would allow the cotton industry to be protected from price fluctuation of the global market and benefit form the advantage of programs such as African Growth Opportunity Act (USA) and Everything But Arms (EU).

Maragra Açucar SARL

A.F. Currie, General Manager
Caixa Postal 2789, Maputo
Tel: + 258 - 1 - 810024 / 028
Fax: + 258 - 1 - 810050
E-mail: tcurrie@illovo.co.za

Founded by the Petiz family in 1968, the original Maragra mill commenced production in 1970, and produced 44,100 tons of raw sugar at its peak in 1972. The Company was nationalized in 1974 and production ultimately stopped in 1984. The Government's privatisation programme saw the estate return to the Petiz family in 1992, and plans for its rehabilitation resulted in the formation, in July 1997, of Maragra Acucar SARL with 50% of the shares being held by the Illovo Sugar Group, the largest sugar producer in Africa, and the balance held by the Petiz family. Today Illovo Sugar owns 72 per cent of the company and the Petiz family 28 per cent. Maragra Açucar SARL cultivates and processes sugar cane. Their markets, in order of importance are: the local Mozambican market, Europe, USA and the world market. Presently the Mozambican sugar industry is working in unison to grow the local market and reduce its exposure to the world market. Maragra Açucar represents approximately 26% of this market and participates fully in the activities of the industry. In terms of growth strategy, Maragra Açucar is now working with various Ministries to develop small Mozambican cane growers by providing management and technological expertise to these growers, in order to increase its cane supply base and hence its annual output of raw sugar. From zero in 1998, Maragra Açucar has planted 4,000 hectares of sugar cane and rehabilitated the factory by December 1999, at a cost of USD 55 000 000. The cane crop was destroyed by the floods of February 2000. By December 2001 the entire agricultural infrastructure had been rehabilitated and the entire 6300 hectares of land replanted at an additional cost of USD 15 000 000. In 2001, 139 000 tons of cane were processed and 16 000 tons of sugar produced, followed by 412 000 tons of cane from which 50 000 tons of sugar were produced, in 2002. This was a record season in terms of Maragra's history. The 2003 season will see 579 000 tons of cane processed to produce 66 700 tons of sugar. Maragra Açucar is working to consolidate and expand its share of the Mozambican sugar industry in parallel with the development of the Mozambican farming community in order to participate fully in the economic recovery of Mozambique.

Moçambique Produce Terminal (Fresh Produce Terminals Group)

Paulo Franco, General Manager
Porto de Maputo - Zona G
Maputo
Tel: + 258 - 1 - 321977
Fax: + 258 - 1 - 30642
E-mail: pf@mptmoz.com

Citrus Board was an association of citrus growers in South Africa that had the monopoly for exporting citrus fruits. It later evolved into OUTSPAN, the company in charge of all fruit exports for South Africa. As the market was then deregulated, consequently many new exporters appeared. To confront this new situation, OUTSPAN and Unifruitti merged and become Capespan. The resulting company is the biggest fruit exporter possessing most of the fruit basket handling facilities. Capespan, which owns various export terminals, decided to get rid of operational activities and concentrate on the core business of exporting. This lead to the creation of "Fresh Produce Terminals" (FPT). FPT is owned 100 per cent by Capespan, but the shareholder structure will be changing soon. The Moçambique Produce Terminal is part of the FPT group. MPT has had a steady growth over the yeasr and has strongly invested in terms of equipment for fruit handling. In the year 2002 they had their cold rooms certified by an international certifying company and this year (2003) they are applying for the ISO 9002 certification. Through these efforts, MPT is increasing the quality of its services and gaining a strong reputation. Thus MPT is becoming more and more competitive.

UGC - União Geral das Cooperativas

Sra. Celina Cossa, Founder & President
Av. Agostinho, N° 714
Maputo
Tel: + 258 - 1 - 430229
Fax: + 258 - 1 - 430459
Email: ugcapm@mail.tropical.co.mz

Founded by poor women during the worst years of Mozambique's civil war, the General Union of Cooperatives of Maputo (UGC) first started as a collective production cooperative. In the mid 1980's, as the government shifted to a policy of economic liberalization, the UGC reorganized itself, placing greater emphasis on financial autonomy and thus transformed into a service cooperative. Today it is one of the capital's premier agricultural businesses, supplying much of its fruit, vegetables and chickens. The UGC works in all aspects of food production and income-generating activities, which are almost never exc usively of economical or of social nature. Sectors of activities include: General Union of Cooperatives SCRL, with Poultry Production, Agriculture (Fruits, vegetables, etc), and workshop services (Mechanic and hydraulic); Support to Development, with Secondary Schools, Technical Institutes, Training Centers, Health Centers, Financial Mediation and Emergency relief services; Saving and Credit Cooperatives SCRL, with Credit and Saving services. UGC functions under a continuous improvement philosophy and thus continuous training is its basis. This philosophy was put in place in order to be able to keep up with the constant evolution of the market and to face any situation that could present itself in the future. Celina Cossa won the Hunger Project's 1998 Africa Prize for Leadership for the Sustainable End of Hunger. UGC is also very proud of its Poultry activity, which receives no subsidies from the government unlike in many other countries. Technological advances and the modernization production processes represent the major challenges for UGC. Nevertheless through the cooperation with local and foreign companies, and the continuous improvement philosophy UGC will continue growing and increasing its aid to the Mozambican community.

FISHERIES OVERVIEW

In Mozambique, the fisheries sector benefits of exceptional natural conditions: 2,500 kilometers of coastline, three important ports (Maputo, Beira, Nacala), several secondary ports (Quelimane, Inhambane, Pemba, Angoche), an exclusive economic zone of 560 000 km_ and various very profitable species (prawns, crabs...). Since the end of the 1970s, the local authorities have invested considerable efforts in the organization and the equipment of the sector, and have put in place incentives to attract investments, in order to stimulate the capture of not only the high value species which are foreign income generator, but also that of the species destined to local consumption in order to reduce the burden of imports.

Ministerio Das Pescas

Hon. Cadmiel Filiane Mutemba, Minister
Rua Consiglieri Pedroso 347 3°
Caixa Postal 1723, Maputo
Tel: + 258 - 1 - 324363
Fax: + 258 - 1 - 325087
E-mail: xikuluvundzu@mozpesca.org
Website: www.mozpesca.org

A young Ministry that was created in 2000 due to the importance of developing this sector for the economy as it accounts for 38% of the exports of the country. It creates income, employment and food supply. The objectives are to organise the fisheries activities, to manage the fisheries resources (they don't offer shrimp fishing licenses anymore)and to promote aquaculture. FDI investment is good, but Pescamar (leader in sector) fishes and exports, doesn't process in the country. They need to promote fishing services inside Mozambique. The investment potentialities are centred in fish, tuna, and aquaculture. Its a Good investment destination because: 1) organising and revising laws for maritime fishing and aquaculture, 2) Reducing bureaucracy 3) Preparing a guide for aquaculture procedures. The priorities in international relations are to cooperate with neighbouring countries and to work on agreements with EU, to strengthen relationships with Norway. Mozambique needs investment in the form of joint ventures locals.

THE SECTOR

The statistic data available on the fisheries products are most of the time incomplete due to, on one side the importance of the traditional sector, and on the other, the lack of technical means to efficiently collect statistical information. The authorities estimate that only 50 per cent of the catches are registered principally because of the uncertainties concerning traditional fisheries. The fisheries sector represents between 3 and 4 per cent of the country's GDP. In 2002, the production resulting from the fisheries industry reached 105 M USD. The annual volume of catches officially registered would situate itself between 30,000 and 35,000 tons. The fisheries sector is composed of 3 sub-sectors.

The traditional fisheries represent 25 per cent of the total production in volume (8,000 tons in 2002). The fleet is composed essentially of veil boats as only 5 per cent of the fleet is motorized. In value, the production of traditional fisheries has reached almost 11 M USD in 2002. This sub-sector is animated by the communities of Mozambican fishermen. The legislation defines traditional fisheries as the one carried out locally, through traditional fishing methods, with or without boat.

Semi-industrial fisheries represent 30 per cent of the total volume of production. The majority of the fleets navigates under Mozambican pavilion and belongs to private Mozambican entrepreneurs. All the embarkations dispose of engines. Before, these embarkations fished and conserved their catch in ice. Today, with the impulse of the new legislation, these embarkations have started to equip themselves with cold rooms. In 2002, the production of semi-industrial fisheries reached 50 M USD.
Industrial fisheries represent 45 per cent of the national production in volume. This production is essentially export oriented (mostly to Europe and Japan). The operators are mixed companies with mostly Spanish and Japanese

capital. Each operator generally utilizes his own technology and equipment. The government, concerned with the sustainability of the exploitation of the sea's natural resources, seeks to develop semi-industrial and traditional fisheries and reduce or at least limit industrial fisheries. Actually, no new licenses for the industrial fisheries of shrimps are being accorded. The production of industrial fisheries reached 90 M USD in 2002.

The total catch officially registered in the industrial and semi-industrial sectors in 2002 elevated to 22,000 tons (94 M USD in value). The principal industry within these 2 sub-sectors is that of shrimps which represents 40 per cent of the catches and 75 per cent of the value.

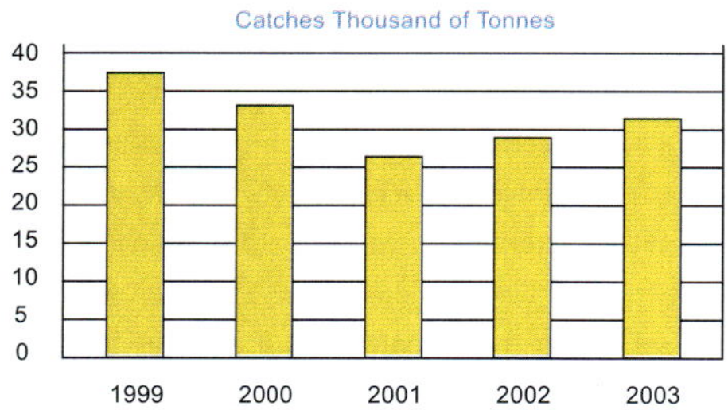

Source: Ministry of Fisheries

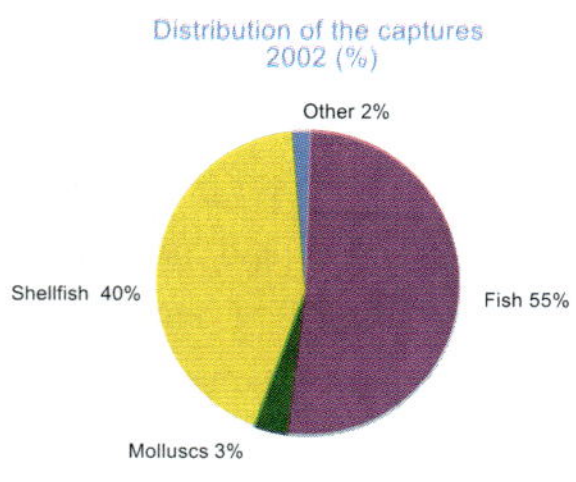

Source: Ministry of Fisheries

AQUACULTURE

Aquaculture, which has a very important potential, is a future growth sector in Mozambique. The principal aquaculture projects concern mostly shrimps. Aquaculture would develop itself in the regions of Maputo, Sofala, Zambezia and Nampula. According to a study realized by the National Directorate of Fisheries, the country disposes of 33,000 hectares for the development of shrimp aquaculture. Fresh water aquaculture is still poorly developed. Concerning the aquaculture of other species, this is done at the moment at an experimental level. The Mozambican Government, conscious of the constraints caused on the shrimp by the increase of fishing effort, is giving privilege to aquaculture for the development of production and export of shrimps. The Ministry of Fisheries estimates that the Mozambican aquaculture production should reach 700 tons of shrimps, 100 tons of fresh water fish and 150 tons of algae in 2003 (which would represent a value of 3 M USD, 3 per cent of total Mozambican production).

FISH PRODUCTS EXPORT

The export of fishery products (principally shrimps and gambas) reached 93 M USD in 2002.

The European market represents 60 per cent of the total export of Mozambican marine products. The principal clients have traditionally been Spain and Japan, and at lower levels, South Africa, Portugal, France, and the Mauritius Island. The sector represents between 35 and 45 per cent of the total traditional exports of Mozambique and directly employs between 70 and 75,000 persons, 60,000 being in the traditional sector. In volume, the total production exported in 2002 reached almost 20,000 tons (against 14,000 tons in 2001).

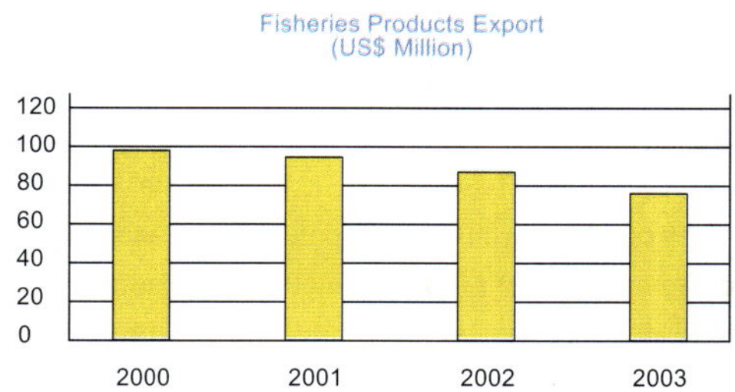

Source: Ministry of Fisheries

ACTUAL PROJECTS

The Mozambican government has a strong will to develop semi-industrial and traditional fisheries. Two projects should contribute for the 6 years to come to the development of the traditional fisheries. The Ministry of Fisheries should start launching soon a project backing traditional fishermen who work in the northern region of the country (Nampula and Cabo Delgado Provinces). This financial aid given by the African Development Bank (ADB), of 23 M USD, should allow to put in place financial facilities such as credits. Another fishery development project in the region of Sofala is being elaborated. This project will be financed by The International Fund For Agricultural Development (IFAD), the Norwegian Cooperation (Norad), the Belgium Fund (BSF) and the Mozambican government. The program involves the development of fisheries, of the communities, the evaluation of resources, the conservation of fisheries products, the access to markets and the concession of credits. The goal of this project is to organize in the long-term the marine resources and to make the activity more profitable for the traditional fishermen. The funds given for these two projects are principally destined to: the acquisition of new equipments; the buying of cold rooms, the construction of small factories for the conservation of the fish; the construction of infrastructures for the commercialization of the fish. Also in October 2002, Mozambique and the European Union (EU) agreed on a deal allowing EU vessels to catch tuna and deep-water shrimps in Mozambican territorial waters over the next three years. A total of 59 EU vessels are to participate in the fishing and Mozambique is to receive a 4 million Euros payment each year.Thus, investment opportunities in the fishery sector lie primarily in the need for a gradual substitution of industrial vessels by semi-industrial freezer boats that can discharge shrimp for further onshore processing. Mozambique currently exports raw products. The Government strategy is to promote value-added activities in this sector and it thus welcomes foreign investors who can provide semi-industrial shrimp vessels as well as processing plants. Furthermore, Mozambique needs to improve its services to the fishing industry. Opportunities exist for the manufacture of rope and steel cable, marine engineering consultancy and marine electronics.

MAIN COMPANIES

Aquapesca

Hervé Ohresser-Joumard, General Manager
Av. Paulo Samuel Kankhomba, n°83
C.P. 1734, Maputo
Tel: + 258 - 1 - 490038 / 494390
Fax: + 258 - 1 - 492789
E-mail: herve@aquapesca.com
Website: www.aquapesca.com

Aquapesca was created in 1994 by three partners, the Reunion-based Armement des Mascareignes, the Mozambican State and the French Development Bank's private investment arm, Proparco. The company is based across the river from Quelimane, the quiet capital of Mozambique's rural Zambezi province. Aquapesca was the first private company to launch itself in the aquaculture of tiger prawns with commercial prawn farms and hatchery. The company has opted for semi-intensive farming, which is said to best balance potential yields with labour and input costs. Also semi-intensive farming reduces the risk of disease and increase the environmental sustainability. Aquapesca started its operations with a pilot project and today is investing in an industrial phase of operations. Their main market being Europe, Aquapesca will operate a processing factory, which will comply with European standards and regulations. Aquapesca is still in its development process. The initial pilot project represented an investment of $5M, and today's industrial phase of operations represents an investment of approximately $40M. When the entire infrastructure will be in place, Aquapesca will produce 2,000 tons of prawns a year and employ 700 people. The cultivated species will be Penaeus monodon, (Tiger Prawn). In fact it is the country's first commercial prawn and hatchery, and according to the initial results from the pilot project future perspectives are encouraging. Mozambique has no tradition of aquaculture but possesses a great potential for its development, and this is not only true for tiger prawns but also for a wide variety of species. Aquapesca strives to strengthen its position as a number of other companies have recently entered the market.

Efripel - Entreposto Frigorifico de Pesca de Moçambique, Lda

Robate Q. Megessane, General Director
Shingo Kokubun, Assistant General Director
Av. Ahmed Sekou Touré, n°1126
Tel: + 258 - 1 - 415557
Fax: + 258 - 1 - 415631
E-mail: megessane@teledata.mz
or efr.mpm@tvcabo.co.mz

After the independence, the fishing companies in Mozambique went through hard times. In an attempt to aid the sector, the Mozambican government asked to foreign investors to come and participate in its functioning through joint ventures with Emopesca, the state fishing company. In 1978, Efripel, which was created several years before, saw its status change has it became a joint-venture fishing company involving Maruha of Japan with 49% of the shares and Emopesca of Mozambique with 51%. Efripel is a fishing company specialized in prawn fishing. They carry out the following activities: Prawn fishing; Process and Storage; Export. Efripel has its own fleet and its unique client is its Japanese mother company, Maruha. Efripel is specialized in prawn fishing. Because of the quotas on prawn fishing Mozambique, possibilities to grown within this market are limited. Thus Efripel is actually studying the possibilities to diversify into the fishing and export of other species. Nevertheless Efripel benefits of a stable market in Japan through its mother company, Maruha. Efripel has contributed to the economic and social development of Mozambique for several years now. In fact it is the second biggest company of the prawn fishing sector, which represents the country's major export and thus Efripel plays a key social role. Efripel's major challenge lies in effectively growing in the fishing sector.

Gambeira - Sociedade de Pesca de Gamba da Beira, Limitada

Lurdes da Coceição M. Cossa, General Director
Rua Tavares de Almeida N° 30
Caixa Postal 1902, Maputo
Tel: + 258 - 1 - 321965
Fax: + 258 - 1 - 323 524
E-mail: gambeira.lurdes@sortmoz.com

Gambeira - Sociedade de Pesca de Gamba da Beira, Limitada was created in 1996 as a fishing company especially dedicated to shrimp and prawn fishing. It evolved from a small fishing company based at the time in Beira, town situated in the central region of Mozambique, to become today part of the biggest companies in the sector. The Mozambican government owns 60 per cent of the shares while Viking Fishing from South Africa owns the rest. Gambeira is a shrimp and prawn fishing company that works throughout the country serving both the local and international markets. Gambeira plans to acquire its own fishing boats in order to grow. In fact Gambeira's growth strategy will be internally focused because externally all the fishing companies are limited by quotas. In terms of quality of their products Gambeira has a world known reputation, which it intends to maintain and strengthen. Gambeira is very proud of having developed themselves from a small fishing company to one of the country's biggest shrimp and prawn company. Today they are part of the country's five biggest fishing company. The challenge lies in maintaining a constant growth, increasing their allocated quotas, accessing new markets and constantly improving the quality of their products.

MAVIMBI, Lda.

Moisés Rafael Massinga, General Manager
Av. 25 de Setembro N° 1171, 1st floor
Maputo
Tel: + 258 - 1 - 423050 / 304509
Fax: + 258 - 1 - 426425
E-mail: mavimbi@emilmoz.com

Mavimbi Lda was created in 1994 with three private shareholders. Today they are five. At its beginnings Mavimbi had two branches: semi-industrial fisheries and industrial fisheries. Today they only work in industrial fisheries and are specialized in prawn fishing. Mavimbi exports its prawns to European markets, Spain being the most important one. They fish across the whole of Mozambique, especially in the region of Sofala Bank. At the moment Mavimbi hires boats for its activity but they plan to acquire their own boats for next year. Growing in the prawn market is difficult because of the restraints imposed by the government through quotas thus Mavimbi has been diversifying its activity line. In fact they have invested in a printer company amongst others. Mavimbi's major achievement will be the acquisition of its own boats next year. The fisheries market is a complicated one but Mozambique offers many opportunities in aquaculture. Nevertheless, Mozambique possesses various advantages: its climate; its land and its uncontaminated sea.

PESCAMAR - Sociedade de Pesca de Mariscos, Lda

Felisberto Manuel, General Director
Largo Manuel António de Sousa, n°6, Beira
Tel: + 258 - 3 - 325821 / 325058
Fax: + 258 - 3 - 325054
E-mail: pescamar@teledata.mz

After having operated in Mozambique for several years, the Pescanova Group decided to created a local company that would serve its needs in prawns. Thus in 1980 Pescamar-Sociedade de Pesca de Mariscos, Lda was created in partnership with Emopesca, the state owned fishing company. Pescamar is registered in Mozambique, 70% of its shares are held by Pescanova and the remaining 30% are held by Emopesca. Today Pescamar is the leading prawn fishing company in Mozambique. Pescamar Lda is a fishing company specialized in prawn fishing. It exports all of its catch mostly to Europe as it supplies the various companies of the Pescanova Group. Today Pescamar Lda accounts for 23% of the prawn exports in Mozambique. It possesses its own fleet of fishing vessels, which are in fact floating factories. Thanks to its experience in prawn fishing, the use of high technology and the possession of the most modern fleet in Africa, Pescamar possesses the leading hedge in its industry. In fact through these various competitive advantages, Pescamar can study the possibilities of diversifying its activities in the near future. Pescamar is also one of the country's major earners of foreign income. Indeed as prawn is one of the major export industries in Mozambique and Pescamar the leading company in this industry, it strongly contributes to the country's economic development. Additionally this economic contribution in strengthened by the fact that it gets all its provisions from local small and medium companies. Finally as it employs around 600 people in the region of Beira, Pescamar has gained a certain importance in terms of the social development for the region. With the development of aquaculture in Mozambique, Pescamar Lda faces difficult times in the near future. Nevertheless thanks to its various competitive advantages and the fact that they are actively investing in their infrastructure, Pescamar will naturally maintain itself as a leading company in Mozambique.

SIP - Sociedade Industrial de Pesca

António Schwalbach, Associate Manager
Av. Zedequias Manganhela, 520. 6° Andar, Flat 601
C.P 2646, Maputo
Tel: + 258 - 1 - 429074 / 6
Fax: + 258 - 1 - 321142

SIP started working in 1994 hiring boats for deep-water prawn fishing. In 1996, SIP added shallow prawn fishing to its activity line. In the year 2000, they bought their own boats and today they operate 3 vessels, which are floating factories. The company's activities include shallow and deep-water prawn fishing plus by-catches. SIP's sells its products to various European markets, namely Portugal, Italy and Spain. SIP is constantly studying investment opportunities to improve its activities. In the European markets, they differentiate themselves from the competition through the quality of their prawns. In fact Mozambican prawns are famous worldwide. SIP's success is based on the efficiency and low cost of its functioning, and the well developed human resources. The year 2000 was the best year ever for SIP in terms of sales and profitability. SIP is also very proud of its work force and the work culture is has put in place which has great impact on the positive result of the company. In the future, SIP will increase its activity lines through the acquisition of new companies and through Joint Ventures.

For a big fish, a big smile

ENERGY & MINING

OVERVIEW

Mozambique possesses a rich and diversified energy resource base capable of meeting both local demand and contributing to large-scale energy exports, including hydropower, natural gas and coal. In addition, there are biomass resources, as well as a proven potential of renewable energy sources such as solar, wind and micro-hydro. In terms of minerals resources both metallic and non-metallic minerals occur in large variety in Mozambique, the most important of these being: coal, rare metals (niobium-tantalum), gold, fluorite tin, heavy minerals, graphite, base metals, phosphorites, and mineralization related to carbonatites and pagmatites, including most notably beryl and other precious and semi-precious stones. Apart from these, kimberlites, in Northern Mozambique and alluvial and diamond potential in the Southern part of the country have been identified.

Until 2000, Energy and Mining was one of the country's less developed sector and this in spite of the abundance of energetic and mineral resources. This is due to the destruction of most of the existing infrastructure during the war, the lack of a solid development strategy for the sector and the lack of geologic and viability studies. Thus during several years, national and international direct investment were significantly low.

Nevertheless as Mozambique is becoming an increasing attractive destination for foreign direct investment and knowledge of the country's wealth of energy and mineral resources is spreading throughout the world, investment in both sectors has strongly increased these last few years. Indeed several large investment projects are being implemented such as the construction of the Mepanda Uncua Dam with 2,400 MW capacity, the rehabilitation of Moatize Coal mines, the SASOL gas pipelines and the Heavy sands smelter in Chibuto.

Today energy and mining is now contributing to the country's increase in GDP and rise in FDI, and signs are that the influx is far from over. Actually, the energy sub sector grew 13,73 per cent in 2002 while the mining sub sector fell about 5,5 per cent between 2001 to 2002.

Ministry of Energy

ELECTRICITY

Currently the whole production of electricity is based on two entities: the Cahora Bassa Company which manages the Cahora Bassa Dam; and the public company Electricidade de Moçambique (EDM) which controls and manages several power generation stations throughout the country.

Electricity Generation

Mozambique's hydroelectric capacity is considered as one of the most important in Africa and has been estimated at around 12.500 MW with a corresponding annual generation of 60.000 GWh. Nevertheless actual production does not exceed 2500 MW and annual internal consumption of electrical energy (excluding the Mozal aluminium smelter) is of around 200 MW. Today only 10 per cent of its population has access to electricity but as demand is growing at a healthy 8 to 10 per cent annual rate, things will rapidly change. Export demand is strongly growing as well, especially from South Africa (the main consumer of Mozambique's electricity). Studies are also underway to add interconnections from Mozambique to Malawi and Tanzania.

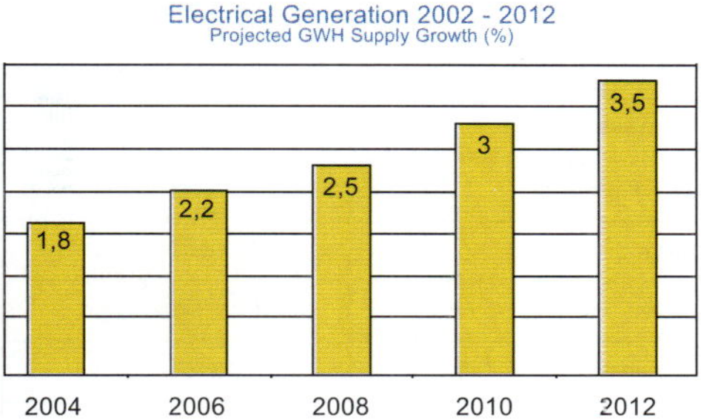

Source: EDM (Electricidade de Moçambique)

The Cahora Bassa Dam, located on the Zambezi River in the North of Mozambique, is considered as one of the largest in the world. It actually produces 1700 M (although its installed capacity is of 2075 MW) and this should increase to 4000 MW by beginning 2004. It is the country's largest producer of electricity with almost 83 per cent of internal production. It exports most of its production to neighboring countries notably South Africa and Zimbabwe. By 2004 exports to Malawi should also be carried out. In the following years the Cahora Bassa Dam will benefit of a $40 Million investment programme for the modernization and maintenance of its installations, which should make it a reliable source of energy for the years to come.

The network of power generation stations is composed of 16 thermal and 5 hydraulic stations. These infrastructures, as well as the equipments, are operated by EDM, which is also their owner and their total production is of around 108 MW. In 2002, EDM produced 296,5 GWh (against 302,7 GWh in 1999). To ensure access to electricity of several regions in the country, EDM imports electricity from neighbouring countries, notably South Africa, Zimbabwe and Malawi and in 2002, these imports were of 1030,1 GWh (against 71,8 GWh in 1999). This is a bit contradictory as Mozambique exports most of its electricity production to these same countries.

In 1997 the New Energy Law 21/97, which regulates the production, transport and commercialization of energy as well as its exportation and importation, was approved and the National Electricity Council (Conselho Nacional de Electricidade), which is the main authority within the sector, was created. The new law has given more dynamism to the industry notably by permitting the entry of new private producers beside the main public company EDM. These private companies have entered at all the different levels of the value chain and today are playing an increasingly important role in the sector. For example, Motraco (Mozambique Transport Company) is a consortium composed of EDM of Mozambique, ESKOM from South Africa and SEB from Swaziland, and it provides power to Mozal and all the Beleluane Industrial Free Zone. As the sector is becoming increasingly dynamic and demand is expected to strongly increase, many investment projects are being studied. The M'Panda Uncua project involves the construction of a new hydroelectric dam on the Zambezi River, downstream from the Cahora Bassa dam, with a production capacity of 2,400 MW. It will be 110 metres high and will have a hydrographic basin of 100 square kilometres and its total construction cost has been estimated at $ 1.8 Billion. The project will follow the BOT model (build, operate and transfer). Other investment projects include the construction of the Cahora Bassa North Dam, the Massingir Dam and the Moamba Major Dam.

Apart from hydropower, Mozambique possesses several alternative sources of electric energy of which the most significant is natural gas (Oil & Gas section).

Rural Electrification

In an effort to reduce poverty and improve the standards of living of the population, the Mozambican government, with the support of international donors, is putting in place an important rural electrification programme. This programme has a total value of $ 200 Million and includes investments in production facilities, and transport and distribution infrastructures. It should notably be carried out through concessions to private companies.

MINING

Mozambique possesses numerous important and high quality minerals resources, which remain mostly untapped. Both metallic and non-metallic minerals occur in large variety in Mozambique, the most important of these being: coal, rare metals (niobium-tantalum), gold, fluorite tin, heavy minerals, graphite, base metals, phosphorites, and mineralization related to carbonatites and pagmatites, including most notably beryl and other precious and semi-precious stones. Apart from these, kimberlites, in Northern Mozambique and alluvial and alluvial diamond potential in the Southern part of the country have been identified.

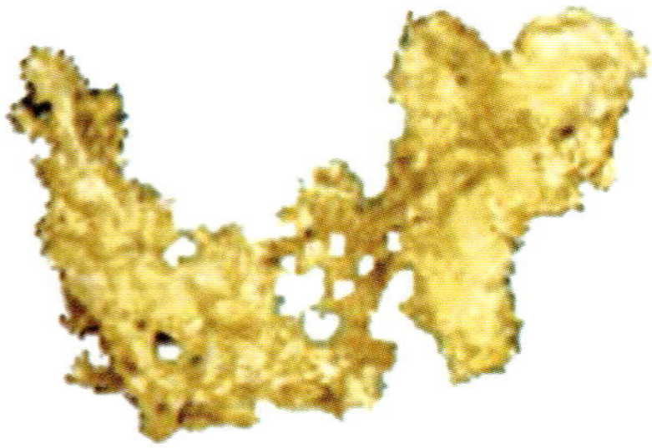

A piece of gold shines like the sun in Mozambique

Known major mineral resources of Mozambique and their reserve estimates:

Apatite	274 million tonnes
Asbestos	500 000 tonnes
Bauxite	6.13 million tonnes
Bentonite	8.45 million tonnes
Black granite	2 million tonnes
Clay	18.3 million tonnes
Coal	15 835 million tonnes
Copper	382 000 tonnes
Diatomite	3 million tonnes
Feldspar	12 000 tonnes
Fluorite	1.45 million tonnes
Gold	47 000 tonnes
Graphite	40 million tonnes
Guano	900 000 tonnes
Gypsum	40.2 million tonnes
Iron ore.	254 million tonnes
Heavy Sands	—
Kaolin	4.4 million tonnes
Marble	30 million tonnes
Mica	72 000 tonnes
Natural Gas	2.7 TCF
Nepheline Syenite	4.3 billion tonnes
Limestone	39.76 million tonnes
Perlite	945 000 tonnes
Silica	11.4 million tonnes
Tantalum ore.	7.5 million tonnes
Titanium ore.	348 million tonnes

Source: Direcção Nacional de Minas

Additionally existing heavy minerals in the region of Moebase (Zambézia Province), Moma (Nampula Province) and Chibuto (Gaza Province) are believed to be world scale deposits.

Despite all these resources, the sector's contribution to the GDP remains very weak with a contribution of 0.4 per cent in 2002. This is mainly due to the lack of infrastructures (destroyed during the war), a poorly developed commercial and legal environment, and insufficient financial resources. The sector is essentially composed of small-scale projects and traditional exploitations characterized by the high degree of illegal sites. Medium and large-scale projects are mostly financed by foreign investment and necessitate exclusive exploration licences, non- exclusive exploration licences or mining concessions. In 2001, 113 licences and certificates were newly awarded which took the total number up to 514.

Under the World Bank's guidance, Mozambique has drawn up a new mining law, fiscal code and a geological mapping of the country. Mozambique is said to have some of the most attractive mineral deposits in the world, attracting interest from various players. Indeed the government is strongly promoting the development of the sector and is consequently putting in place various measures to attract foreign investors including simplified measures for the approbation of investment projects, tax exemptions, and tax-free imports of equipment among other incentives. Consequently the number of projects within the mining sector has been progressively growing these last few years. Nevertheless the obsolescence of existing sites and machinery is resulting in a closure of several activities, which is giving way to new-large scale projects.

Mozambique's rich mineral resources are indeed attracting an increasing number of new projects. Southern Mining Company of South Africa and Australia's WMC Ltd. are advanced in their study of the $1.3 billion heavy mineral sands mega-project called "Limpopo Corridor Sands", for titanium dioxide and smelting, near Chibuto (Gaa Province). Another major project is the construction of a Titania slagsmelter at the port of Nacala that would process ore from the TiGen heavy sands projects in Moebase, in Zambézia Province. The Moatize mine, in Tete Province, is one of the world's largest coal sites with more then 6 billion tonnes. JCI Coal Project - Johannesburg Consolidated Industries, an Anglo-American spin-off, has promoted a project to export Moatize coking coal via the Sena line and Beira Port to Brazil. At Moma, a $100 million is being financed by Kenmare Resources from Ireland with the aim to annually produce 600 000 tonnes of ilmenite, 13 000 tonnes of premium-grade rutile and 52 000 tonnes of premium-grade zircon - all titanium minerals used in the hi-tech, plastic and paint industries.

The Government is actively encouraging the development of this sector and is putting in place favourable legislations as well as tax regimes. Mozambique is thus slowly taking advantage of its resources and most certainly the mining sector will become in the near future one of the country's most important contributor to economic development and poverty reduction.

OIL AND GAS

The sector is composed of 2 types of activities: the exploration and the distribution. The exploration activity is controlled by ENH (National Company of Hydrocarbons), a public company wholly owned by the government created in 1981. Its role consists in promoting and attracting investments for oil and gas exploration in Mozambique, appraising and developing the known natural gas reserves and putting together projects for the production and export of natural gas, as well as manage the sales of the resulting products. Indeed it possesses the monopoly in terms of exploration rights and can exercise these rights through joint-ventures with international investors. Privatization of ENH is being studied.

Distribution of petroleum products is carried out by various public and private companies, both national and foreign. A private procurement company owned by the Industry, Imopetro, manages all the petroleum imports. In fact it guarantees the supply of petroleum to all the companies within the country. The government has also established price structures for the sector.

Petroleum Exploration

There are currently no petroleum exploitations in Mozambique. All the country's needs are being covered by imports, which proceed principally from South Africa (40 per cent in 2000). The total imports of mineral combustibles amounted to 450,000 tonnes in 2001.

The Evolution of Consumption

Product	2000 Qty	2001 Qty
LPG	7780 (TM)	8622 (TM)
Diesel	334 288 (m-)	352 930 (m-)
Petrol	64 413 (m-)	94 722 (m-)
Jet A1 / Kerosene	117 852 (m-)	77 804 (m-)
Fuel	10 829 (m-)	16 863 (m-)

Source: Impetro

Natural Gas Exploration

Mozambique possesses several important reserves of natural gas throughout its territory. They are principally located in Pande (70 billion m2), Temane (30 billion m2) and Buzi (79 billion m2), and are currently poorly exploited. But the Government of Mozambique, ENH and Sasol signed in 2002 two contracts for the Pande and Temane gas fields and exploration acreage with a total value of $1.1 billion. A Petroleum Production Agreement was signed for the unified Pande and Temane gas reservoirs, together with a Production Sharing Agreement, which granted Sasol the rights to explore for hydrocarbons in the remaining acreage around the two fields. Today ENH and Sasol are partners in the development of the Pande and Temane reservoirs. The gas in these reservoirs will be dedicated to a gas sales agreement with Sasol Gas for on-selling to customers in Mozambique and South Africa. Sasol and the Government of Mozambique also agreed on the terms of a Pipeline Agreement. A subsidiary company of ENH, Sasol and iGas, a subsidiary of South Africa's Central Energy Fund, is building a pipeline from Temane to Ressano Garcia to take 120MGJ per annum to South African customers. Provision has also been made for the supply of gas to the Maputo Iron and Steel project (MISP), as well as the free transportation of a share of the Government's royalty gas to up to five points along the pipeline route. The gas pipeline terminates at Sasol's Secunda Petrochemical Complex, in South Africa. The project should be fully operational by June 2004.

Increasing Exploration

Thus explorations are being carried out, with Sasol in the unified Pande-Temane block, the American Company Wilrusco in the Inhaminga block and the Malasian Petronas in a joint-venture with ENH, finalizing an exploration and production contract for an offshore block in the Zambeze Delta.

In fact, in June 2002, Petronas, together with ENH was awarded the exploration and production contract for the offshore Zambezi Delta Block by the government of Mozambique. The Exploration Production Contract for the block was signed in Maputo, Mozambique between Petronas and ENH as partners, and Mozambique's Ministry of Mineral Resources and Energy. Under the terms of the EPC, Petronas, through its wholly owned subsidiary Petronas Carigali Mozambique E&P Limited, will hold an 85 percent interest in the block while ENH will own the remaining 15 percent interest. Petronas Carigali Mozambique has been designated the operator for the block. In the event of commercial discovery, ENH has the option to increase its participation up to 20 percent during the development and production phase of the block. The Zambezi Delta Block, covering an area of approximately 29,054 square kilometers, is located offshore of the Zambezi Delta in water depth of up to 2,000 meters. The basin within which the block is located has proven hydrocarbon system with discoveries of several onshore gas fields.

Therefore Mozambique's future in terms of oil and gas seems very promising and the structure and pace of its economic growth can drastically change with the development of these sectors. All the companies within both these sectors benefit of duty free imports and re-export for equipments and material used in their activity, an exemption from VAT, and a reduction of 25 per cent on the tax over revenues during the 8 first years of activity.

Distribution

Petromoc is the leading petroleum company in Mozambique. In fact it is the national gas and petroleum marketing and distribution company, and 80 per cent of the company is owned by the government and the remaining 20 per cent is owned by the company's employees. Actually the government is studying the possibility of reducing its involvement in the company in order to increase that of the private sector. Indeed in November 2001, the Government of Mozambique hired the IFC (International Finance Corporation), a multilateral institution, which promotes the development of the private sector, as lead advisor on the privatization of Petromoc. This privatization will be the first large-scale privatization in Mozambique and will, therefore, serve as role-model for further privatizations in strategic sectors of the economy. The gas and petroleum marketing and distribution sector is additionally composed of several private companies.

MARKET SHARE FOR 2001

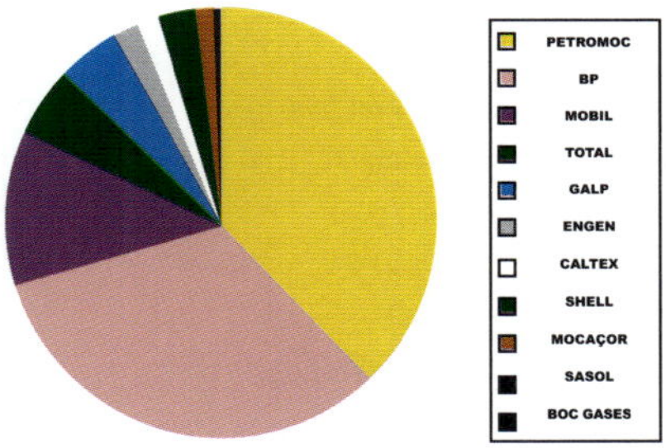

According to Imopetro, market shares in 2001 were as follows:

PETROMOC: 38,19%
BP: 32,19%
MOBIL: 11,45%
TOTAL: 5,03%
GALP (PETROGAL): 4,85%
ENGEN: 2,28%
CALTEX: 2,07%
SHELL: 2,03%
MOÇACOR: 1,42%
SASOL: 0,44%
BOC GASES: 0,05%

During the colonial times, there used to exist a refinery in Matola that produced 17000 barrels per day but it closed in 1984. Actually, Mozambique neither possesses refining infrastructures nor a petrochemical industry in the country. Nevertheless Sasol is planning to invest $1.7 billion project for the production of petrochemical products (methanol, diesel and derived products) in the city of Beira for the local and regional market. This project, "Complexo Petroquimico da Beira", should start sometime between 2004 and 2005.

MAIN COMPANIES

BP Moçambique, Lda

António Macamo, General Manager
Av. Mártires de Inhaminga, nº 170
P.O.Box 854, Maputo
Tel: + 258 - 1 - 325021 / 5
Fax: + 258 - 1 - 326042
E-mail: Antonio.macamo@mz.bp.com
Website: www.bp.com

BP Started operations in Mozambique in the 1920s and today it is the leading private sector oil company with 28% of the market share and a major industrial force in the emerging post-war economy. BP Mozambique is a fully owned subsidiary of BP - Amoco PLC, which is incorporated in the United Kingdom and managed by BP AFRICA - located in Cape Town, RSA. BP Moçambique is a Petroleum Marketing and Distribution company. It has 38 branded service stations located throughout the country and three ocean installations at the Mozambican port cities of Maputo, Beira and Nacala. The company controls eight airfield depots and supplies Jet A1 and aviation fuel at eight airports. In fact Air BP supplies the national airline for domestic flights and international carriers. Lubricants are also an important aspect of business for BP Mozambique, which has the largest market share. The company works with several major clients including CFM (Harbours and Railway Company), the Electricity Company (EDM) and Mozal (aluminium smelter). Finally the company has contracts to transit most of Zimbabwe's requirements of refined petroleum products and also services Malawi in this regard. Indicating growing confidence in the economy and an ongoing effort to align the company with the country's needs, BP Moçambique invests on average US$5 million per year in its marketing and distributing infrastructures. BP Moçambique is also actively developing its retail network along the Maputo Corridor, and the Beira Corridor into Zimbabwe. BP Moçambique differentiates itself from competition through the fact that they have been present in Mozambique for over 80 years and thus have extended experience and knowledge of the local culture and well-developed infrastructure. BP Moçambique has been able to provide services and products of a high standard in Mozambique throughout the years. Its staff, mostly Mozambican, is highly professional and represent the key factor in the multinational's success in Mozambique. Its objective is to keep the BP Moçambique's growth aligned with that of the country and to continuously contribute to the country economic and social development.

Caltex Oil (S.A.) (Pty) Limited

Joáo Sacadura Botte, Country Manager
Av. 25 de Setembro, nº 916, 2º Andar
Maputo
Tel: + 258 - 1 - 325061 / 3
Fax: + 258 - 1 - 427318
E-mail: caltexmz@virconn.com
Website: www.caltex.com

Caltex Oil (S.A.) (Pty) Limited is today a wholly owned subsidiary of Chevron Texaco. Its origins go as far back as 1914 when the Texas Company (S.A.) LTD established itself in Mozambique. It was changed to Caltex (Africa) LTD in 1941, Caltex Oil (S.A.) Limited in 1964 and Caltex Oil (S.A.) (Pty) Limited in 1972. Caltex Oil (S.A.) (Pty) Limited is a petroleum and lubricants marketing and distribution company. In fact Chevron Texaco, the world's fourth largest publicly held company in terms of oil and gas reserves, refines and markets its products in Southern and Eastern African under the Caltex brand. Today Caltex Oil (S.A.) (Pty) Limited owns two ocean terminals located in Maputo and Beira and has a 2,5% share in the refined fuel business and 6% share in lubricant sales in the domestic Mozambican Market. Chevron Texaco have named Caltex has a key strategic brand for Southern Africa. Caltex Oil (S.A.) (Pty) Limited through high quality products, efficient services and strong customer focus strives to continuously delight its customers. In 1981, as Mozambique became a central planned economy, Caltex Oil (S.A.) (Pty) Limited sold most of its assets to the newly created National Petroleum Company, Petromoc.

It continued to operate in transit trade and foreign marine bunker business. In 1997, Caltex Oil (S.A.) (Pty) Limited re-entered the domestic refined fuels and lubricants market after an absence of sixteen years.

To effectively grow within the Mozambican economy by focusing in the most strategic sectors in order to achieve its targets in terms of shareholder returns.

ENH - Empresa Nacional de Hidrocarbonetos de Moçambique E.P.

Issufo Abdula, Chairman
Av. Fernão Magalhães, 34
P.O.Box 4787, Maputo
Tel: + 258 - 1 - 429456 / 427634
Fax: + 258 - 1 - 324808
E-mail: iabdula@emh.co.mz
Website: www.emh.co.mz

ENH - Empresa Nacional de Hidrocarbonetos de Moçambique E.P (Public Company) results from the transformation of the old ENH National Company of Hydrocarbons, E.E. (State Owned Company) under the terms defined in the Decree Law n° 39/97 of 12 of November 1997. In fact the old ENH was created in 1982 with the mission of studying evaluating, appraising, and developing a project for the production and utilization of oil and natural gas. The transformation to the new ENH as seen today, a public company wholly owned by the government, came into effect on the 01 of January of 1998. Today ENH is the national gas and oil company which has the objective to promote and attract investments to the oil and gas exploration in Mozambique, appraise and develop the known natural gas reserves and put together a project for the production and export of natural gas, and manage the sales of the resulting products. In fact it promotes oil and gas exploration through joint ventures with international companies such as Petronas and Sasol. ENH also participates in major projects through the creation of specialized companies such as CMH SARL (Companhia Moçambicana de Hidrocarbonetos) and CMG SARL (Companhia Moçambicana de Gasoduto). Finally ENH offers specialized services within the oil and gas sector. Mozambique possesses very high potentials for both oil and gas production and many inland and offshore sites still remain to be explored. Indeed international companies have understood this potential and are now actively involved in developing these sectors in Mozambique. Today the country's second largest investment, namely the gas pipeline agreement between ENH and Sasol involving the Pande-Temane natural gas, is reaching its finalization stage and by 2004 will become operational. Potential is here, expectations are high and benefits extensive. Mozambique will benefit not only by expected substantial improvements in the economy, but it will also derive the benefits of jobs and other opportunities created by development of oil and gas exploration and exploitation.

ENH strives to successfully commit to its continued mission: promoting and exploring for oil and gas in the country and bringing forward the Pande-Temane natural gas mega-project.

Mobil Oil Moçambique Lda.

António de Almeida Catoja, Managing Director
Av. 25 de Setembro, 1725 - 2° Andar
P.O.Box 207, Maputo
Tel: + 258 - 1 - 307230 / 3
Fax: + 258 - 1 - 307232 / 4
E-mail: tony.a.catoja@exxonmobil.com

Mobil Oil has a long history in Mozambique. In fact its presence can be traced back to the beginning of the 1900s. Mobil Oil Moçambique Lda was created in 1992 and is today amongst the leading petroleum companies in the country. It is a fully owned subsidiary of ExxonMobil. Mobil Oil Moçambique has 6 branches in Mozambique with four branches in the Capital city Maputo, one in Beira and one in Matola. It has 13 service stations and 2 terminals. Mobil Oil Moçambique is a petroleum products marketing company and thus distributes and markets oils and lubricants. They are the third largest petroleum company in the country. Thanks to its relatively small size and its restraint number of clients it can offer very high quality services and products. Mobil Oil aims to grow on its focused market through investments and innovation. Mobil Oil Moçambique participates in the country economic development through its petroleum activities but also participates in its social development through several educational, health and community programs as well as in environmental education.

MOGÁS - Sociedade Moçambicana de Gases Comprimidos, S.A.R.L.

Eng. José Esteves, General Manager
Avenida de Moçambique N° 1870
Maputo
Tel: + 258 - 1 - 475058 / 195
Fax: + 258 - 1 - 475196
E-mail: mogas@mail.tropical.co.mz

Mogás finds its roots in the year 1954 in its sister company Angases, SARL, an Angolan company. Mogás was created in 1957 as a Portuguese family business. It produces and markets industrial and medical gases (Oxygen, Dissolved Acetylene, Carbon Dioxide, Argon, etc); it markets materials for the welding industry (autogenic, oxyacetylenic and electric); and produces and markets fire extinguishers. As the sole producer of this type of product in the country, Mogás has four industrial complexes in Maputo, Beira, Nacala and Tete. Growth areas for Mozambique are directly linked to the growth of the industrial and hospital sectors. One of the major achievements for Mogás is to be the only national producer of respiratory oxygen, and thus the only supplier of oxygen to the hospitals. Their future challenge is to combat the entrance of new competition from neighbouring countries into Mozambique.

Petromoc - Petróleos de Moçambique SARL

Mr. Casimiro Francisco, CEO
Praça dos Trabalhadores, n° 9
Maputo
Tel: + 258 - 1 - 427191 / 7
Fax: + 258 - 1 - 430181
E-mail: petro.casimiro@teledata.mz
Website: www.petromoc.co.mz

Petromoc - Petróleos de Moçambique SARL was created in January 1999. Its origins can be traced back to 1977 when Petromoc E.E. - Empresa Nacional de Petróleos de Moçambique was created from the integration of SONAP/SONAREP's activities and infrastructures. Today, the government owns 80% of the company and the remaining 20% is owned by the company's employees. The government is actually studying the possibility of reducing its involvement in the company in order to increase that of the private sectors. This process should end at the beginning of next year. Petromoc is the leading petroleum company in Mozambique and is the national petroleum marketing and distribution company. It commercialises oils and lubricants across the whole of Mozambique. In fact the company possesses 19 depots and a wide range of service stations across the country. The company is also involved in several related areas such as Gas development, transport, and pipelines as well as in other non-related strategic investments as for example in real estate. The company's overall mission is to continuously satisfy its customers needs with the best quality products and services, actively participate in the country's economic and social development, and constantly respect the environment. Thanks to its extensive infrastructure and commercial network, Petromoc covers the overall Mozambican territory including the major cities as well as the rural areas and small cities. Additionally Petromoc benefits of 26 years experience which is of great value in these parts of the world. Finally a major strength of the company is its labour force. Petromoc's strategy is to focus on the petroleum business and attract investments to benefit of the country's many opportunities. Through this Petromoc strives to increase its productivity and consequently grow nationally as well as internationally. Petromoc benefits of an image as a friendly, caring, open minded and socially responsible company, which represents the values of Mozambique. Petromoc has managed to create a very good and strong image of itself through the high quality of its products, services stations and management. The company has successfully grown over the year in terms of financial benefits as well as technical capacity and today it is positioned as the 4th company in the country. Petromoc strives to become a major player in the region and participate in the region's integration, economic and social development.

Total Moçambique SARL

Antoine Tournand, General Director
Matola Lingamo Parcela n° 729
CP 2073, Maputo
Tel: + 258 - 1 - 720015 / 404 / 407
Fax: + 258 - 1 - 720311 / 722342
E-mail: antoine.tournand@totalmozambique.co.mz

Total has a long history in Mozambique. Following the company's commitment to being present on the African continent, Total has established itself in Mozambique with a long-term vision. Total Moçambique SARL is fully owned by TotalFinaElf, the Multinational Petroleum Group. Total Moçambique SARL is a petroleum marketing company and thus it is fully dedicated to the distribution and marketing of its products. Through its 16 service stations spread throughout the country it distributes its oil, lubricants and other petroleum related products and carries out maintenance services. Additionally, Total Moçambique offers personalized services to individuals and groups with specific needs. Total Moçambique is still relatively small in Mozambique and thus possesses the capacity to react efficiently to sudden changes in the market and to successfully adapt its services to emerging needs. Also Total Moçambique benefits from the technical assistance of the TotalFinaElf Group presents in most of the neighbouring countries. Today, Total Moçambique might be relatively small but it is extremely innovative. In fact it has commercialised the unique prepaid TopCard, which offers an alternative payment method. As part of a socially responsible group, Total Moçambique is engaged in the social development of Mozambique. Indeed the company actively participates in the educational program "un Olhar de Esperança". Total Moçambique strives to maintain and strengthen its position in Mozambique, increase in coverage, and improve shareholder's return.

FINANCE

BANCO NACIONAL ULTRAMARINO
MOÇAMBIQUE
B789704
MIL ESCUDOS
BANCO DE MOÇAMBIQUE
1000
PAGÁVEL EM MOÇAMBIQUE
MIL ESCUDOS

OVERVIEW

Mozambique's financial sector is one of the most dynamic in the country. Since 1991 and 1992, the government has been putting in place a significant restructuring process in the country's financial system. In fact most of these restructuring processes are correlated with the National Action Plan for the Reduction of Absolute Poverty (PARPA) set up with the IMF.

Fiscal Policy, Tax Reform, and Public Expenditure Management

Fiscal policy in 2003 continued to support macroeconomic stability and the objective of reducing aid dependence in the medium term. The government's fiscal program in fact envisages a further increase in tax revenue relative to GDP, a slight increase in the domestic primary deficit, and a decline in the net indebtedness of the government with the banking system. At the same time, with no further outlays for bank re-capitalization - other than debt service on bonds already issued for this purpose - and lower external assistance, total government spending and the overall fiscal deficit after grants would both decline to 28.7 percent of GDP and 3.9 percent of GDP, respectively, in 2003.

Total revenue was projected at 14.3 percent of GDP in 2003. Tax receipts were expected to rise by 0.7 percentage point of GDP, with most of this increase accounted for by the new income tax introduced this year, while non-tax revenue would fall owing to lower receipts from privatisation and an expected decline in the recovery of non-performing loans. In addition, the government is confident that the smaller deductions envisaged in the new tax law will do more than compensate for any loss arising from the decision to reduce the rate of the corporate tax from 35 to 32 percent. Further administrative gains are also expected in VAT collections because of recent efforts to combat smuggling. These gains, however, will be partly offset by the impact on customs revenue of a reduction in the top import tariff rate from 30 percent to 25 percent. The government has taken all necessary steps to ensure that the new income tax law is fully applicable to incomes generated from January 1, 2003.

The fiscal program for 2003 envisaged an increase in the nominal wage bill of 25.8 percent relative to 2002 owing to an adjustment of 21 percent in the minimum wage effective April 1, 2003, which translates into an average wage increase of 17 percent for government employees; automatic promotions under the new career system; the hiring of 6,900 people in the PARPA priority areas of health, education, and security, which in line with current practices will be certified by the administrative tribunal; and full compensation of tax payments for those employees who became subject to the income tax this year. Because of the above, the wage bill is expected to rise to 7.6 percent of GDP in 2003, from 7.3 percent in 2002. The fiscal program also provides for an increase in spending on goods and services to 3.9 percent of GDP to meet the cost of opening new schools and health posts and the local elections scheduled for October 2003. Capital spending would fall by 11/2 percentage points of GDP, to 12.7 percent of GDP, largely because of a decline in external project financing, while net lending would decline by 4 percentage points of GDP owing mainly to the completion of the bank restructuring program and lower assistance to public entities. The domestic primary deficit would be contained at 3.7 percent of GDP in 2003.

Reforms are also continuing in tax administration. Key steps have been taken to ensure that the customs service keeps on operating effectively now that the three-year program of management support from Crown Agents expired in mid-2003.
Additionally the government is in the process of establishing a central revenue authority (Autoridade Tributária de

Moçambique) (ATM) that will comprise the Domestic Tax Administration Directorate (DNIA) and the General Directorate of Customs (DGA).

The government gives high priority to implementing the new financial administration system (SISTAFE), which is expected to play an important role in improving transparency and efficiency in the management of public resources.

Ministry of Finance

Fiscal revenues	1999	2000	2001	2002	2003
As percentage of GDP (real prices)	11.00%	12.10%	13.50%	13%	14.3%

Source: INE

Financial institutions (November 2003)

Commercial banks	10
Credit cooperatives	3
Financial location societies	3
Investment societies	2
Foreign exchange agencies	29
Stock exchange	1

BANKING

At independence, the Bank of Mozambique (BM) was created as the new central bank on 17 May 1975 by transforming the former Portuguese Central Bank, the Banco Nacional Ultramarino. The government nationalized all but one of the remaining banks on 31 December 1977. Four banks were merged into BM and two were merged to form the People's Development Bank (Banco Popular de Desenvolvimento, BPD); only Banco Standard Totta de Moçambique (BSTM) remained private. The BM became the only bank that could deal in foreign exchange on 1 September 1978. It was the treasury, central bank, the controller of the execution of the state plan, and a commercial bank.

With the reforms of the public sector and the economy in general which started in 1987 with the PRE (Economic Rehabilitation Program), the banking sector was liberalized and in 1992, through the law n°1/92, BM was declared Central Bank and separated from its commercial branch which became Banco Comercial de Moçambique (BCM).

BM introduced the Inter bank Money Market (MMI) in 1997. This was an important step in making the indirect instruments for monetary control operational. In addition to the commercial banks lending each other liquidity, the central bank conducts open market operations on the MMI. Treasury bills and securities of the Bank of Mozambique itself are traded on this market.

There is also an Inter-bank Foreign Exchange Market (MCI), supervised by the central bank, where foreign exchange operations are transacted among the commercial banks, bureaus de changes and other economic agents, with significant volumes of translations in foreign exchange.

Since 1992, the government has pursued its aims of creating a strong and dynamic private banking sector. International donors, notably the World Bank, have been supporting the government of Mozambique to resolve some financial difficulties in the banking sector and reduce the government's role in the financial sector, opening it up to private participation. The sector has been steadily growing although it went through a certain period of crisis during the years 2000- 2001 following the insolvency of the two privatized banks due to extensive non-performing loans made to politically connected individuals and then inherited with privatization in the late 1990s.

Nevertheless the Credit Institution Law (1991), the liberalization of interest rates (1994), the privatization of financial institutions (1996-1997) and the start of the use of indirect control instruments by the central bank, among other mechanisms, were determinant to the sophistication and competitiveness of the banking industry and even the modernization of the payment system. With the ongoing important steps that are being taken to improve the different banks' financial positions and their operational efficiency monitored closely, the industry is growing and practices are reaching international standards. In fact the government has remained committed to implementing International Accounting Standards (IAS) for banking institutions, a complex process that will be carried out gradually and will require substantial technical assistance. Indeed by end-July 2003, BM had identified training requirements for its staff and assessed the next steps to implement IAS, including the establishment of a steering committee with representation from the BM, audit firms, and the commercial banks, in line with recommendations made by the Financial Sector Assessment Program (FSAP) mission.

"The goal is to promote competitiveness in the financial sector with a view to cutting costs and to maintaining a spread between interest on loans and on deposits at the level recommended by international practice"

Governor of the Central Bank of Mozambique, Adriano Maleiane

The sector remains dynamic and continues to show traces of nominal growth, although with decreasing rates when compared to previous years.

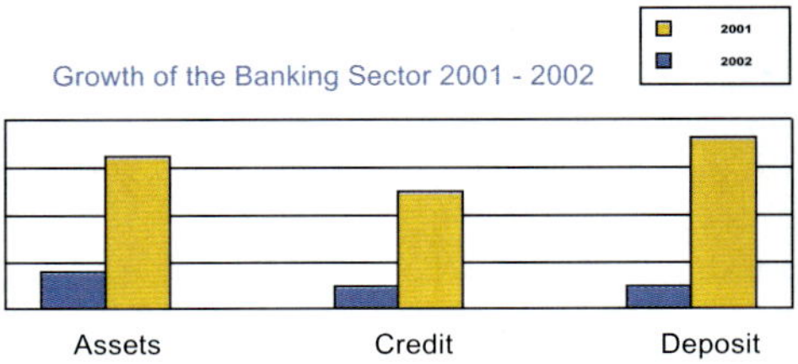

Source: Top 100, KPMG (2001)

Banking activity, in terms of volume assets, registered for the period 2001/2002 a growth of 10.99 per cent, reaching about 1.34 billion US dollars, which was mainly financed by an increase in clients' resources both in domestic and foreign currencies. This compared with a 34 per cent growth in 2001 - but much of that merely reflected the sharp devaluation (by about 36 per cent) of the metical against the US dollar that year.

The sector's activity measured by volume of deposits showed an increase during 2002, although at a lower rate then 2001. The total deposits in domestic currency increased by 12.7 per cent (39 per cent in 2001). Emphasis is made of the 20 per cent growth of local currency deposits, and the nominal 6.4 per cent growth deposits in foreign currencies.

The gross credit in the economy was 13,738 MM MZM at the end of 2002, 721 MM MZM more than the previous year, which implies a growth of 5.56 per cent (27.59 per cent in 2001). Credits in local currency have decreased by 10.3 per cent, while credits in foreign currency have increased by 14.2 per cent. In fact the reduced appreciation of the dollar and the high interest rates for credits in local currency are the reasons for the increased appetite for credit in foreign currency.

There are various opportunities within the banking sector especially in terms of rural development as the government has set priorities to increase the banking sector's coverage of rural areas.

Banco Standard Totta

CAPITAL MARKET

The Mozambican capital market is still young and reflects the economy, which is still in a consolidation phase. Financial Markets started being liberalized in 1991 and only in 1999 with the approbation of the Law of Credit Institutions and Financial Corporate was there sufficient conditions for the creation of the Mozambican Stock Exchange. Indeed Mozambique's first stock exchange, the "Bolsa de Valores de Moçambique" (BVM) started operating on the 14th of October 1999. It was successfully launched with the support of the Lisbon Stock Exchange and the World Bank. Today the Bank of Mozambique acts as the supervising institution, and the stock exchange remains under the control of the Ministry of Planning and Finance.

Four years after it was opened, BVM counts with five companies (Banco Internacional de Moçambique; Banco Standard Totta; Telecomunicações de Moçambique; Cimentos de Moçambique; Cervejas de Moçambique). The Stock exchange activities are based mainly on treasures Bills transactions and only one of the five companies, namely Cervejas de Moçambique, is a listed company but others are to come. The capital base requirement for listing is $1.5 million (down from the initial proposed $3 million, because of Mozambique's fragile private sector). Government bonds of nearly US$5 million were launched in May 1999. In the first phase, the bonds will be reimbursed in three years at varied interest rates and also adjusted to the re-discount rate of the Central Bank.

After a weak performance on the first two years, the Mozambican Stock exchange is assisting a light improvement in its activities and in the accumulated negotiated values.

The Mozambique Stock Exchange proposes world-class services and is equipped with the lasted telecommunication technology. At the moment it is carrying out a extensive marketing, education and training campaigns throughout the country in other to promote the benefits of the stock exchange for private companies as well as for individual investors. In fact the Stock Exchange is studying the possibility of opening in the near future a second market. The "Bolsa de Valores de Moçambique" is proud to have successfully developed in such a short time and to have become self-sufficient. Today it has a Market Capitalization of $123 millions, which demonstrate the amplitude it has acquired. At the moment it is working for the introduction of "pension funds". But Mozambique still has many major companies that can be listed on the stock exchange and thus the major challenge facing BVM is to effectively promote the benefits these companies can gain. Also Mozambican companies have specific organizational structure and needs, and thus BVM has to adequately adapt itself to their needs.

INSURANCE

The Mozambican insurance legislation is mostly inspired by the Portuguese Law. Insurance in Mozambique was nationalised in 1977, with the creation of a state owned monopoly called Empresa Moçambicana de Seguros (EMOSE). Although insurance was de-monopolised in 1991, EMOSE still remains the leading company with around 45 per cent of the market. This share however, is gradually shrinking due to increasing competition. There are five insurance companies operating in Mozambique, writing a combined gross premium income (GPI). In 1999, following strong pressure from the sector's companies, the Instituto Geral de Seguros was created as the sector's regulatory body. It is composed by the different insurance companies and depends on the Minister of Planning and Finance. Today there are five insurance companies operating in Mozambique, writing a combined premium income (GPI) of around $30 million. Ranked by non-life market share, the companies are as follows: EMOSE, Seguradora Internacional De Moçambique (SIM), CGSM, Hollard, and Moçambique Companhia de Seguros (MCS). The latter two entered the market during mid-to-late 2001.

MARKET SHARE FOR 2002

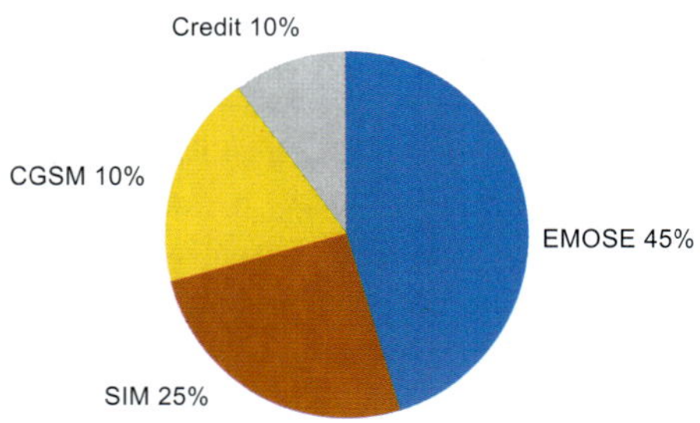

Source: KPMG

Insurance activities are controlled by the Inspector General of Insurance (IGS), established in 1999. A new law was passed by the parliament in June 2003. Key issues in this new law include the separation of life and non-life operations, the introduction of compulsory motor insurance dealing with third party injury and property damage, consumer protection and solvency requirements (these have not been set as yet). A levy of 1.5 per cent of premium is payable to the IGS by the licensed insurers.

Brokers play an important role in facilitating insurance in Mozambique. There are currently 13 licensed insurance brokers, many of these with Portuguese, South African and local shareholders. However, brokers are aggrieved by the high transactional administration fees charged by the insurers, ranging from 15 per cent to 20 per cent, on top of risk rates and surcharges (1.5 per cent levy and 5 per cent stamp duty). This effectively adds 27.5 per cent to the base risk premium.

The average reinsurance premium cession for the industry was around 31 per cent in 2001, up from 14 per cent in 1999. Participating re-insurers include Munich Re of Africa, Swiss Re Southern Africa and African Re Mozambique is also a member of African Re (BBB+ internationally rated)

Overall, the insurance sector has been showing significant growth in revenue. In 2001 it reported a real growth of 4.4 per cent. In real terms, the total premium charged in 2001 rose to 719.8 billion meticais. Additionally EMOSE continued to lead the sector with revenue estimated at 436 billion meticais, more than 70 per cent increase from the previous year. In 2000, the insurance industry's contribution to GDP was 0.03 per cent, compared to around 17 per cent for South Africa.

Indeed Mozambique's insurance industry still has an important growth potential as cultural constraints are decreasing with the significant flow of information and education put in place these last few years. The majority of the operators in the sector have adopted "niche" strategies with the objective of reaching specific segments, through the introduction of new products or development of existing ones The recent entry in the market of new players sends confidence signals on the existence of potentially attractive market segments. In fact potentials are strong in short-term products related to education, marriage and funeral, which are areas of considerable costs to African families.

MAIN COMPANIES

ABC - African Banking Corporation (Moçambique) SARL

Zandile M. Chireshe, Managing Director
Prédio 33 Andares, 1st floor - Av. 25 do Setembro, 1230 Maputo
Tel: + 258 - 1 - 306700
Fax: + 258 - 1 - 306305
E-mail: zmchireshe@africanbankingcorp.com

The bank started operating in the year 2000. It was created as a joint-venture between BNP and Nedbank but was then sold to ABC Holdings Limited in August 2002. The major shareholder is ABC Holdings Limited, which has a primary listing on the Botswana's and a secondary listing on the Zimbabwe's stock exchange. ABC offers a wide range of financial services to its clients: Corporate Banking; Structured Trade Finance; Private Banking; Treasury; International Banking; Investment Banking. Growth areas for Mozambique are centred in large corporations and as Mozambique opens up, the bank will continue to focus on providing efficient and innovative banking services to its customers. In terms of products, ABC plans to increase its activities in investment banking, corporate banking and trade finance. As a group, ABC strives to enter key markets in Africa in order to become the premier pan-African bank. ABC's quality of service, the provision of advisory services for investing in Mozambique, and exchange control have been outstanding and have gained a good reputation in the market. ABC prides itself in offering World Class Financial Solutions for Africa thanks to the international skills and the local knowledge of its Human Resources. ABC will continue assuming the leadership role in helping develop the market to world-class standards, whilst taking into account their customer needs and objectives. This will be achieved in partnership with local industry and other stakeholders.

Austral Consultoria e Projectos Lda

António A. Matos, Chairman
Predio 33 Andares - 3°
P.O.Box 2242, Maputo
Tel: + 258 - 1 - 322780
Fax: + 258 - 1 - 307369
E-mail: austral@austral.co.mz or amatos@austral.co.mz
Website: www.austral.co.mz

Austral Consultoria e Projectos Lda is part of the greater Austral Group, which was established in 1986 with the creation of Sociedade Austral de Desenvolvimento. Austral Consultoria e Projectos was created in 1991 and is today one of the leading enterprises in Mozambique. Austral Consultoria e Projectos provides a wide range of complementary consulting services such as Project Management, Human Resources Development, Transport & Communications Services, Socio-Economic Analysis, Environmental Studies, Market Research, Conferences and Seminars Organization. Additionally they provide ISO certification services and were the first company to propose such services in the country. Finally Austral Consultoria e Projectos is also actively involved in social projects of great importance such as the information and prevention on HIV/AIDS. Although its main client is the government and indirectly international donors for whom they manage socio-economic development projects, Austral Consultoria e Projectos offers invaluable support to investors in their investment making process. They are present in various countries of the region but are truly specialized in the Mozambican and Angolan markets. Austral Consultoria e Projectos benefits from years of African knowledge and experience, highly trained and motivated staff. Unlike most of their competitors, they are present in the whole of the country and thus offer a unique and efficient option for projects in remote areas of Mozambique. Their actual strategy is to concentrate on their current activities in order to continuously improve their services. Austral Consultoria e Projectos is proud to have developed a very good local capacity within its team. Indeed it is the only truly Mozambican consulting company that offers world-class services. Austral Consultoria e Projectos strives to maintain and strengthen its current position. It will concentrate on consolidating and growing its current activities.

BCI - Banco Comercial e de Investimentos, SARL

Abdul Magid Osman, Chairman of the Board
Av. 25 de setembro, Prédio John Orr's, n° 1465
CP 4745, Maputo
Tel: + 258 - 1 - 307777
Fax: + 258 - 1 - 307152
E-mail: amagide@bci.co.mz
Website: www.bci.co.mz

BCI - Banco Comercial e de Investimentos, SARL resulted from a joint venture between a Mozambican Group of Investors and a Portuguese banking institution. In Fact BCI, whose board is headed by former Mozambican Finance Minister (1986 - 1991) Abdul Magid Osman, has as its main shareholder the Portuguese state bank, the Caixa Geral de Depositos (CGD) which has been widely acknowledged as Portugal's leading banking institution for 127 years. BCI's mission is to be a major player in the financial, economic and social development process of Mozambique and to become a sustainable institution, which generates sustainable shareholder value. BCI, as a Commercial and Investment Bank, offers Universal Banking services. This means it offers a whole range of banking services normally restricted to merchant banks, commercial banks and governmental banks. Nevertheless BCI's main business activity is located in retail banking. In terms of geographical location, BCI covers most of the country. The likely merger in the near future between the Fomento Bank (BF) and BCI demonstrates the bank's will to grow. In fact, since its creation BCI has gone through organic growth. Today, having reached a significant size, they are starting to focus on external growth and through the merger, BCI will become the country's second largest banking institution. Their vision is to become the country's best bank, especially in terms of services and customer satisfaction. In its few years of activity, BCI has become a solid bank with a very high reputation and trust from its customers. Today it possesses 15% of the market. Additionally BCI formalized its commitment to social responsibility at a ceremony in Maputo in June 2003 by signing on to the Global Compact, an initiative by UN Secretary-General Kofi Annan that asks businesses and other organizations to support principles related to human rights, labour and the environment. The bank's growth will naturally depend on the economic growth of Mozambique but BCI strives to improve its performance and obtain assets of $1 billion in the next 10 years.

BIM - Banco Internacional de Moçambique

João Figueiredo, Vice - President
Av. 25 de Setembro, n° 1800
P.O.Box 865, Maputo
Tel: + 258 - 1 - 307512
Fax: + 258 - 1 - 303795
E-mail: Joao.Figueiredo@bim.co.mz
Website: www.mundobim.co.mz

Banco Internacional de Moçambique was created in 1995 through a joint venture between Banco Comercial Português (BCP), the biggest financial group in Portugal, and local partners including the Mozambican Government, EMOSE (Empresa Moçambicana de Seguros), INSS (National Institute of Social Security), and FDC (Foundation for Community Development). In 2000, BCP became the major shareholder of another Mozambican Bank, namely the Banco Comercial de Moçambique. Later on the two giants decided to unite and this gave birth, in November 2001, to the new Banco International de Moçambique, which became the biggest financial institution in Mozambique. Consequently the BIM Group was created, which includes the bank as well as a number of complementary and specialized subsidiary companies. Today BCP - Internacional II, Sociedade Unipessoal, SGPS, Lda owns 66.69 per cent of the bank's Social Capital, the Mozambican Government 23.13 per cent, INSS 4.95 per cent, EMOSE 4.15 per cent, and FDC 1.08 per cent. BIM is currently the leading bank in Mozambique and the BIM Group, the leading financial institution. The BIM Group is composed of Banco Internacional de Moçambique (BIM) the country's biggest bank; Seguradora Internacional de Moçambique (SIM), the leading insurance company, BIM Investimento, the only investment bank in Mozambique; BIM Leasing, a leading leasing company; NovoBanco, a major micro-finance bank; CrediCar (ALD), a long term credit company. All of this gives the BIM Group the possibility to offer to its clients a wide range of specialized and complementary services and products. Today the group's effective cross-selling strategy allows it to constantly satisfy its clients' demands while being cost effective. Focusing on the banking sector, BIM offers an extensive array of personalized services. In fact it has successfully segmented the market into four different activity lines: BIM Expresso for low-income individuals; BIM Particulares & Empresas for middle income individuals and companies; BIM Private for high income individuals; and BIM Corporate for major companies. Through this segmentation, BIM is able to effectively cover the whole of the market and satisfy the different needs of its clients. The bank's network is spread throughout the whole country and connected to an online system. Through its various companies, the BIM Group benefits of economies of scale and scope. Its strategy is based on an effective cross-selling of its different services and products. Additionally the BIM Group is strongly focused on continuously improving its offerings through innovation and technology. Today it offers an extensive network of ATMs and POS throughout Mozambique, Internet Banking services, and correspondent banks throughout the world. Indeed, the BIM Group is the engine behind the financial sector's development. The BIM Group truly contributes to the modernization and development of the financial system and the Mozambican economy. Through its constant efforts to improve its services and products, it is encouraging the entire country to move forward. The BIM Group is proactively working in order to maintain and strengthen its position as the leading financial group n Mozambique. It is here to serves its clients needs, as well as to participate in the country's economic and social development by offering world-class services to national and foreign investors.

BVM - Bolsa de Valores de Moçambique

Jussub Nurmamade, C.E.O
Av. 25 de Setembro, n° 1230, 5°Andar, Block 5
Maputo
Tel: + 258 - 1 - 308826 / 8
Fax: + 258 - 1 - 310559
E-mail: jussub@bvm.co.mz
Website: www.bvm.co.mz

Mozambique's first stock exchange, the "Bolsa de Valores de Moçambique" started operating on the 14th of October 1999. It was successfully launched with the support of the Lisbon Stock Exchange and the World Bank.

Today the Bank of Mozambique acts as the supervising institution, and the stock exchange remains under the control of the Ministry of Planning and Finance. The stock exchange started operating with 2 sessions per week. Today this has increased to 3 sessions per week. It also started with one government bond and today it proposes 9 security leases. Various companies from the telecommunication, cement, financial and industrial sectors are now listed on the stock exchange. The capital base requirement for listing is $1.5 million (down from the initial proposed $3 million, because of Mozambique's fragile private sector). The Mozambique Stock Exchange proposes world-class services and is equipped with the lasted telecommunication technology. At the moment it is carrying out a extensive marketing, education and training campaigns throughout the country in other to promote the benefits of the stock exchange for private companies as well as for individual investors. In fact, the Stock Exchange is studying the possibility of opening in the near future a second market. The "Bolsa de Valores de Moçambique" is proud to have successfully developed in such a short time and to have become self-sufficient. Today it has a Market Capitalization of $123 Million which demonstrate the amplitude it has acquired. At the moment it is working for the introduction of "pension funds". Mozambique still has many major companies that can be listed on the stock exchange and thus the major challenge facing BVM is to effectively promote the benefits these companies can gain. Also Mozambican companies have specific organizational structures and needs and thus BVM has to adequately adapt itself to their needs.

CGSM - Companhia Geral de Seguros de Moçambique

Piet Nel, General Manager
Rua de Imprensa, 183 - R/C
Caixa Postal N°2659, Maputo
Tel: + 258 - 1 - 313280 / 9
Fax: + 258 - 1 - 313291
E-mail: pnel@cgsm.co.za

Companhia Geral de Seguros de Moçambique (CGSM) was registered as an insurer in 1992. The company is registered as a joint stock company (S.A.R.L), with a maximum shareholder liability equal to vested share capital. The holding company is CGSM Holdings, a limited liability company in South Africa. After having been part of the Truck & General Holdings from 1995 to 2001, CGSM Holding was purchased in 2001 by RWA Lewis, which now holds 98.4% of the Company. Today CGSM is one of the dominant insurers in the local market with 25% of the market share. Although CGSM is licensed to transact both short term and life insurance, the company is predominantly a short-term insurer. The bulk of its business is sourced from the corporate market, which includes the large multinationals and several large parastatals. CGSM has more recently branched out into personal insurance, life insurance and also offers bank assurance products to the Mozambican market. CGSM has offices in both Maputo and Beira. CGSM has competitive advantages in the high quality of its services and the modern IT system. Additionally, CGSM benefits from a very strong South African backing. For CGSM its main assets are its people and its services. All of this is reflected in the new rating CGSM has received this year. In fact CGSM is now rated as an A- company, previously being a BBB+ company. Today CGSM, which remains a young and dynamic player in the Mozambican market, strives to actively participate in the industry's overall development by creating effective regulative institutions and putting in place an up-to-date legal framework. Recently CGSM has managed to create a very strong and positive image of its services characterized by its professionalism. Also CGSM has been carrying out an extensive training programme for its employees as well as the industry as a whole. Definitively CGSM is having an important role in Mozambique economic and social development.

Insurance in Mozambique is primarily broker driven and CGSM has effectively gained a high level of broker acceptance. Therefore in order to continue on this successful trend the company strives to increase its market share. Also CGSM is actively studying the possibility of diversifying its services into other insurance related areas such as pension funds.

Ernst & Young Moçambique

Ibraimo Ibraimo, Managing Partner
Rua Belmiro Obadias Muianga, N° 179
C.P. 366, Maputo
Tel: + 258 - 1 - 353000 / 324043
Fax: + 258 - 1 - 321984
E-mail: ern.young@teledata.mz
Website: www.ey.com

Ernst & Young started its operations in Mozambique in 1991 with two employees, Dr. Ibraimo Ibraimo, the actual Managing Partner, being one of them. The company first only offered Audit services but as it grew, it expanded its range of services. Ernst & Young is a market leader in Mozambique providing professional services and a strong contribution to the Mozambican economy. They have a labour force which is composed of 90% Mozambicans and 10% foreigners. In the near future, Ernst & Young Mozambique will be fully owned by Ernst & Young Global. Ernst Young Mozambique provides the following services: Auditing; Management Consulting; Financial Consulting; Corporate tax, legal and human resource services. Ernst & Young Mozambique offers high quality services that outmatch the competition. In order to continuously fulfil all the market needs and to contribute to the country's economic development, they constantly invest in developing new products, which are adapted to the market demands. Ernst & Young Mozambique responds quickly and successfully to its clients needs, delivering value that their clients care about. Ernst & Young is very proud of the market share and reputation it has acquired in Mozambique. They are market leaders. Ernst & Young Mozambique strives to pro-actively support the country's economic development and institutional reforms.

Ernst & Young building in Maputo

GAPI SARL

António Souto, Chief Executive Officer
Rua de Mukumbura, n°434
Maputo
Tel: + 258 - 1 - 491505
Fax: + 258 - 1 - 491827
E-mail: fasouto@gapi.co.mz

In 1984, the Friedrich Ebert Foundation (FEF) from Germany started a small project for the promotion of small industries in order to stimulate local economic development. This project became known in Portuguese abbreviation as GAPI: "Gabinete de Consultoria e Apoi à Pequena Industria". As Mozambique switched to a market oriented economy, the government realized the importance of developing national entrepreneurship and the private sector through small and medium sized enterprises and thus the project was transformed into a financial institution. Therefore GAPI Limitada was created in 1990. In 1999, GAPI was officially and legally registered as a joint-stock company: GAPI SARL. Its equity capital is held by two main shareholders: the Friedrich Ebert Foundation and the Ministry of Planning and Finance. GAPI is a small investment company. Its objective is to foster economic development through the promotion of small and medium enterprises as well as strengthening micro-finance institutions. GAPI wants to achieve this objective through a combination of financial services, business development services (BDS), and technical assistance. GAPI is also a second-tier banking institution. Their main financial products are loans to SMEs, wholesale credits for micro-credit institutions (MFIs), and venture capital. These services are complemented with business and management training services. GAPI provides its services through its 6 regional offices spread out through the country. GAPI aims low income markets in all sectors. They provide SMEs with the necessary basic services for them to launch themselves and grow to become the basis of Mozambique's future sustainable economic and social development. In fact GAPI continuously reinvests all of its benefits into its activity. GAPI plays the intermediary between investments and local SMEs. GAPI is a financial institution with a human face. GAPI has contributed to the economic and social development of Mozambique and has proven to the world that developing SMEs is possible in Mozambique. GAPI strives to increase its activity as a wholesaler in order to expand its financial services, as well as to reinforce its decentralization process, all of this with the objective to contribute more strongly to the growth of the low income markets in Mozambique.

Novo Banco SARL
Banco de Microfinanças

Koen Wasmus, General Manager
Av. Olof Palme, n° 112
Maputo
Tel: + 258 - 1 - 313344
Fax: + 258 - 1 - 313345
E-mail: novobanco@teledata.mz

Small and very small enterprises in Mozambique lack access to formal financial services of all kinds and thus two thirds of Mozambique's population are unable to development any kind of business. Consequently IMI (Internationale Micro Investitionen AG), the IFC (International Finance Corporation), the FMO (Nederlandse Financierings-Maatchappij voor Ontwikkelingslanden NV), and Stichting DOEN-Postcodeloterij/Sponsorloterij, together with the largest Mozambican bank, Banco International de Moçambique (BIM), and the State of Mozambique through its housing development fund, Fundo de Fomento da Habitação (F.F.H.), resolved in 1999 to found NovoBanco, a bank created specifically to meet the needs of micro and small enterprises, and thereby to contribute to the rebuilding of

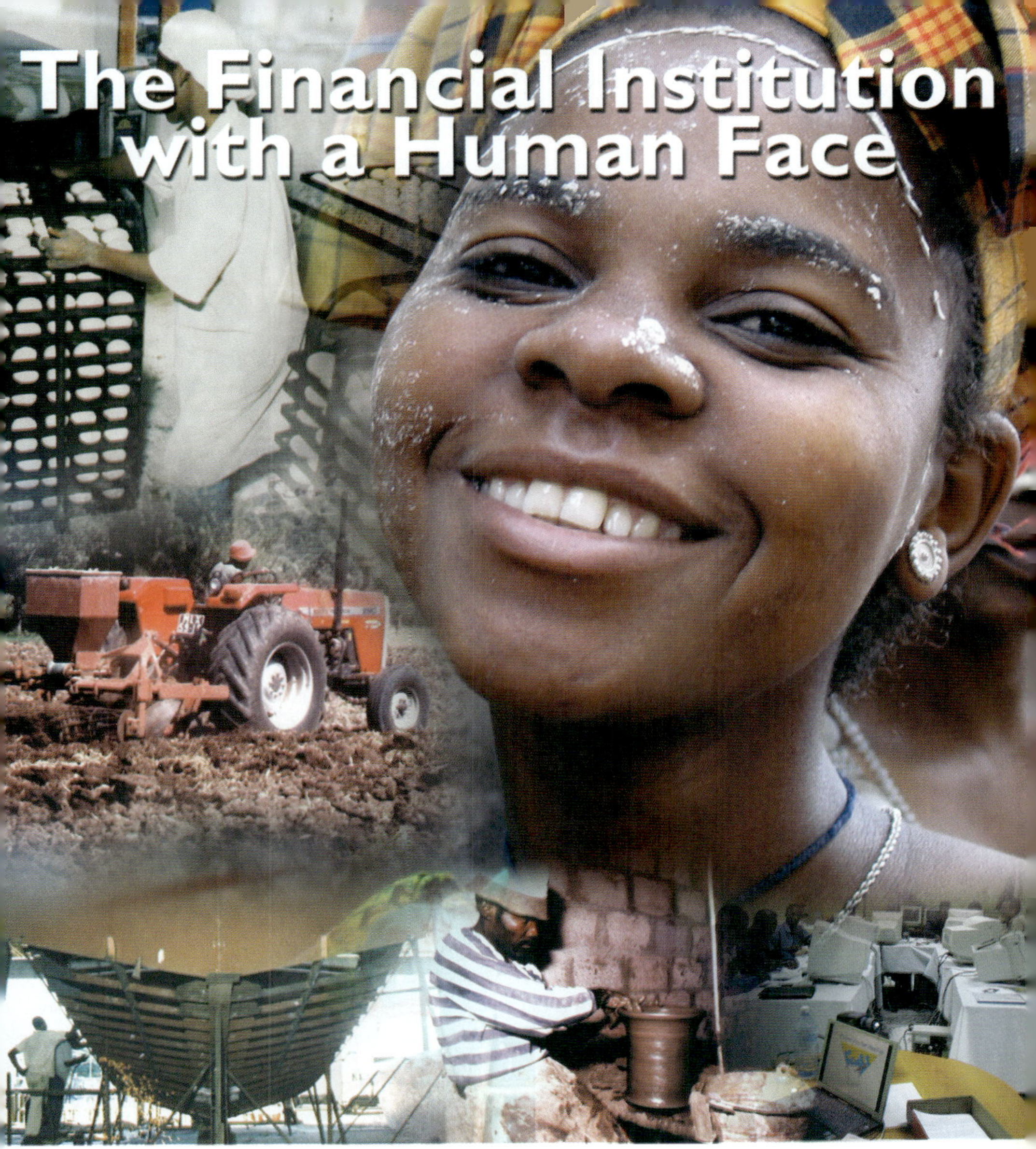
The Financial Institution with a Human Face

Mozambique's economy, to the development of its financial market and to the reduction of poverty levels. NovoBanco differs from the micro-finance organisations that have previously been active in Mozambique in that it is a commercial bank. As such, it is explicitly profit-oriented. NovoBanco began operations in November 2000 and today is the leading micro-finance bank in Mozambique. NovoBanco provides loans, which in 94% of all cases, do not exceed USD 1,000. The vast majority of these loans have been provided to traders and small trading enterprises. Also in November 2001, NovoBanco began to introduce deposit facilities. The bank now has six branches, with four in Maputo, one branch in Beira and one in Nampula. NovoBanco offers flexible and efficient financial services that meet the specific demands of each individual client. In fact NovoBanco's services are accessible and have a human touch. Thanks to the vast network its partners operate and the resulting experience, NovoBanco can effectively and continuously adapt itself to the needs of its customers. The objective now is to become a fully commercial bank characterized with a wide range of financial services. Small and very small enterprises are the basis for true economic and social development, notably in Mozambique, which remains one of the poorest countries in the world. NovoBanco therefore plays a significant role in reducing poverty levels in the country. NovoBanco aims to become a full service bank for the low-income segment of the Mozambican population.

União Comercial de Bancos (Moçambique) SARL

Robert Cantin, General Manager
Av. Friedrich Engels, n° 400
Maputo
Tel: + 258 - 1 - 481900 / 499900
Fax: + 258 - 1 - 498675
E-mail: robert.cantin@ucbmoz.co.mz
Website: www.mcb.co.mu

União Comercial de Bancos (Moçambique) SARL (UCB) was created on the 16th of August 1999. UCB is part of the Mauritius Commercial Bank Group, which is the leading banking institution in the region, with activities in the Reunion Island, Mayotte, the Seychelles, Madagascar and Mozambique and is represented in Paris. The Mauritius Commercial Bank Group possesses 81.25% of the bank and Proparco possesses the remaining 18.75%. UCB is a leading bank in Mozambique and is actually ranked number one in terms of return on investments.
UCB is a Corporate Bank, which offers a wide range of financial services. As part of an international group, UCB clients are very diversified in term of size and sectors. Indeed UCB selects its clients according to strict criteria enabling it to assure itself an effective customer relationship. Since 1999, UCB's activities have constantly grown. UCB benefits from a very large network, which expands through Europe, with partners such as the Société Générale & the Lloyd's Bank, and the Indian Ocean region, with the Mauritius Commercial Bank Group. UCB offers very high quality services and a different approach to business. In fact UCB strives to remain specialized, effective and flexible in order to continuously meet its customers' needs. The banks final objectives are to effectively grow, promote and facilitate investments, participate in the economic and social development of Mozambique, and constantly improve shareholder returns. In its few years of activity in Mozambique, UCB has managed to make a name for itself and gain a significant share of its market. It has become a leading banking institution in the country and has continuously improved its results over the years. Thanks to its strict client criteria, UCB has managed to avoid bad debts. Although results for the banking sector depend on the economic activity of Mozambique, UCB is certain it will keep on improving its activities over the years.

INDUSTRY & TRADE

OVERVIEW

Mozambique's industrialization process started in the early 1890s with the entry of concessionary companies through British Investment capital. Industries mainly appeared because of the necessity to process agricultural products like sugar cane, coconut, cotton, tea and sisal for export. It is only after 1914 that Portuguese industries started to develop.

From 1960 to 1974 Mozambican industries was at its highs. The country had a well-developed petroleum industry, steel foundries, and alcohol and plastics production facilities, just to name a few. In fact in 1973 Mozambique was considered the eighth most important industrial country of Africa, producing 4 percent of the continent's total production.

It is important to note that under the Portuguese colonial rule it was forbidden to develop industries, which could threaten the Portuguese industrial system. In fact Mozambique had to remain a market for Portuguese exports and as a consequence, the country's industry concentrated on the basic transformation of raw materials, which would then be exported to Portugal to be processed.

Mozambique's industrial system suffered a great blow with the independence in 1975. It is estimated that 185 000 of the 200 000 Portuguese inhabitants, about 90% of the Portuguese population in Mozambique, left the country in less than a year. This led to great problems as the factories felt short of skilled workers. Consequently most factories found themselves in the incapacity to function effectively and many closed down.

In an effort to rescue the failing industrial system, the government of Mozambique launched itself in an extensive nationalization of production capacities in the country. The government introduced its own management system and Mozambique became a centrally planned economy. However, production and productivity never regained the pre-independence levels.

Total Production and Trade Indexes 1973-86 (billion dollars)

	1973	1974	1977	1981	1986
Total production	4.353	3.755	2.322	2.346	1.411
Agriculture	1.440	1.306	0.960	0.866	0.630
Industry and fishery	1.634	1.429	0.867	0.950	0.378
Transports	0.467	0.449	0.217	0.251	0.101
Exports	0.226	0.296	0.153	0.280	0.079
Imports	0.465	0.460	0.336	0.801	0.543

Source: National statistic institute

The Mozambican situation was worsened by two interrelated factors. The beginning of the civil war that led to the destruction of many factories and the fall of production of raw material, and the decision by the Mozambican authorities to end all relations with the South African Apartheid regime which led to the loss of the country's main technical material and equipment supplier as well as its main export market.

In the mid 80s the situation started to change. In fact in 1984, with the recommendation of the IMF (International Monetary Fund) the government introduced the Program for Economic Rehabilitation (PRE) also called "Programa de Reabilitação Economica" which would accelerate the economic recovery of the country. This program was composed of a package of measures such as the gradual liberalization of the economy, the review of price and exchange mechanisms, and the privatisation of production facilities owned by the government. Additionally in 1987 relations with South Africa were re-established. Finally the PRE program was fostered with the peace agreement between the rebels and the government in 1992, which brought some confidence to national and international investors.

Consequently foreign direct investment inflows (FDI) strongly increased. From 1990 to 2001, they increased from approximately 21 millions to 925 millions.

The government is fostering measures to create a more favourable environment for national and foreign investments. Indeed the government has developed a favourable tax regime with tax exemptions and Industrial Free Zone, for export-oriented industries, where, in addition to other advantages, the investment is exempt from VAT and custom taxes on the import of inputs.

Foreign investors have responded favourably to this new economic environment and the country has experienced a huge increase of national and foreign investment.

"The shorter the process, the more simplified it is, the better benefit for the economy. What we have been trying to do, through a governmental program, is to make the legal system much easier. Thus to create a company, we are going to establish a 'one stop shop' facility. You can get in one shop everything: certificates, import authorization cards, tax card, etc. Today this is a huge challenge because we need to change the culture of the people and traditions... but we believe that it is a crucial issue."

Honourable Carlos Morgado, Minister of Industry and Trade.

Foreign Direct Investment

	1999	2000	2001	2002
Investment (000s USD)	80 727	248 865	925 412	557 351

Today the Mozambique's manufacturing sector is slowly redeveloping itself but there exist many untapped opportunities.

Ministry of Industry and Trade

INDUSTRY

The Mozambican industrial sector is rapidly growing in terms of production and revenues through the consolidation of investment made these last years. Total production grew by 21 per cent from 2001 to 2002.

According to the World Bank, Industry in Mozambique accounts for 27.7 per cent of total GDP. Industry employs about 4 per cent of Mozambique's labour force but although total production has increased in volume, it has diminished in value due to the devaluation of national currency against the US Dollar and the South African Rand.

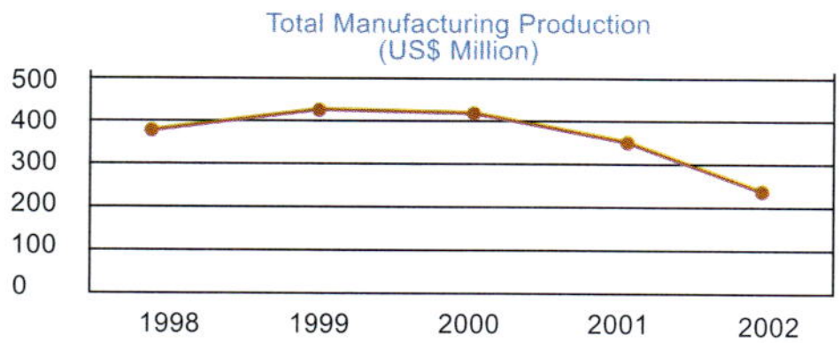

Source: National statistic institute

The Manufacturing sector, also called the transformation Industry, is the sub sector that has known the most considerable growth these last two years. The growth and development of privatised factories and the macroeconomic stability contributed to the overall development of the manufacturing sector which registered in 1997 a growth rate of 39.1 per cent, with construction materials, and consumer goods being the principal growth engines, notably with the creation of Mozal. Today Manufacturing accounts for 15.4 per cent of GDP (World Bank).

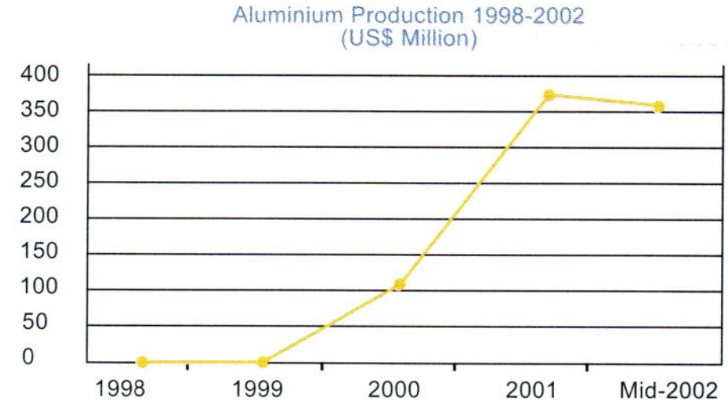

Source: National statistic institute

Aluminium production has strongly increased, notably with the expansion of Mozal production capacity which has doubled the smelter's output of primary ingots from 253 000 tons per year in 2001 to 506 000 tons per year in 2003.

Cement production, which is a reliable index in showing the dynamism of the country's economy, has also strongly increased these last few years. In 5 years, cement production in terms of value has grown by 31 per cent.

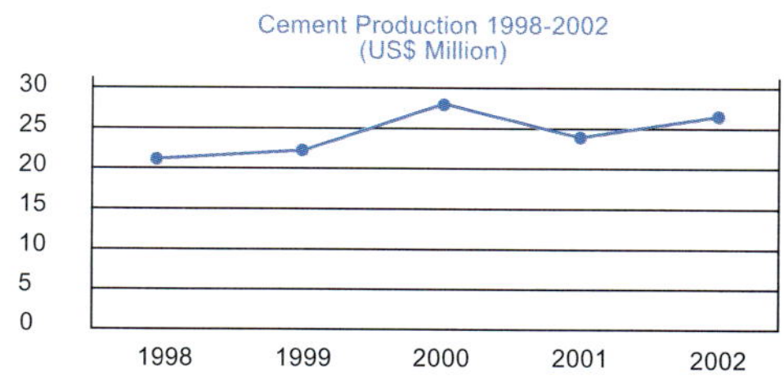

Source: National statistic institute

The extractive industry is going through a very strong development, especially in terms of the investments it is receiving. SASOL, a $1.1 billion dollars-mega gas project that will start its activities beginning of 2004, represents one of the largest investment until date and further major projects are planned to commence in the following year. Amongst these figures the 1.3 billion-mega projects on Heavy Minerals Sands by Southern Mining Company of

South Africa. The project will be localized in Chibuto, in the Gaza province, known for its richness in heavy sands minerals used for the production of titanium.

Thus a vigorous privatisation programme, combined with strong foreign investment is having its impact on the manufacturing sector and the extractive industry. Long neglected, there is a tremendous need for the upgrading of old plant, and investment in new sectors. The strong growth in the domestic economy, and not inconsiderable market of 18 million is currently under-served, and consumer goods industries should blossom. The low cost electricity, the relative abundance of water resources, considerable mineral resources, combined with highly competitive wage rages should act as a major catalyst for industrialisation. To support this process, generous investment incentives exist and the government has introduced a legislation allowing the establishment of free-zones for export oriented investments. Mozambique's preferential access to major markets in the US and EU should act as a powerful magnate for many labour intensive industries. Mozambique's industrial sector should strongly develop in the years to come, completely altering the structure of the Mozambican economy. Priority sectors identified for development include: Food Processing and Agro-industries (High priority - salt, sugar, copra, cotton, processed fish, processed fruits and cashew nuts; Lower Priority - milling, sisal, tea, bakery products, pasta, processed meat, tobacco, animal feed, dairy products and liqueurs); Textile and clothing industries (which do not face any quota restrictions); Edible Soaps and oils; Chemical Industry; Metallurgy (downstream of Mozal, and other products); Metal working industry (construction materials, heavy equipment, furniture, structures, tools and parts); Packaging Industry (wooden boxes, glass bottles, corrugated board, flexible packaging).

Indeed the Mozambique's industrial sector is thus growing and developing itself, and today's main challenge for the government consists in spreading this development to all the regions of the country, consolidating policies and attracting additional foreign investment to untapped industrial sectors.

TRADE

Because of the relative weakness of its manufacturing sector, Mozambique remains essentially an import-based economy and consequently its trade balance with neighbouring countries tends to be negative. This tendency has been further enhanced by the world economic recession since 2001 and the international depreciation of real prices on agricultural products and raw materials, which are Mozambique's main exports. Also until recently, agricultural trade for Mozambique has generally meant exporting a readily available, little processed commodity such as cotton, raw cashew or sugar. Many of these agricultural products are of low value. In addition they are frequently vulnerable to swings in the world market price, which can leave the country's economic base in a very precarious position. Therefore, diversifying exports and switching to higher-value goods have been identified by the government, the IMF and the World Bank, as an economic priority.

Export and import levels (US$ mill.)

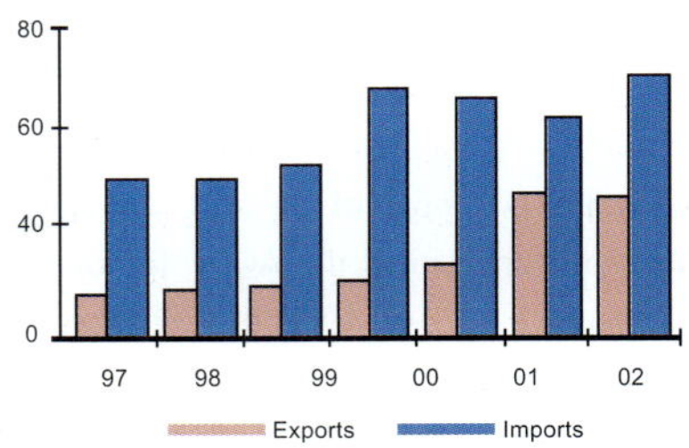

Source: World Bank, 2003

Growth of exports and imports (%)

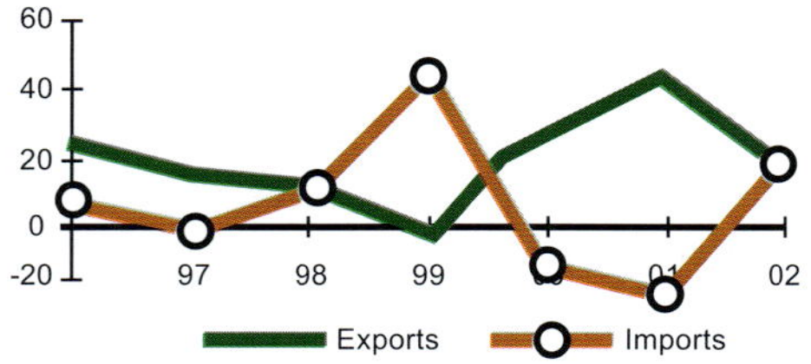

Source: World Bank, 2003

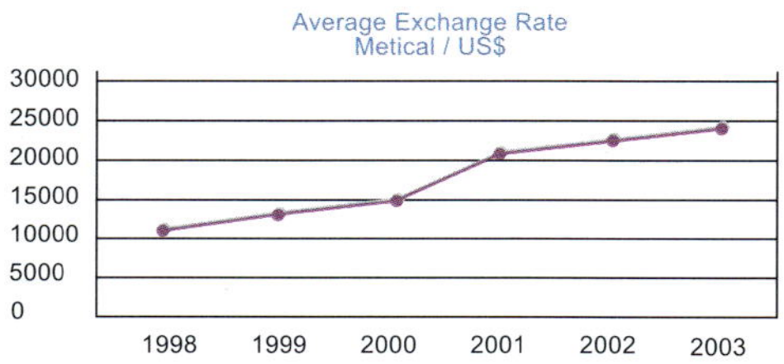

Source: Central Bank

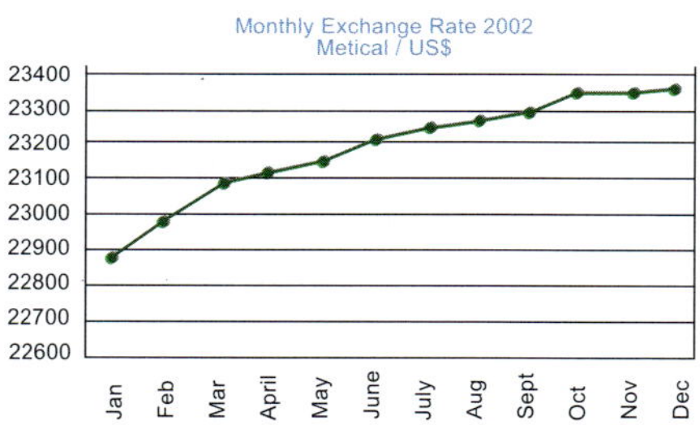

Source: National statistic institute

Today Mozambique is part of the SADC (Southern Africa Development Community), the AGOA (African Growth Opportunity Act), the Everything but Arms Initiative (EBA) with Europe, the Preferential Trade Area for Eastern and Southern African States (PTA), and others. All these agreements and organizations aim to promote economic cooperation between member states, particularly in the areas of agriculture, industry, transportation, and communications. They also aim to facilitate international trade through the lowering of tariff barriers between states and offer tangible incentives for Mozambique to continue their efforts to open their economies and build free markets.

EXPORTS

Main Products

The export structure of Mozambique strongly changed with the introduction of aluminium exports since 2001. Mozal has strongly contributed to Mozambique's exports, providing for US$400 million in foreign exchange earnings per annum and today aluminium is the main export product with 36.4 per cent of total exports. Prawns represent the country's second export product, followed by electric energy (notably through the Cahora Bassa Dam), cashew nuts and cotton.

Main export gains 1998 - 2001 (Million USD)

Export product	1998	%	1999	%	2000	%	2001	%
Aluminium	0.0	0	0.0	0	60	7.8	383	36.4
Prawn	72.7	12,5	65.7	11	60	7.8	92.3	8.7
Electric energy	34.3	5.9	75.4	12	67	8.7	57.3	5.4
Cashew nut	19.1	3.2	35.8	5.8	24.7	3.2	22.6	2.1
Cotton	22.4	3.8	20	3.2	19.2	2.4	18.3	1.7
Sugar & molasse	2.6	0.4	6	1	4	0.5	8	0,8
Total	**580.7**	**100**	**621**	**100**	**769**	**100**	**1 052**	**100**

Source: national statistic institute

Mozambique's export structure will most certainly change further as the country's government is putting in place various incentives for diversifying exports and switching to higher-value goods. The Instituto de Promoção de Exportação (IPEX) is the main institution promoting the development of national export oriented industries. To attract investments, which fulfil this priority, the IPEX has been creating Industrial Free Zones that are export oriented (more that 85% of total production must be for export) and job creative. In addition to other tax exemptions, Industrial Free Zone investments enjoy tax exemption on VAT and customary bill on the importation of production inputs, construction material and equipment for implementing the investment.

Exports: Main destination 1999 - 2002 (thousands USD)

Destination	1999 (USD)	2000 USD	2001(USD)	2002 (USD)
South Africa	70 954	54 643	107 635	120 412
Belgium	******	****	808	282 611
Japan	14 683	15 670	29 185	4 851
Spain	34 491	39 055	26 971	19 053
Portugal	24 491	42 401	28 214	29 824
Malawi	4 771	10 980	11 713	10 369
Hong Kong	103 607	64 500	5 197	2 839
USA		5 900	6 678	10 751

Source: national statistic institute

South Africa and Mozambique have been consolidating their strategic, diplomatic and economic relations over the past years. In fact South African economic investment in Mozambique is enormous, and that is why economic cooperation is being strengthened. Indeed South Africa and Mozambique's economic relationship is the strongest in the Southern African region, and trade between the two countries is on the increase. About 26 percent of Mozambique's exports are destined for South Africa.

IMPORTS

As Mozambique's industrial sector remains relatively small, the country imports a great deal of processed products as well as petroleum products, industrial machinery, and transport equipments. Additionally, with the development of various mega-projects these last few years, these imports have increased as well as those of construction materials.

Main imported products 1999-2002 (1000 US)

Main products	1999	2000	2001	2002
Mineral and Chemical Products	120185	232280	236118	221644
Machinery, equipment	109 852	262 306	140 182	136 097
Transport equipment	177 761	173 814	77 733	135 510
Vegetal products	78 221	75 184	83 721	80 091
Rubber and plastic products	15 985	32 974	54 003	63 214
Paper prods, printing & publishing	13 337	34 287	24 510	43 433
Food, beverage & tobacco Prod.	51 487	31 923	39 461	22 555

Source: national statistic institute

As for the exports, South Africa is Mozambique major trade partner in terms of imports. Indeed about 57 per cent of Mozambique's imports come from South Africa (18 percent of South Africa's exports to Africa).

Imports: countries of origin 2001

Country	1999	2000	2001	2002
South Africa	392 110	450 916	432 302	342 179
Portugal	38 225	88 753	90 133	77 534
USA	45 544	40 266	19 165	55 611
India	10 558	20 368	25 176	53 606
Japan	26 774	53 197	6 937	42 417
China	15 134	22 433	21 739	16 935
Pakistan	18 332	18 322	30 915	6 845

Source: national statistic institute

As part of the effort to liberalize trade in Mozambique, exchange controls have been relaxed. The exchange market has been opened to market forces based on supply and demand, which has made redundant the control of exchange operations in terms of documentation and approval. At the same time, UTRA (Technical Unit for the Restructuring of Customs) was bearing its responsibilities to carry out the minimum supervision necessary, in order to control and register fiscal revenues collected in places of customs jurisdiction. As for imports and exports, a single document (DU) has been established to serve as the support for all foreign trade operations undertaken in the country. This is part of the reforms carried out in several spheres of the economy which aim, among other objectives, to simplify administrative procedures so as to promote a good climate for economic activity, without damaging the functions of control, establishing norms and collecting revenues which should be undertaken by the state. Indeed the government is putting in place simplified procedures for import, notably of goods and materials which are necessary for the successful implementation of investment projects within the country. Also, through various bodies, it has improved the protection of intellectual property and other issues related to international trade.

MAIN COMPANIES

ABB Tecnel, Lda

Johan Kesson, President
Av. das Indústrias, Parcela 760.
C.Postal 99, Machava, Maputo.
Tel: + 258 - 1 - 750750
Fax: + 258 - 1 - 750850
E-mail: abbmztec@virconn.com
Website: www.abb.com

In 1986 was created Electromoc EE, a state owned service company for the energy sector. In 1992 it changed its name into Tecnel SARL, with 75 per cent of its share owned by private investors and the rest held by the government. In 1996, ABB Tecnel Lda was created as the result of the joint venture between ABB, the international engineering company, and Tecnel SARL. The joint venture is 60 per cent owned by ABB and 40 per cent by Tecnel SARL. ABB Tecnel Lda is a sales and services company, which works mostly in the electrical engineering sector. It offers sales and services for the following products: Electrical motors; Transformers; Gen-sets; Medium voltage equipment. ABB Tecnel's growth strategy depends on the overall economic growth rate of the country, as economic development and electrification go hand in hand. Nevertheless through its strong local presence and experience, its worldwide brand name reputation and its well-established clientele, ABB Tecnel strives to strengthen its position in Mozambique. Today it is the main supplier of EDM, Electricidade de Moçambique.

Africom Lda. / Merec Industrias Lda

Mr. Mhamud Charania, Chief Executive Director
1107 Av. do Trabalho
Maputo
Tel: + 258 - 1 - 401850
Fax: + 258 - 1 - 401695
E-mail: mcharania@sasseka.com

AFRICOM was created in 1995 and started importing food products, packaging them and supplying them to different domestic markets. In 1998 MEREC, with an 1800m2 factory complex in Machava, in the outskirts of Maputo, was created for the production of wheat and maize flour and coconut oil. Since then AFRICOM and MEREC have become major players in the commodities trade in Mozambique and the region. AFRICOM is a Marketing Company that has an increasingly wide range of products at accessible prices under their brand name "SASSEKA": products such as rice, sugar, spaghetti and other alimentation products. It is specialized in Importation, Packaging, Distribution, and Marketing. Merec Industrias Lda produces wheat and maize flour plus coconut oil that are then distributed by AFRICOM. In terms of investment projects, MEREC plans to increase its production rate with the expansion of its 3 production plants. They will also distribute new products such as sardines, soap and paint. In terms of strategy, AFRICOM is focused on its brand name "SASSEKA" which has a good reputation and a wide geographical presence. Already present in Kenya, they wish to expand their presence. AFRICOM's competitive advantage lies in the quality of their distribution network, their after sales service and their organizational structure. In 5 - 10 years, AFRICOM will be present in neighbouring countries and this will represent their major challenge.

Cimentos de Moçambique SARL (CM)

Francisco Ilídio Diniz, Administrator
Av. Fernão de Magalhães, n° 34, 2nd floor
Caixa Postal 270, Maputo
Tel: + 258 - 1 - 350906
Fax: + 258 - 1 - 307458
E-mail: idiniz@mz.cimpor.com
Website: www.cimpor.pt

Cimentos de Moçambique SARL (CM) was privatised in 1994 but was actually created in the 1940s through Portuguese investments. In fact when its Portuguese owners left Mozambique after independence in 1975, the government nationalised the company. It was not until 1994 that the idea of privatisation appeared. Today CIMPOR - Cimentos de Portugal, the largest Portuguese cement group, owns 67% of the company, the local government owns 22%, the employees own 6.8% and the remaining is owned by local companies. Cimentos de Moçambique SARL is Mozambique's biggest cement producer. It possesses 1 Cement Plant in Matola (Maputo), and 2 Cement Milling Facilities in Dondo (Beira) and Nacala (Nacala). The company has a total production capacity of 990 thousand tons per year. Cimentos de Moçambique SARL produces and sells its cement directly from its production sites mostly to local traders. The company works with the latest production technology and is especially well equipped in terms of IT systems. Additionally it possesses a very well trained and professional labour force. Also what makes the company's real strength is its cost effective structure and organization.

Finally it offers a very high quality product, which is certified ISO 9000. Cimentos de Moçambique SARL is based on continuously satisfying the customers' needs and constantly improve its facilities through investments. As Mozambique will go through economic and social development, the demand on cement is going to increase and thus potential for this sector remains very important. Therefore Cimentos de Moçambique SARL strives to maintain and strengthen its position.

Coca - Cola Sabco (Moçambique) S.A.R.L

Hansie Koen, National Financial Director
Av. 24 de Julho, N° 3549, 29 Andar
Caixa Postal 1441, Maputo.
Tel: + 258 - 1 - 404840 / 402062
Fax: + 258 - 1 - 402061
E-mail: hkoen@ccsabco.co.za
Website: www.ccsabco.co.za

The South African Bottling Company (SABCO) (Pty) Ltd was established in Port Elizabeth (South Africa) in 1940. In 1995 SABCO merged its South African franchises with those of The Coca-Cola Company in East Africa, to form the venture company Coca-Cola Sabco (CCS). CCS operations in Mozambique started in Maputo on 25th May 1994 with 80 employees and 1000 cases produced per hour. Since then operations have known tremendous growth and development. CCS carries out bottling and distribution activities in Mozambique. They operate plants in Maputo, Chimoio and Nampula. Maputo is the capital, Chimoio is strategically located on the Beira corridor route, and Nampula serves the Northern provinces. They also have various depots across the whole country. CCS possesses excess production capacity at the moment and therefore is in a favourable position to consistently and effectively meet the increase in demand. It possesses also well-established distribution channels all across the country but may include in the near future third parties for these matters. CCS has strongly participated in the economic and social development of Mozambique and is one of the country's main investors. During the floods in the year 2000, Coca-Cola Sabco was one of the first companies to offer relief funds. Finally the company has a strong commitment to taking care of its employees who are considered as its main resource. For the years to come, CCS strives to continuously increase the effectiveness of its operations in Mozambique while effectively meeting the demand for its products.

Diname - Distribuidora Nacional de Material de Escolar

Antonio Chambal, General Manager
Av. Zedequias Manganhela, N° 1278
Maputo
Tel: + 258 - 1 - 303142
Fax: + 258 - 1 - 321118
E-mail: chambal@diname.uem.mz

The company was created in 1986 by the Ministry of Education with the financial aid of the Swedish government as a warehouse. In 1986, it developed into a school material distribution company and since then it has had monopoly of this market. In 1996, it started distributing free school books through the government's Caixa Escolare Program (one child one book). The company's activities include the distribution, editing and production of schoolbooks. In 2004, the company will be privatised and the market will be liberalised. Thus, as new local and foreign companies will enter this market, competition will strongly increase. But thanks to its extensive experience, its important infrastructure, its local knowledge, and geographical spread DINAME observe a bright future. As DINAME will go through a privatisation process, the 3 different activities that are the ones of edition, production

A book... A seed!
Diname is the only company editing and publishing the national school books in the country. We keep on increasing our performance in order to ensure that our products reach our clients with efficiency and on time.
Maputo • Gaza • Inhambane • Sofala • Manica • Tete • Zambézia • Nampula • Niassa • Cabo Delgado
Diname
Distribuidora Nacional de Material Escolar.

and distribution will be separated into 3 different companies.

DINAME will focus on what has been its core com petency since its creation: the distribution of school material. DINAME has a truly promising future.

Medimoc SARL - Empresa de Importação e Exportação de Medicamentos

Dr. Renato Ronda, Chief Executive Officer
Av. Julius Nyerere, N° 500
Maputo
Tel: + 258 - 1 - 491211
Fax: + 258 - 1 - 490168
E-mail: rronda@medimoc.imoz.com

Medimoc was created in 1977 by the Government of Mozambique for the import and distribution of medicines and until 1998, it was a public company. In fact until its privatisation, Medimoc had the monopoly of the market but this market was liberalised and competition increased very strongly. Today, Medimoc SARL is the third largest importer and distributor of medicines in Mozambique. It is owned 70 per cent by its workers and 30 per cent by the government. Medimoc SARL works both with the public and the private sector. When it comes to the public sector it is the official importer and distributor of the government for all the health related products and equipments and thus it is very closely linked to the Ministry of Health. Regarding its relationships with the private sector, Medimoc imports and sells various products and equipments according to the demand. It possesses offices in Maputo, Beira and Nampula and works with a large number of pharmacies, NGOs and private companies. Medimoc SARL is also involved in the trade of veterinary products.

Medimoc SARL is studying various projects for the future, as for example the creation of a strong line of pharmacies through the establishment of a separate company, or local production of medicines through a joint venture with an international company. Medimoc is an employee-focused company that offers health insurance and other benefits to its labour force. It is an especially socially committed company. Medimoc strives to achieve a stable and strong position within the health sector.

Mozal Aluminium Smelter

Peter Wilshaw, General Manager
Beloluane Industrial Park, Boane District
P.O.Box 1235, Maputo
Tel: + 258 - 1 - 735002
Fax: + 258 - 1 - 735082
E-mail: pete.wilshaw@bhpbilliton.com
Website: www.mozal.com

Mozal is one of the world's leading aluminium smelter. It initially started operating in 2000 with a single Potline, with a capacity of 253 000 tonnes per annum (tpa) but in 2003 a second potline was introduced, which increased the total production capacity to 506 000tpa. Today Mozal is one of the largest of its kind in the western world. The total investment of US$2 billion used to build Mozal (Mozal I) and its recent expansion (Mozal II) significantly boosted the economy of Mozambique. It was the first major project to be implemented in Mozambique over the past 50 years. Mozal's shareholders are: BHP Billiton (47% and the smelter operator), Mitsubishi Corporation of Japan (25%), the Industrial Development Corporation of South Africa (IDC, 24%) and the Government of Mozambique (4%). Mozal produces re-melted aluminium ingots for the export market. In fact it imports alumina liquid pitch and petroleum coke, processes it and exports the resulting aluminium ingots to Europe where it is purchased by its shareholders. Mozal, together with Bayside and the expanded Hillside smelters in Richards Bay, forms an aluminium axis in southern Africa, which will have a combined capacity of over 1.3 million tpa, constituting some 7% of world aluminium production. Mozal produces one of the world's best aluminium in terms of quality. In fact in its few years of operation, it has already gained a very strong reputation across the world markets. Additionally thanks to the expertise and technical know-how of its partners and the high quality of its management team, it is also one of the world's lowest cost aluminium producer. Mozal's strength also lies in its highly qualified and efficient labour force. The company participates very strongly in Mozambique's economic and social development, and is notably the biggest contributor to the country's GDP and the principal source of foreign earnings. On the social side, it has put in place several programs as for example the Small and Medium Enterprise Empowerment and Linkages Programme (SMEELP), which was established for the upliftment of local businesses by linking local SMEs. Mozal strives to maintain and strengthen its position as one of the world's leading aluminium smelter.

Nobilis Holding - SDL

Mrs. Deolinda Wicht, General Manager
Av. 25 de Setembro, num. 420 3rd floor
Maputo
Tel: + 258 - 1 - 308950
Fax: + 258 - 1 - 314588
E-mail: sdl@virconn.com

The company Nobilis is owned by 3 partners: Swiss, French and Mozambican. It has established itself in Mozambique with a long-term vision and with the aim to develop its activities in various sectors. Nobilis is a holding company. It is present in a variety of sectors such as trade, construction and tourism. In the tourism sector, it owns a travel agency in Maputo (SDL), a hotel in Namaacha and it is currently working on various projects, notably the construction of a resort in Ponta d'Ouro, which should be operational in three years time. The strategy of the company is based on diversification, as a key element to a successful business. They are active in the trade sector but are mainly looking for opportunities in a sector full of potential: the tourism sector, where they are investing a lot. They are looking at expansion in the regions. As part of a socially responsible group, Nobilis is engaged in the social development of Mozambique. Indeed the company actively participates in educational programs such as "um Olhar de Esperança". They also work in collaboration with ISPO; provide assistance to students to graduate and also provide equipment to schools. Nobilis strives to strengthen its position in Mozambique, as well as build effectively the new resort in Ponta d'Ouro. They are also eager to create good conditions for investment in the country, as an aim to reduce poverty and make regions more accessible.

Setec Auto LDA

Gerry J. Wigglesworth, Executive Manager
Avenida Acordos de Lusaka 118
Maputo
Tel: + 258 - 1 - 417000
Fax: + 258 - 1 - 417040
E-mail: gerry.wigglesworth@setecauto.com

The company was born in 1983. It was created by a Dutch multinational who then sold it to a British company in 1991. Since then it has been in the same hands. Setec Auto initially distributed Leyland Daf, but in 1991 it started distributing Land Rover. In 2002 it acquired distribution rights for Mazda as well. At its beginnings it only had branches in Maputo and Beira. Today it has moved into additional regions around the country, mainly into Quilimane, Nampula and Pemba. Its activities include: Sales and repair of Land Rover and Mazda vehicles; Sales of spare parts for Land Rover and Mazda vehicles; Sales of 4 x 4 accessories for Land Rover and Mazda vehicles. In the recent past, Setec Auto has invested approximately 500,000 USD in buying premises in Nampula and Beira. It is now in the process of upgrading its installations in Maputo, with a total investment of 1,5 million USD. Setec is very proud of the service level that it has managed to achieve, which is due to the large emphasis they give to training. In fact they have special training programmes in South Africa and a high percentage of their fixed costs is reserved for training purposes. Mozambique has high import duties on New Motor Vehicles and consequently Setec Auto faces strong competition from importers of Japanese second hand cars. It is therefore actively working to regain its lead of this new competition.

Visabeira Moçambique

Paulo Varela, President of the Administration Council
Av. Kenneth Kaunda, n°403,
Maputo
Tel: + 258 - 1 - 483300
Fax: + 258 - 1 - 495026
E-mail: paulovarela@visabeiramoz.co.mz
Website: www.grupovisabeira.pt

The Grupo Visabeira began its activity in 1980 within the telecommunication sector and quickly became Portugal's leader for this market. Later on, the Grupo diversified its activities in terms of sector and location. In 1990, Grupo Visabeira created its first company in Mozambique called Televisa through a partnership with TDM (Telecomunicações de Moçambique). Then followed the civil construction company Sogitel and several other companies. Today Grupo Visabeira is present in several sectors of the Mozambican economy. Visabeira Moçambque is the company responsible for the management of the group's different companies present in Mozambique, although each company is an independent entity. In fact Visabeira Moçambique manages and coordinates the different companies offering them accounting and treasury services amongst other services. The following companies are a few of the many companies within the group: Real Estate & Construction: Sogitel, Imovisa; Agriculture and forestry: Agrovisa, Alamo, Industry: Marmonte, Celmoque; Services & Trade: Autovisa, Mercury, Hidroafrica; Tourism: Girasol, Bahia Hotel, Rodizio Real, Indy Village, Bahia Restaurante; Telecommunication: Televisa, TV Cabo, Teleserve. Visabeira Moçambique benefits of several advantages such as their know-how in different sectors, their experience and their geographical spread throughout Mozambique. And Grupo Visabeira and Visabeira Moçambique strive to continuously grasp the growth opportunities that arise and that follow their philosophy "we do what we know". In fact the group has various ongoing projects in the telecommunication, real estate and tourism sectors. Visabeira Moçambique is proud to have continuously contributed to the economic and social development of the country over the years. Visabeira Moçambique is today a unique company in Mozambique. Visabeira Moçambique strives to effectively grow in this stable and peaceful country called Mozambique.

Maputo fresh produce

Nobilis Holding
Mozambique

Invest in Mozambique

Av. 25 de Setembro, 420
Prédio JAT, 3° andar
Caixa Postal 2412
Maputo, Moçambique

Tel. +258 1 30 89 52
Fax + 258 1 31 45 88
Email: sdl@virconn.com

PUBLIC WORKS

OVERVIEW

The availability of basic infrastructure is the key to obtaining sustainable economic growth and poverty-reduction. Although nationwide infrastructure is still fragile, efforts put in place by the government are substantially changing the situation.

Indeed, since peace returned to Mozambique in 1992, the government has focused on giving significant technical assistance through Public Works for the reconstruction of the country and its economy. This effort became even more important after the 2000 - 2001 floods. Technical assistance, combined with important foreign investments, has resulted in an increase of engineering activities in Mozambique.

Mozambique's Minister of Public Works and Housing is responsible for the development of infrastructures across the country. It works through and with various Ministries, governmental institutions and public and private companies such as the Ministry of Transport and Communication, the National Directorate for Roads and Bridges, the Mozambican National Road Administration (ANE), and the Ports & Railway company (CFM) just to name a few. The rehabilitation and construction of roads, railways, ports, hospitals, schools, factories, residential buildings, offices, commercial centres and other rural and urban infrastructures have accentuated these last years the growth of the Civil Engineering and Construction Materials industries. Investment opportunities in these sectors are numerous.

Public Works are mainly financed by international institutions through bilateral and multilateral agreements, but the private sector is playing an increasing important role especially through public-private partnerships.

PUBLIC WORKS

To benefit from the privileged geographical situation of the country which commands access to sea for various hinterland countries, public authorities have focused on the development of national transport infrastructures such as roads, ports, railways and airports notably through the rehabilitation and construction of East - West transversal corridors and North - South liaisons.

Maputo Corridor

In 2000, the Maputo Corridor (Johannesburg - Maputo) was enhanced with the creation of the transnational highway EN-4. This highway will be part of a whole transport system, which includes railways that link Maputo to South Africa, Zimbabwe and Swaziland as well as the port of Maputo. Rehabilitation of the railway and port is actually undergoing notably through private management agreements.

Nacala Corridor

The concession of the Nacala Corridor, made in 2001, to the private consortium Edlow should allow for an effective development and promotion of the railway and road liaison between the deep water port of Nacala and Malawi.

Beira Corridor

A similar concession should soon be awarded for the Beira Corridor that links the port of Beira to Zimbabwe. The port of Beira is managed by Cornelder de Moçambique SARL, which resulted from the partnership between the Dutch Company Cornelder B.V. and the Mozambican public company CFM. Additionally the concession of the Sena railway line should soon be awarded.

WATER SYSTEM

Following the establishment of the national water policy in 1995, the liberalization of the sector and the decentralization of water resource management in 1998, the water sector in Mozambique is going through radical changes.

In fact, access to potable water has become one of the key vectors of government actions aimed at improving the population's living standards. Given its crucial importance for the country's socio-economic development, the government seeks to promote sustainable water use, increase the supply of potable water and provision of low cost sanitation in urban areas. The establishment of a Strategic Integrated Plan for the Management of Water Resources, the expected reform on the water policy as well as the development of the water treatment sub sector should attract major investments in urban and rural areas (PNDA I & II). In 2002, 1171 drinking-water fountains (standpipes) were constructed and/or refurbished. This corresponds to an average national coverage of 35 per cent. Thus there is still much to be done.

Local capacities remain limited in comparison to the needs (qualified labour force, Technical Research Centres, NGOs) and consequently the sector's development is relatively slow. Still, private consortiums, such as Aguas de Moçambique, are moving into this still untapped sector. Indeed this Portuguese-Mozambican consortium manages the water supply in the major Mozambican cities and has concessions in Maputo, Beira, Quelimane, Nampula and Pemba. It is responsible for the water and wastewater of more than 2.5 million people and for expanding the networks in these cities.

ENERGY WORKS

In the domain of energy, various studies are being carried out for the improvement of transport and distribution of electricity produced by the Cahora Bassa Dam, on the Zambezi River. Also a project for the construction of an additional dam is currently being studied in order to respond to the growing need of electricity, especially from South Africa. In terms of distribution, the government is strongly involved in electrifying the whole of the country. In fact, Mozambique is one the least electrified countries in East Africa with less then 8 per cent of its population having direct access to electricity. The finance of these electrification programmes have been fully ensured by the international community including the World Bank, the IMF, the European Union and several countries. The Ministry of Public Works, the Ministry of Energy and Mineral Resources and EDM (Mozambique Electricity Company) have formed partnerships with private companies for an effective rural electrification of Mozambique. Various programmes have been successfully carried out these last few years. Others are still ongoing and many remain to be done.

EDUCATION AND HEALTH WORKS

These two sectors are considered priority by the government and should induce a strong and rapid growth of the Public Works and Construction sectors thanks to the construction and rehabilitation of a great number of schools and hospitals. Indeed, following the government's Action Plan for the Reduction of Absolute Poverty (PARPA) put in place in collaboration with the IMF and the World Bank, education and health have become the centre of attention. Therefore an important amount of capital is being poured into these two sectors and throughout the country. A total of 424 new schools were opened in 2001 (an additional 6 per cent over the total number of schools in 2000), distributed mainly in the provinces of Zambezia, Niassa, Inhambane; another 275 were opened in the first half of 2002 (51,5 per cent over the total schools in 2001), benefiting mainly Zambezia, Gaza and Inhambane. Thus the number of new schools built per year has significantly increased and a great number of construction and civil engineering companies are increasingly involved in these sectors. Nevertheless Mozambique remains a rural country and schools' geographical repartition is still not adequate.

Alongside education, the health sector also has an important place in government policy and budget, given its mission to promote and preserve a healthy population. The 2000 - 2004 government programme stresses the need to universalise basic healthcare throughout the population, in conjunction with universal access to primary education, in order to have a healthier, better trained and more motivated labour force throughout the country. In keeping with the Strategic Health Plan (PESS), the government strives to improve access to healthcare and thus a number of rehabilitation and construction projects are being undertaken across the whole country.

BIG PROJECTS

With the recent expansion of the Mozal Aluminium smelter with 506 000 tons production capacity, the SASOL and the Pande and Temani Gas and Pipeline projects gas that will start its activities beginning of 2004, and various major investment projects, the engineering and construction sector is set to growth rapidly over the next few years.

RESIDENTIAL AND NON-RESIDENTIAL BUILDINGS

For the last 20 years, urban population has considerably grown in Mozambique. In fact due to an elevated population growth rate (2.2%) and strong population migration from rural areas to major cities, urban population represents today 34 per cent of total population. This causes certain problems as demand for housing has strongly increased and the capacity to respond still remains limited.

Types of Housing in Mozambique, 2002

Total	3 540 700	100%
Residences	315 122.3	8.90%
Apartments	42 488.4	1.20%
Other	3 183 089.3	89.90%

Source: the national statistics Institute

Types of Housing in Urban Areas, 2002

Total	894 200	100%
Residences	245 905	27.5%
Apartments	38 472	4.3%
Other	608 056	68.8%

Source: the national statistics Institute

Consequently the Government liberalized the sector and privatised various state-owned companies. Today the sector is composed by about 105 large and medium sized companies and an important number of NGOs. Additionally the Government and the National Directorate for Housing have established a National Housing Fund to provide land and financial credit to housing construction and rehabilitation for low-income people and young couples. On the other hand, the Government has also transferred about 70% of its real estate stock to Mozambicans at highly subsidised prices, and the income generated from the sales has been allocated to the National Housing Fund. A National Council for Sustainable Development, which comprises government institutions, civil society, and the private sector, has been established within the country, with a view to supervise the implementation of the Habitat Agenda in coordination with the United Nations.

The Mozambican construction industry is currently experiencing a boom period due to the renewed impetus given to national reconstruction programs following the return of peace and internal stability. Housing construction and renovation is strongly underway in the major cities, as well as the development of commercial and industrial property. The boom in new hotels will have also provided a strong boost to the local construction industry. The needs of Mozambique in terms of new rural and urban infrastructures are enormous, and it offers tremendous opportunities for civil engineering firms. They include road, rail and port rehabilitation programs, and reconstruction of social services such as schools, hospitals, water systems and electricity. Thus there are opportunities for private contractors (both foreign and Mozambican) to tender for contracts incorporating government and international donor funding.

OVERALL

Construction and Rehabilitation of Infrastructures, 2002

Description	Percent (%) of values
Construction of General	2.5
Rehabilitation of General Infrastructure	1.5
Construction of non residential buildings	6.8
Rehabilitation of non residential buildings	5.5
Construction of mixed buildings	2.0
Rehabilitation of mix buildings	0.7
Construction of residences	0.7
Rehabilitation of residences	0.2
Construction of Roads	2.6
Rehabilitation of Roads	77.3
Construction of Bridges	0.1
Rehabilitation of Bridges	0.0

Source: the national statistics Institute

Downtown Maputo

MAIN COMPANIES

Aguas de Moçambique, SARL

José Mestre, General Director
Av. Eduardo Mondlane, 1352, 5° Andar
Caixa Postal 2952, Maputo
Tel: + 258 - 1 - 302431 / 2
Fax: + 258 - 1 - 324675
E-mail: jmestre@adp.pt

Aguas de Moçambique SARL was created after a consortium including SAUR and IPE/Aguas de Portugal won the Mozambique multiple water concession in 1999. Today Aguas de Portugal (AdP) is the leading shareholder with 73% of the company's shares and the remaining 23% are in hand of a grouping of four Mozambican companies, Mazi-Mozambique. Aguas de Moçambique is a private consortium, which manages water supply in the major Mozambican cities. In fact it has concessions in Maputo, Beira, Quelimane, Nampula and Pemba, and is responsible for the water and wastewater of more than 2.5 million people and for expanding the networks in these cities. Aguas de Mozambique's priorities include expanding the production capacity at the Maputo water treatment station on the Umbeluzi river, and studying possible complementary sources for the capital. Additionally, the company aims to reduce losses of water caused by obsolete piping and improve the collection of money owed by customers. In fact, the consortium intends to promote the economic and environmental sustainability of the system. Currently Aguas de Moçambique is renewing its image in accordance to its efforts to improve their services, guaranteeing supplies of safe, good quality water. The result should be a more efficient Customer Relationship Management system.
Aguas de Moçambique is going through an important restructuring phase at all the different levels of the company. This process should give the company the necessary basis for a strong and sustainable development of its activity in Mozambique.

Ceta Construção e Servicios S.A.R.L

A. Romeu Rodrigues, General Director
Av. 24 de Julho nº 2549, 1° Andar
P.O.Box 2783, Maputo
Tel: + 258 - 1 - 302160
Fax: + 258 - 1 - 301855
E-mail: romeur@ceta.co.mz

As a result of the independence many construction companies were left unmanaged and on a virtual shut down. In 1980 the government regrouped various small and medium sized construction companies, which it nationalized and created the state owned company, CETA e.e. Although it was strongly affected by the civil war in the mid 1980s, CETA managed to effectively grow over the years and gain a certain reputation. In 1999, the company was privatised leading to the creation of CETA Construção e Servicios S.A.R.L with 49% of its shares belonging to MINCO, a Venture Capital Fund and 51% belonging to the Managers and Workers. Today CETA is the only fully Mozambican construction company in the construction sector. CETA Construção e Servicios S.A.R.L is a construction company with specialization in school, hospital, water systems & sewerage, and roads & bridges. In fact most of their works are carried out on the latest, which account for the bulk of their activity. CETA has worked on various major projects in Mozambique and repeatedly formed joint-ventures with leading international companies such as Teixeira Duarte, LTA (S.A), C.M.C di Ravenna, HBG and CFG. CETA operates throughout Mozambique and has permanent offices in Maputo, Beira and Nampula. The company differentiates itself from its competitors by the fact that it is the only true Mozambican construction company, created by Mozambicans for Mozambicans. Thus its local knowledge, labour force and expertise represent CETA Construção e Servicios S.A.R.L's main competitive advantages. And as the only local company CETA Construção e Servicios S.A.R.L strives to maintain and strengthen its presence in the country.

Cimbetão - Cimpor Betão de Moçambique SARL

Carlos Lima, General Director
Estrada de Lingamo, Estaleiro da Fábrica de Cimentos de C.M. - Matola
Maputo
Tel: + 258 - 1 - 720150
Fax: + 258 - 1 - 720261
E-mail: cimbetao@teledta.mz
Website: www.cimpor.pt

CIMPOR - Cimentos de Portugal is the largest Portuguese cement group, operating in eight countries - Portugal, Spain, Morocco, Tunisia, Brazil, Mozambique, Egypt and South Africa, involved in manufacturing and marketing cement, hydraulic lime, concrete and aggregates, precast concrete and dry mortars. CIMBETÃO - Cimpor Betão de Moçambique SARL is owned at 99% by CIMPOR International and 1% by its managers. CIMBETÃO was created in 1998 in order to satisfy the increasing demand in mixed concrete. Today it is the leading concrete company in Mozambique. CIMBETÃO manufactures and markets ready-mixed concrete. It is the leading company in its sector and supplies 85%-90% of the demand in concrete in the Capital City of Maputo. CIMBETÃO has participated in the construction of the capital's major building and infrastructures. As the rest of Mozambique is slowly developing itself, CIMBETÃO is planning to expand its activity to the neighbouring provinces. CIMBETÃO has reached the leading position in the concrete market thanks to its competitive advantages and its effective strategy. CIMBETÃO benefits from the Group's experience in the cement and concrete sector. Additionally CIMBETÃO offers a very high quality product and notably being certified with ISO 9001. In terms of strategy, CIMBETÃO operates with a very aggressive commercial strategy, which makes it the undisputed heavy weight champion of its sector. Geographical expansions plans are being studied and projects like the rehabilitation of the national road linking Maputo to Beira can contribute in the sense. CIMBETÃO has notably provided concrete for the construction of the Cimpor Centro, the new Foreign Affairs' building and the Maputo Conference Center. Also most of the hotels and other major buildings recently built in the Capital obtained their concrete from CIMBETÃO.

Ergogeste, Lda - Construções e Obras Públicas

Justino Pereira, General Manager
Av. Zedequias Manganhela, n° 564
P.O. Box 1465, Maputo
Tel: + 258 - 1 - 305162 / 72
Fax: + 258 - 1 - 305167
E-mail: ergomo@mail.tropical.co.mz

When ErgoGeste was created in 1996, it actually started as an import-export company. Then through a partnership with the ECOP Group from Portugal, it turned into a construction company. In fact by 1997, ErgoGeste had already started building. Currently 51% of the company's shares are held by Mozambican private investors and 49% by the ECOP Group. Today ErgoGeste is a leading construction company in Mozambique. ErgoGeste - Construções e Obras Públicas is a construction company specialized in the construction of buildings. Today ErgoGeste is the 4th company in the construction sector in terms of revenues.

It is classified as the country's 36th largest company. ErgoGeste is present throughout the country, from Niassa to Punta de Ouro and this gives it a considerable advantage over its competition. Additionally, it has a strong international backing through the ECOP Group. Finally it offers flexible and high quality services. ErgoGeste will have to prepare itself to the effects of the increasing regional integration within the construction sector. Therefore it is currently studying various possibilities including partnerships and creating international operations, notably in Angola.

Padilha Construçoes Lda.

Francisco F. Padilha & Maria José L.M. Padilha
General Director & Financial Director
Rua Ismael Alves da Costa N°1280 - 1290, Machava
C.P. 2966, Maputo
Tel: + 258 - 1 - 750066
Fax: + 258 - 1 - 651532

PADILHA CONSTRUÇÕES LDA. was created in 1998 with a total capital of 10 million Meticais which allows it to tender for a wide range of construction projects. PADILHA CONSTRUÇÕES LDA. is a Mozambican company whose employees are in majority Mozambican. 51 per cent of the company shares are owned by Mr. & Mrs. Padilha and the remaining shares are in the hands of private Mozambican investors. PADILHA CONSTRUÇÕES LDA. is a Civil Constructions and Public Works company which carries out a whole range of construction projects. They have built hotels, schools, public buildings amongst others. The company is actually involved in projects in various provinces, namely Maputo, Gaza, Inhambane, and Niassa. They have their own installations in Machava where they carry out carpentry, mechanical and storage activities.

PADILHA CONSTRUÇÕES LDA. has several competitive advantages including a local labour force, vast experience in the construction sector, an extensive infrastructure, collaboration agreements with various construction equipment manufacturers and very good customer relationship management.

Teixeira Duarte Engenharia e Construçoes (Moçambique), Lda

Fernando Garção, Director Financiero
Avenida Julius Nyerere, 130
Maputo.
Tel: + 258 - 1 - 491401 / 496980
Fax: + 258 - 1 - 491400
E-mail: tdmoc@isl.co.mz

Teixeira Duarte is Portugal's biggest construction company. Its administrative headquarters has always wanted to be present in Africa and this has been part of the company's strategy for several years now. Since 1992, they have been present in Mozambique as well as in Angola. The company's activities include: Civil Construction (They built Maputo's biggest and most functional buildings); Hotels (They own three of Maputo's major hotels); Commercial Centers; and Real Estate. Teixeira Duarte is actually looking to open other hotels in the rest of the country following their belief that there is a market for such hotels. They recently opened the Hotel Avenida after a series of rehabilitation processes. Teixeira Duarte's main advantage lies in its size in Portugal, which guarantees the quality of its services.

TRANSPORT & COMMUNICATION

OVERVIEW

Due to its exceptional geographical situation, Mozambique has benefited, since colonial times, of significantly well-developed communication and especially transport infrastructures. The situation is such that it is ideally suited as a transit country for international trade to its neighbours. Both sectors will increasingly form the main backbone of Mozambique's economy, and become major foreign exchange earners.

Indeed, even before colonial times, Arab traders established various settlements within Mozambique and on its coastline to serve as trading post for the flourishing trade in gold, silver, slavery and ivory with the interior, and notably with Kilwa, near present-day Tanzania, the hub of Arab trade in East Africa.

When the Portuguese realized the value of trade with the interior and inland countries, they took over the control of numerous trading posts originally managed by the resident Arabs traders and developed routes that would transport the goods to the ports.

Since then, Mozambique's transport and communication sector has been at the forefront of development efforts and slowly it became the main transit area for trade with and from Malawi, Zimbabwe, Swaziland, and to a certain extent Zambia and the Northern provinces of South Africa. In fact most of these countries became dependent of Mozambique railway-port system for their external trade.

In 1973, two years before independence, Transport and Communication activities contributed to 90 per cent ($110 Million USD) of Mozambique trade balance surplus. This shows the important economic potential that transports and communications represent and the natural transit function of Mozambique. Nevertheless several years of war have considerably reduced the sector's activity and have damaged existing infrastructure.

Today the transport and communication sector is undergoing significant changes, resulting from the fact that the government recognizes that the sector plays a vital role in all aspects of economic and social development, particularly in the development of exports and of tourism.

With the support of international donors, notably the World Bank, a number of reforms have been put in place resulting in concessions of the ports and railways, management agreements, privatisations and public-private partnerships.

The whole of Mozambique's transport and communication system is being developed in an integrated manner. Indeed the government of Mozambique, with the support of international donors, is concentrating on developing transport and communication Corridors that will serve internal and external movement of goods and people in order to obtain significant economic and social development for Mozambique and the whole region. In fact, under the SADC agreements, Mozambique is responsible for the Transport and Communication sectors.

"In an under developed country, you can not talk of economic development without the development of an adequate infrastructure. By this, I mean roads, railways, telecommunications amongst others. Because the most important thing is to have access to markets at low cost. This is the key point to successful economic development".

Honourable T.A. Salomão, Minister of Transport & Communication

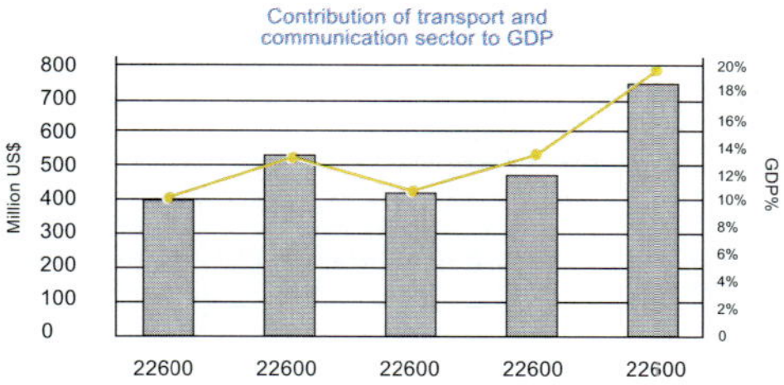

Source: National statistics Institute

TRANSPORT

In its current situation, Mozambique's transport system, which falls under the Ministry of Transport and Communication authority, is essentially comprised of:

- A 30,400 Km road network, with only 5,685 Km of tarred road.

- 3 major ports: Maputo (South), Beira (Centre), and Nacala (North); and 16 smaller ports including Quelimane and Pemba.

- 3 distinct railway lines.

- 19 airports including 5 international airports (Maputo, Beira, Chimoio, Nampula, and Pemba).

Roads & Bridges

The road system plays an important role for the movement of goods and people across Mozambique. Indeed it is a crucial mean of transport as it handles about 98.8 per cent people movements and 16.27 per cent of goods movements.

Total road network, 2002

Total	30 400 km
Main roads	6 212 km
Secondary roads	7 880 km
Tertiary roads	13 184 km
Unclassified roads	3 124 km

Source: Ministry of public works and Housing, National Directorate of Roads and Bridges, department of Planning

Type of Surface of roads, 2002

Total	30 400 km
Tarred	5 685 km
Gravel	9 082
Dirt	15 633 km

Source: Ministry of public works and Housing, National Directorate of Roads and Bridges, department of Planning

MAIN SECTORS OF THE ECONOMY: TRANSPORT & COMMUNICATION

Today Mozambique has a total road network of 30,400km with one main national road, the N 1, which runs through the whole country, from North to South, and from which diverts various other principal roads that spread along the country. The EN2, 3 and 4 are roads from Maputo to the west, southwest and northwest (EN2 to Swaziland and EN4 to South Africa). EN6, 7 and 8 link the coast to the hinterland: EN6 runs from Beira to Zimbabwe, EN7 from Quelimane to Malawi and EN8 from Nacala to Malawi. Of this road network, only 5,685km are tarred.

Under the new Policy and Strategy for Roads (Politica e Estrategia de Estradas) a new national road administration, called the "Administraçâo Nacional de Estradas" (ANE), was approved for the management, maintenance and development of Mozambique's road and bridge systems. The government also created an auxiliary companies, the Empresas de Construção e Manutanção de Estradas (EMCEP) for roads construction and maintenance through partnerships with the private sector. All private sector involvement is based on the BOT model (Build, Operate, Transfer).

Over the past decade, three programmes have been put in place for the rehabilitation of the sector. ROCS I (Roads and Coastal Shipping Project) took place from 1993 to 1997. This $150 Million programme focused on the central and provincial management of road networks, on the training of personnel, and feasibility studies. ROCS II was implemented from 1994 to 1998, and was extended until 2001. The main objective of this $850 Million programme was the improvement of the whole Mozambican road network. Finally ROCS III, which started in 2001 and should terminate in 2010, is a $1,7 Billion programme. It should be implemented through 3 phases and focuses on various rehabilitation projects, periodic maintenance, and construction of additional roads. For this programme, an international fund (Road Fund) was established by international donors and is managed by ANE, the National Roads Administration. More than 40 projects have and will be implemented throughout this 10-year programme. Several parallel programmes are also being implemented.

Type of activity	Investments 2000 (US)	Investments 2001 (US)	Investments 2002 (US)
Construction of roads	4 479 020.00	7 698 953. 59	20 598 415.07
Rehabilitation of roads	26 969 388.22	46 830 713.63	518 131 000.21
Construction of bridges	286 924.70	3 926 924.69	468 584.27
Rehabilitation of bridges	445 079.11	507 329.24	160 745.34

Source: National statistics Institute

Port and Railway

The Ports and Railways of Mozambique E.P. (Portos e Caminhos de Ferro de Moçambique; CFM) is the Mozambican public company, which owns and manages the country's ports and railways. Its origins can be traced back to the 1930s. CFM is actually undergoing a restructuring process and is in fact privatising the management of the port and rail system in order to undertake the large-scale investments necessary for their rehabilitation and development so that it may be modern, competitive, efficient, market-guided and financially viable.

Main Sectors Of The Economy: Transport & Communication

Mozambique has a railway system of 3700 km length linking the ports of Maputo, Beira and Nacala to South Africa, Zimbabwe, Botswana, Zambia, the Democratic Republic of Congo and Malawi. In fact, Mozambique's Transportation Corridors, are mainly composed of railways and ports.

"The model for port and rail development is private sector concessions"

Honourable T.A. Salomão, Minister of Transport & Communication

There are three main Transportation Corridors: the Southern Maputo corridor west of Pretoria; the Central Beira corridor from the port of Beira to the Zimbabwe capital of Harare; and Northern Nacala corridor, which runs west to Lilongwe, in Malawi.

CFM Headquarters

The Southern Maputo Corridor runs through one of the most industrialized and productive regions of Southern Africa and is composed of the Maputo and Matola ports, several railway lines and one transnational road (EN4). Maputo's port is one of Africa's biggest deepwater ports capable of receiving ships weighing 100,000 tonnes and above. It was conceded on the 14th of April 2003 for a period of 15 years, with a 10-year extension option to the Maputo Port and Development Company (MPDC) a registered Mozambican company and backed by a consortium of European (EU) investors with Mozambican partners. The Maputo Corridor is also composed of three railway lines. The 88 kilometres Ressano Garcia Line which links the Port of Maputo to the Republic of South Africa and which is managed by Ressano Garcia Railway SARL. The 522 kilometres Limpopo Line which links the Port of Maputo to the Republic of Zimbabwe. And the 78 kilometres Goba Line which links the Port to Swaziland. Thus Maputo, already the centre of most of the country's business activity, will grow as an international trade centre.

The Central Beira Corridor is composed of the port of Beira, the Machinpanda Railway and the Sena Railway. It is a Corridor that presents a lot of growth potential. Indeed the port of Beira is the most modernised port in Southern Africa and is operated by Cornelder de Moçambique SARL, a joint venture between Cornelder B.V. from Holland and CFM. Ideally situated on the East African Coast, the port of Beira's main strength is the short transit time it offers to Zimbabwe, Malawi, Zambia, Botswana and Congo - formerly Zaire, as well as part of Mozambique itself. In fact the port is directly linked by road and by the 317 kilometers Machipanda railway line to the border of Zimbabwe and will soon have a direct rail link to Malawi with the 600 kilometers Sena line.

The Northern Nacala Corridor is more than a series of rail and port infrastructures under development since the first decade of the last century. It is a window open to investment opportunities, an axis that will stimulate the exploitation of the natural resources available in the areas. It will also encourage the implantation of various undertakings and businesses, generating employment and economic and social development. In the regional context, the Nacala Corridor plays a particularly important role for the economies of Malawi and Zambia, who have no direct access to the Indian Ocean, but have in Nacala a gateway open to international trade, at substantially lower costs. Indeed the Corridor is composed of the port of Nacala, the deepest port in Oriental Africa a depth ranging from 15 to 40 meters. That condition provides great advantages of navigability and safety permitting the entry of all size of ships. Additionally the existence of modern and essential infrastructures with capacity to handle 2,000,000 tonnes annually gives the port a strong growth potential. The corridor is also composed of the Nacala - Malawi and the Nacala - Lichinga railway line. The whole of the Nacala Corridor is being managed by the Northern Development Corridor consortium, formed by the Nacala Corridor Development Company (SDCN) and CFM.

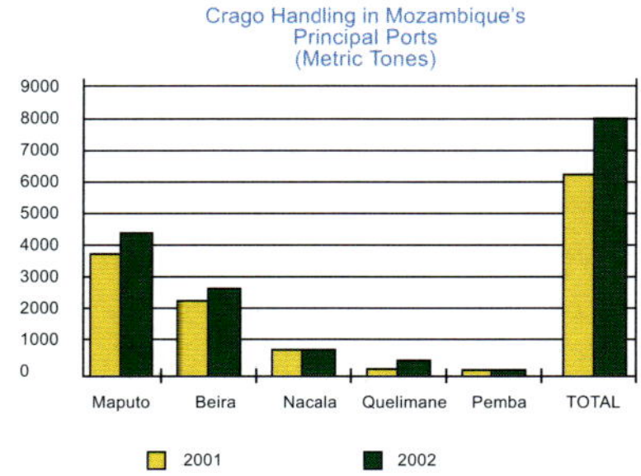

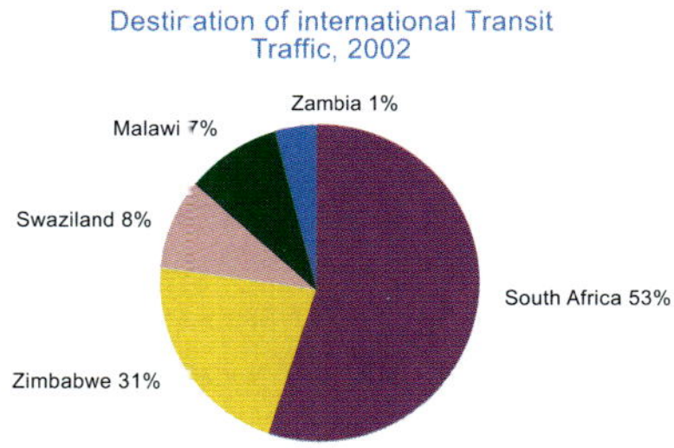

Source: Ministry of Transport and Communication

Maputo, a main port for the whole region

Airports

Mozambique's air transport system is actually going through important reforms with the introduction of private partners to manage and improve the infrastructures. The national flag carrier, Linhas Aereas de Mozambique (LAM) services 9 provincial capitals from Maputo and has international flights to South Africa, Portugal and Zimbabwe. The privatised firm Empresa Nacional de Transporte e Trabalho Aereo (TTA) has scheduled services and offers charter flights in light aircraft and helicopters. Light aircraft services are also provided by international feeder airlines to Nelspruit and Durban in South Africa as well as Manzini in Swaziland. The airports and aerodromes in Mozambique are operated by Aeroportos de Moçambique (ADM), which also operates the air navigation services of the country. ADM is a state owned corporation, operating on a self-financing basis. Maputo Airport is the main gateway to Mozambique and has approximately 430,000 passengers per year. The terminal and other facilities at the airport are in serious need of upgrading. The government has decided that an upgrade will be achieved by way of a concession and in fact various airports are expected to go through concessions. "We are waiting proposals for a 25 year concession to operate Maputo airport" says Honourable T.A. Salomão, Minister of Transport & Communication. The airports' system is also assisting an important growth with the increasing internationalisation of several airports. The country possesses 19 airports including 5 international airports (Maputo, Beira, Chimoio, Nampula, and Pemba). There are additional plans to privatise and liberalize the air transport market. Indeed, studies are being carried out to privatise LAM (Linhas Areas de Moçambique), the national airline. Actually air links to other countries remain limited, expensive and productivity levels are very low. Through all these reforms, Mozambique expects to change this situation and one immediate payback Mozambique expects, is the increase of international tourists notably thanks to cheaper flights resulting from improved management and competition levels.

International flights from/to Maputo

Companies	Weekly frequency
LAM	16
S. African Airways	7
TAP	2

TELECOMMUNICATIONS

The Government of Mozambique is in the process of revolutionising its telecommunication industry. The privatisation and liberalisation of the telecommunication sector is beginning and the government is convinced that only access to and use of information and communications technologies by an increasing large segment of the population will pull the country decisively out of its current situation of underdevelopment.

Indeed, the telecommunication sector is one of the sectors undergoing the most important developments in terms of reforms. In 1992 the Mozambican parliament introduced a legislation re-defining the telecommunications sector policies, strategy and objectives and this reform process is still ongoing. The main company within the sector is Telecomunicações de Moçambique E.E. (TDM) which is the main telecommunication operator and has for principal objective the establishment, the management and the exploration of Mozambique's telecommunication network. Today the Mozambican telecommunication sector is being liberalized and consequently TDM is going through a restructuring process. Nevertheless, the Grupo TDM still controls 60 per cent of the companies in the sector, contributing to 91 per cent of the sector's revenues. Indeed TDM is known as one of the best-run companies in Mozambique, though it is still a state-owned entity. To make sure the company continues its aggressive infrastructure development programme, the government will sell at least a part of its shares on the Mozambique stock exchange or to a strategic partner. In 1999, the Telecommunication Law 14/99 was approved for opening the telecommunication market to private entities and the promotion of access to telecommunication and information technologies.

TDM building

Telecommunication companies function under the regulation of the Instituto National das Comunicações de Moçambique (INCM), namely the National Institute of Communication of Mozambique, which is a body of the Ministry of Transport and Communication. In an effort to revitalize the sector the INCM is opening up the market to free competition. Indeed in a bid to introduce and encourage private sector competition, the government has defined areas of competition under the Telecommunication Law 6/2001. TDM is obliged by law to keep the public telecommunications network open to all users. It must provide access to the public transmissions network, to all telecommunications service providers on an equal non-discriminatory basis in respect of access, pricing and quality. The company may provide complimentary or value added services in competition with other operators and service providers, however it is prevented by law from taking unfair advantage of its dominant position as the public operator. TDM has put in place a strategic investment plan, over a five-year period, which began in 2001 for the construction and improvement of broadband connections throughout Maputo as well as the whole of the country.

Fixed Phone

International telephone services as well as fax services are available in most towns. TDM is the only fixed line operator and although it is actively increasing the number of fixed lines across the country there is still lots to do in order to reduce the huge rural disparity that exists within the telecommunications industry. Around 65 per cent of all lines are concentrated in the capital city Maputo and the 2nd and 3rd largest cities only have 11 per cent and 7 per cent of all lines leaving the expansive rural areas with no telecommunications network. To increase the accessibility of telephone system in the country, the company as introduced a pre paid card system all around the main cities of Mozambique. TDM expects to increase the number of users to 120,000 in 2004. TDM is also the first telecommunication company in the SADC to have set up a full digital exchange system.

Fixed telephone indicators

	1999	2000	2001	2002
Coverage	78,2	78,7	78,7	78,7
Subscribers	78 072	85 714	89 488	85 488
Teledensity /1000hab	4.3	4,7	4,9	4,7

Celular phones

Currently there is only one mobile phone operator in Mozambique, namely M-Cel. In fact in 1997 TDM created the cellular mobile telephone service M-Cel that was managed by Telecomunicações Móveis de Moçambique, Lda. (TMM) owned 100 per cent by TDM. At the beginning of 2003, with the privatisation and liberalization of the sector, the Mozambican government converted TDM into a limited company, and separated it from its cellular mobile telephone service. TMM thus ceased to be a wholly owned subsidiary of TDM and is now a limited company, which has taken the official name of Moçambique Celular (M-Cel) and whose shares are, for the time being, owned by the state. Today Mozambique has 350,000 mobile phone users with 90 per cent on using pre-paid services. In September 2002, VODACOM from South Africa was named as second mobile operator. It should enter the market by beginning 2004 at the latest and eventually invest an estimated $180 Million, thus contributing for the development of the sector. Through this increase competition coverage should rapidly increase as for now the majority of mobile phone users is mainly concentrated in Maputo and the surrounding areas.

Mobile Phone Indicators

	1999	2000	2001	2002
Contract	12 234	21 969	25 088	26 389
Pre payment		29 096	169 900	232 970
Density / 1000 hab	0,7	2.8	11.0	14.0

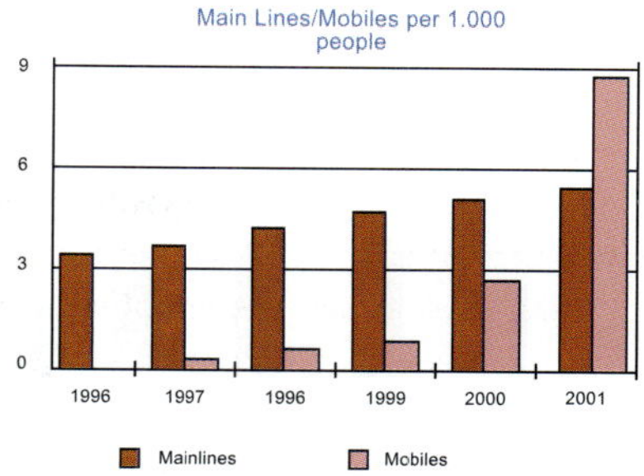

Source: World Bank, 2003

Internet

Over the past 2 years Mozambique's Internet usage has more than doubled from 5500 to 12000. Up until now over 75 per cent of the users were based in the Maputo area with the remaining 25 per cent based in the provinces. Although Mozambique is a poor country, Maputo has several Internet cafés, which charge $3 per hour for access and $30 for a dial-up and over 10 Internet service providers. The newly created fibre optic (see above) highway has promised to deliver information technology access to rural communities where the majority of Mozambicans live. Internet usage has dramatically increased and promises to duplicate yearly for the foreseeable future. With the improvement in bandwidth, telecommunication infrastructures and the expansion of ISPs through out the country it is expected that Internet usage will boom. The National Commission on Information is to focus on information technology policies. This is a government body headed by the Prime Minister Honourable Dr. Pascoal Mocumbi that formulates national policy for the Internet, information technology, research and the future of commerce on the Internet. It also raises national awareness on the importance of information technology in the areas of education, science, health and entertainment. The sector functions under the Information and Communication Technology Policy approved on the 27th of June 2002.

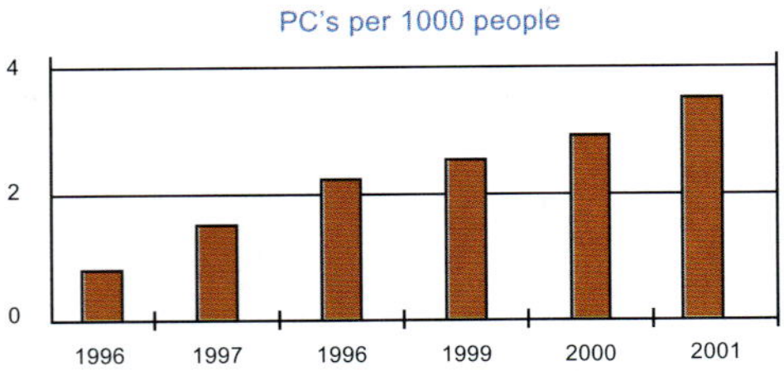

Source: World Bank, 2003

MAIN COMPANIES

Agrofresco (Mozspan group)

Dave Walker, Operations Manager
Estrada Nacional n°2 ao Km 5,5 Matola
P.O.Box 2605, Maputo
Tel: + 258 - 1 - 751122 / 23
Fax: + 258 - 1 - 750632

AGROFRESCO is a young and dynamic company that operates in the fresh product industry. It belongs 100 per cent to MCT (Matola Cargo Terminal) and operates throughout the country. AGROFRESCO carries out the following activities: local and International Procurement of fresh products; Processing of fresh products; local and International Marketing of fresh products. In fact AGROFRESCO carries out the trade of various fresh products such as mangos, tangerines, bananas, lychees, papayas and pineapple, just to name a few, as well as vegetables. AGROFRESCO was built on MCT experience with the handling of fresh products. Today the company is unlocking the fresh product potentials that exist in Mozambique. Thus AGROFRESCO's activity is slowly spreading to all the different fresh products available in Mozambique as well as to all those products needed in the country. In just a few months of activity, the company has already air freighted lychees to Portugal and supplied fresh products to major European players. AGROFRESCO is proud of successfully meeting the needs of a growing industry. AGROFRESCO strives to effectively grow with the industry and continuously meet the various needs of its existing and future clients.

FCL - Freight Care Logistics (Mozspan group)

Philippe de Maeyer, Operations Manager
Estrada Nacional n°2 ao Km 5,5 Matola
P.O.Box 2605, Maputo
Tel: + 258 - 1 - 751122 / 23

Freight Care Logistics (FCL) belongs 100 per cent to the Matola Cargo Terminal (MCT). FCL carries out freight forwarding and project logistics services and possesses expertise in fresh product logistics. Its services are for both inbound and outbound goods. FCL has very strong assets, as it possesses its own trucks, warehouses and forklifts. FCL is ideally situated on the Maputo Corridor, close to the Matola Port and at the International road Terminal, which operates as well as the clearing house for the customs. FCL possesses a strong asset basis and carries out all the work itself. It possesses a very good reputation and FCL is the only true fresh product logistic company. FCL is actively working with major international players such as Vodacom and Siemens in the telecom industry and Capespan in the fresh product industry. Because of the high quality of its services a number of companies prefer to route their cargo through Mozambique with FCL services. FCL strives to actively participate in Mozambique's economic development by offering best value for money services. FCL aims for the future to be amongst the leading logistics companies in the country.

King & Sons (Moçambique) Lda

Liam McKenzie, General Director
51 Praça dos Trabalhoras - 4° Andar
P.O.Box 2902, Maputo
Tel: + 258 - 1 - 430021 / 2 / 3
Fax: + 258 - 1 - 322262
E-mail: mckenzie@virconn.com
Website: www.kingandsonsmoz.co.za

The name of King & Sons has been synonymous with shipping in Southern Africa for over a hundred years. From beginnings in Durban in 1891, King & Sons is now a major operator in the region, and is represented in all shipping centres in Mozambique, South Africa and Namibia. As part of the network of Southern African Port Agents who share the historic name, King & Sons Mozambique is an independent locally registered and operated company that has been active in freight and general Ships Agency business in Mozambique for over thirty years. The company has as main shareholders Grindrod Freight Investment (PTY) Ltd, which is part of the Grincor Group of Companies, the largest South African Shipping Group. With full port agency offices in Maputo, Beira and Nacala, and sub-agency offices in Pemba and Quelimane, the company currently focuses on the provision of Non-Liner Port Agency, Clearing and Forwarding and Inspection services. The company draws on the strength, integrity and expertise of its local and international shareholder companies, as backup to the services of King & Sons Mozambique. King & Sons is one of the few Mozambican ship and cargo agencies with an established regional network and committed international shareholder support. King & Sons strives to develop, maintain and increase the business of customers through the provision in all areas of agency Services at levels that meet and exceed International Standards. By doing this King & Sons has a view to become the dominant player in the sector.

Linhas Aéreas de Moçambique (LAM)

José Ricardo Viegas, MD & Chairman
P.O. Box 2060, Maputo
Tel: + 258 - 1 - 465074 / 5143
Fax: + 258 - 1 - 465134
E-mail: jrviegas@lam.co.mz
Website: www.lam.co.mz

LAM started off as a company named DETA (Divisão Esploraçao Transportes Aereo), and as a domestic airline before the independence, the only international flight it had being Johannesburg. At the time, intercontinental flights were under the monopoly of TAP (Transportes Aereos Portugueses). DETA operated several types of airplanes before the independence, the biggest one they had was 727-200. Thus in 1980, with the new restructuring of the company, the government decided to turnaround the situation. As an independent country, they needed a national carrier able to penetrate other countries, so the government decided to invest in the expansion of the Maputo International Airport by extending the runway of 1000 metres. It was then that LAM started creating intercontinental flights with a DC-10. LAM's different segments include a domestic market (70,000 passengers per annum); a regional market (75,000 passengers per annum to Johannesburg; Pemba); a secondary regional market (Harare, Mayette Island, Durban); an intercontinental market (Lisbon); and it operates on a franchise basis with other Mozambican operators. They focus on domestic operations, (without forgetting the intercontinental flight) and prepare the airline for competition. Until 2001 LAM had the exclusive rights to operate in Mozambique. Since then the government has decided to liberalise air transport by giving traffic rights to other operators. Consumers will benefit from the fair war, thus LAM has decided to centre its efforts in the domestic area and invest in its equipment. Staff at LAM is 100 per cent Mozambicans and they give elevated results and great success.

In order to maintain the leadership on the national market, LAM strives to improve the quality of their service, open up new markets and engage in regional marketing.

Manica Freight Services (Moç) SARL

Fernando Amado Couto, CEO
Praça dos Trabahadores, n°51
P.O.Box 292 or 557, Maputo
Tel: + 258 - 1 - 324023
Fax: + 258 - 1 - 430674
E-mail: fcouto@manica.co.mz
Website: www.manico.co.mz

Manica Freight Services (Moç) SARL was created in 1892 in Beira, in the Province of Sofala. In 1940, it was bought by South African investors. In the year 2000, several private investors bought Manica and today the company is 100% Mozambican. It is the leading maritime transport company in Mozambique. Manica Freight Services SARL offers maritime-based freight transportation services: Shipping Agency; Freight Management; Forwarding & Clearing; Container Handling; and others. Indeed it is the leader in Mozambique with more than 60 per cent of the market share and it is present in the six most important ports of Mozambique, namely Maputo, Matola, Beira, Quelimane, Nacala and Pemba. It is also an active sponsor in various projects across Mozambique such as the Corridor of Nacala where, with two other companies, it runs the railway line to Malawi and Zimbabwe. Manica strives to consolidate its current market share and grow in the regional market through partnerships and the possible creation of sister companies in neighboring countries. Manica works at all the different levels of the economy where it offers high standard services. They have received the ISO 9002 certification and they actively train their employees. Manica Freight Services differentiates itself from the competition by its undeniable experience in Mozambique, its adaptability and flexibility, and its leadership. "Manica is the Mozambican link in the global market of transport". Manica Freight Services (Moç) SARL has managed to effectively and successfully sustain its activities throughout the years. Since its creation, it has constantly lead the transport market in Mozambique and this demonstrates its capacity to continue doing so in the years to come. Manica will face the challenges in order to maintain and strengthen its position as leader in Mozambique through their understanding of local and global needs, innovation, and the respect of the different cultures present in the country.

: : Moçambique Celular : :
International Roaming
More than 150 operators worldwide
GSM 900/1800 Mhz
Best coverage in Mozambique
Telecommunication Market Leader
Innovative products and services
Customer Care Line
111 Free on 082 network
131 Free on 082 network
Headquarter: mCel Building Av. 25 de Setembro PO Box 1483
Tel: +258 1 35 11 00 Fax: +258 135 11 01 Maputo - Mozambique
www.mcel.co.mz
you first
082
mCel
Moçambique Celular

MCT - Matola Cargo Terminal, SARL (Mozspan group)

J.C. Strauss, Managing Director
Estrada Nacional n°2 ao Km 5,5 Matola
P.O.Box 2605, Maputo
Tel: + 258 - 1 - 751122
Fax: + 258 - 1 - 750632
E-mail: mct@virconn.com

Matola Cargo Terminal (MCT), which is also called the International Road Terminal, was created in 1993. In 1996 Outspan International Limited, an citrus trade company, bought MCT in a joint venture with Manica Freight Services. Today its major shareholders, with 90% of the shares, is the Capespan Group, a specialized world class leader in the marketing of fresh fruit internationally. It is part of the Mozspan Group. MCT serves as the Mozambican Clearing House for the Customs Office for all cargo transported by road. Additionally MCT works as holding depot for fruit exported through the Maputo port and in fact offers the following services: Warehouses; Cold rooms; Trucking door to door. MCT offers high quality and safe services. In fact it possesses armed security guards which watch all cargo on a 24 hour basis. Additionally the Matola Cargo Terminal is ideally located on the Maputo Corridor a short distance away of the Matola port.

M-Cel (Moçambique Celular)

Peter Correia, CEO
Stanley Henning, Commercial Director
Edificio mCel, Av. 25 de Setembro
Caixa Postal 1483, Maputo.
Tel: + 258 - 1 - 351100
Fax: + 258 - 1 - 351117
E-mail: pcorreia@mcel.co.mz or shenning@mcel.co.mz
Website: www.mcel.co.mz

Fax and Data Service; Short Message Service (SMS); Call Barring; Electronic Invoice. M-Cel is a competitive customer-focused operator, which offers high quality services at reachable prices. In fact although their services are locally adapted, these are complemented with a wide range of up-to-date value added services. Additionally their services are present in all the country's provinces. Today the M-Cel brand and its giro brand have become household names. In fact since 2001, they have increased the number of subscribers from 50,000 to 350,000, and to many analysts, M-Cel is a success story. Last but not least, M-Cel is a socially active company, which is involved in various community-based projects in education and infrastructure just to name a few.

M-Cel strives to strengthen its position in Mozambique as a World Class Mobile Operator and a top brand name and to create superior network services backed by superior client care while offering competitive prices.

Maputo Port Development Company (MPDC) SARL

Alec Don, MD
Port Director's Building, Port of Maputo
PO Box 2841, Maputo
Tel: + 258 - 1 - 313920
Fax: + 258 - 1 - 313921
E-mail: info@portmaputo.com
Website: www.portmaputo.com

On the 14th of April 2003 the Maputo Port Development Company (MPDC) SARL started operating the deepwater port of Maputo. In fact the port of Maputo has been conceded to MPDC for a period of 15 years, with a 10-year extension option. MPDC is registered in Mozambique and is backed by a consortium of European (EU) investors with Mozambican partners. Finance has been sourced from the consortium's own resources and an international group of merchant banks. The consortium, which holds 51% of the equity, consists of the Mersey Docks & Harbour Group (UK), owner and operator of the Port of Liverpool, Skanska (Sweden) one of the world's leading construction companies, and the Portuguese terminal operator Liscont. The Mozambican partners are led by Portos e Caminhos de Ferro de Mozambique (CFM), which holds 33% of the equity, and the balance of 16% is retained by the government, for future disposal to regional investors. Under the Agreement MPDC has been granted the rights to finance, rehabilitate, operate, manage, maintain, develop and optimise the port concession area, which includes the ports of Maputo and Matola. In fact MPDC operates as the Port Authority and therefore is responsible for marine operations, towage, stevedoring, terminal and warehousing operations as well as port planning and development. MPDC's development project has commenced with the implementation of a 3 year US$70m rehabilitation programme designed to enable importers and exporter to "add value' to their trade by using a secure, modern and cost efficient alternative to South African Ports. In fact the Maputo Corridor, which provides the shortest transit route to the sea for all the northern provinces of South Africa and the neighbouring regions, ends at the deepwater port of Maputo. Compatible road and rail networks link all the productive hinterland areas, and significant new investment projects, aimed at modernizing the cross-border transport systems, are now in progress and will give the Port of Maputo strong competitive advantages. MPDC's objective is to re-establish the port of Maputo as a key economic growth centre in Mozambique. It strives to successfully implement its investment programme, attract businesses from all over the world and participate in the economic development of the country as well as the region.

Mocargo - Empresa Moçambicana de Cargas, S.A.R.L

Manuel Amaral, Managing Director
Rua Consiglieri Pedroso, N° 430
P.O.Box 888, Maputo
Tel: + 258 - 1 - 428318 / 321440
Fax: + 258 - 1 - 302067 / 305263
E-mail: msamaral@teledata.mz
Website: www.mocargo.co.mz

In the early years following independence the government of Mozambique controlled all the imports and exports activities. Mocargo - Empresa Moçambicana de Cargas, then a public company, was created in 1982 to assist the system with shipping services. With the privatization and liberalization wave of the mid-1990s, Mocargo was privatized in 1995. Today, 80 per cent of Mocargo's shares are in hands of its workers and Mozambican investors, and the remaining 20 per cent, are in those of a private Danish shipping company. It is a private logistics company which provides services through specialized Business Units: Mofrete-Mocargo Fretes: shipping & forwarding of Mozambique import/export; Motran-Mocargo Trânsitos e Navegação: services for cargo in transit and ship's agency; Air Cargo Division: services in shipping & forwarding of cargoes by air. Mocargo attends and represents all the logistics interests of their clients in the region and neighbouring countries. They possess branches in the main ports of Maputo, Beira and Nacala. Mocargo's offers cost effective operations with a delivery of services of high standard. In fact thanks to their flexibility they ensure personalized and client oriented services. Through their international connections with major players in the transport industry they are able to offer a wide range of logistics services. Mocargo has been involved with the MOZAL Aluminum Smelter Project providing them with their logistics needs as well as major projects with the most reputable international and regional companies.

Move (Mozspan group)

Philippe Franco, General Manager
Estrada Nacional n°2 ao Km 5,5 Matola
P.O.Box 2605, Maputo
Tel: + 258 - 1 - 751122
Fax: + 258 - 1 - 751075

Matola Cargo Terminal (MCT), the holding depot for fruit exported through the Maputo port, found that it did not use its forklift during the low citrus season and thus started renting them to the industrial sector. As the business picked up, MCT decided to create a separate company in charge of this business activity. Thus in 2000 MOVE was created. Today it belongs 100 per cent to MCT. MOVE is a material handling company, which offers forklift rental services. In fact it possesses the country's biggest fleet of forklifts. MOVE carries out the following services: Forklift rentals; Sales and maintenance of the forklift from the Clark Brand; Sales of tools related to materials handling; Sales of water pumps; Transport services for the industry through their partner "Corredor Transport"; Service centre for forklifts and trucks; and crank rentals. MOVE is strongly focused on delivering the best material handling services to the industrial sector. It is strongly focused on this segment of the industry as it aims to become, in the near future, the biggest supplier and operator of material handling products in Mozambique. MOVE benefits of a strong asset base, expertise in the area, and the fact that it operates from the International Road Terminal. MOVE is the major material handling company in the fresh product industry.

MOVE strives to continuously meet the needs of its customers through high quality products and services.

Mozline, Empresa de Transportes Marítimos e Rodoviários de Moçambique, S.A.R.L

Liam McKenzie, General Manager
Av. Karl Marx, 478, 2° Andar
P.O.Box 2902, Maputo
Tel: + 258 - 1 - 303076 / 8 / 9
Fax: + 258 - 1 - 303073
E-mail: mozline2@virconn.com
Website: www.mozline.com

Mozline started operating in 1997 with the objective of serving the domestic shipping market with efficient, reliable and regular maritime-based freight transportation services. Unifeeder (Pty) Ltd, formerly known as Unicorn Lines Ltd, from South Africa owns 40 per cent of the company's shares. Grupo Tertir Investimentos SARL from Portugal owns 35 per cent of the shares, and the remaining 25 per cent are owned by local private Mozambican investors. Today Mozline is the major player in the domestic shipping market and in 2000 was ranked as the 48th largest company in Mozambique. Mozline offers maritime-based freight transportation services both along the Mozambican coast and regionally. It is active in eight regional countries and it provides freight services through established relationships with many major Mozambican and South African companies. Mozline strives to continue growing through the expansion of regional pier to pier shipping services as well as the development of landside freight logistics services in the region. Mozline plans also to increase its presence throughout Mozambique with the creation of regional offices. Their main competitive advantage lies in the cost efficiency, the reliability and the frequency of their services. Having started from zero, Mozline enjoyed rapid growth and today is the largest shipping company in Mozambique. Mozline's major challenge lies in the regional market as they strive to sustain their growth in a very competitive market.

Privest Training (Mozspan group)

Sonia Smith, General Manager
Rua José Mateus, n°75, Maputo
Tel: + 258 - 1 - 485022 / 24
Fax: + 258 - 1 - 485021
E-mail: privest@emilmoz.com

PRIVEST belongs 100 per cent to MCT (Matola Cargo terminal) and is specialized in the training for the material handling industry. It offers training in material handling, driving of forklifts and other related fields. PRIVEST also offers training in the following fields: Languages (English & Portuguese); Social Re-integration Programs for retrenched miners or demobilized soldiers; Health & Safety Training and ISO certification; Middle Management Training Programs; Sourcing, Placement of Technical Staff; Technical Training (welding, etc...). PRIVEST TRAINING offers complete and effective training programs in various crucial fields. It is actively working in order to increase its influence on companies' performance levels by extending its range of training services, including for example Middle Management Training Programs. PRIVEST TRAINING continuously improves, and maintains its training technology through various institutes in South Africa. PRIVEST TRAINING is proud to participate in Mozambique's economic and social development. In fact it is giving the Mozambican population the opportunity to develop the skills necessary for them to craft their own future. PRIVEST TRAINING strives to become Mozambique's main Human Capacity Building Company.

South African Airways

Femao-Gil de Passos, Country Manager
Rua Fernao Melo e Castro N°. 287
Maputo
Tel: + 258 - 1 - 499914
Fax: + 258 - 1 - 499808
E-mail: femiesaa@teledata.mz
Website: www.flysaa.com

South African Airways started operating in Mozambique over 40 years ago but ceased operations during the civil war in the mid-1980s. When the war ended in 1992, South African Airways restarted its flight operations between Maputo and Johannesburg and slowly increased their frequency. Today they have 10 flights per week and are actively strengthening their presence in the Mozambique. South African Airways offers several services in Mozambique: Passenger flights between Johannesburg and Maputo, their hub; Freight/Cargo Services; SA Airlink between Durban and Maputo, and between Johannesburg and Beira. South African Airways is working to put in place a code share agreement with Lineas Aeras de Moçambique (LAM) in order to increase capacity to Mozambique. Through Johannesburg, their hub, South African Airways offers flights to the whole of South Africa and to various regions in all five continents. In fact through code share agreements with several major airlines, such as Cathay Pacific, Delta Airways and Quantas, it offers flight destinations across the whole of the globe. South African Airways has greatly contributed to the economic development, the increase of investments and the reconstruction of Mozambique, as most of their clients flying to Maputo are business related. Thus South African Airways has served as a link between Mozambique and the rest of the world. The main challenges facing South African Airways concerning Mozambique are: to attract an increasing number of tourist-related passengers; to increase their capacity and the number of entry points into Mozambique.

STA - Sociedade de Transportes Aéreos SARL

R. Walter Carreira, Chairman Board of Directors
Rua de Tchamba, 405
Maputo
Tel: + 258 - 1 - 491765 / 492022 / 495107
Fax: + 258 - 1 - 491763
E-mail: sta.tta@sta.co.mz
Website: www.sta.co.mz

STA - Sociedade de Transportes Aereos SARL was created in 1990 as a domestic carrier in a moment where the avia-

MOZSPAN Group
MATOLA CARGO TERMINAL S.A.R.L T/A
MOVE
• Forklift Rental / Sales
• Full Maintenance plans
• Trucking Long - Short Distance
• Service Centre
FCL
FREIGHT CARE LOGISTICS
• Project Logistics
• Import / Export Documents
• Container Handling
• Storage: Ambient and Refrigeration
AGRO FRESCO
'Fresh from the farm'
PRIVEST
TECHNICAL TRAINING
GENTE • PRODUTIVIDADE • DESEMPENHO
• Fresh Produce Processing
• Fresh Produce Exports / Imports
• Banana Ripening and Sales
• Agricultural Project Development
• Technical Training
• Language Training
• Social re integration of redundant staff
• Health and Safety
• Agricultural Training
Estrada Nacional N° 2 ao Km 5,5 • Matola - Moçambique P.O. Box 2605 Maputo
Tel.: +258 (1) 75 11 22 • Fax. +258 (1) 75 06 32 • Cel.: +258 (82) 30 96 39
E-mail: jota_ce@mozspan.co.mz

tion market was being liberalized. It started with a fleet of small aircrafts and today it has grown to be the second largest national airline. STA's network of services in Mozambique is extensive, carrying an average of 6,000 passengers and 150,000 tons of cargo annually. STA serves the needs of thousands of travelers to the different provinces every year. Its reputation has grown and is visible today in the large number of clients who use STA as their preferred domestic and regional carrier. STA also operates intercontinental charters.

The company's activities include: Freight and passenger transport; Regular Flight destinations are: Maputo, Beira, Quelimane, Nampula, Chimoio, Tete, Songo, Nacala and the connection Johannesburg - Vinlankulo; Charters flights for domestic, regional, and intercontinental destinations; Helicopter services. Like for any airline, the growth of the company's activities relies on the development of the national economy and the infrastructures across the different provinces. STA is constantly adapting its products and services to the needs of its customers and this is what differentiates it from its competitors. In fact as a customer-focused company they offer customized - high quality flights. STA has of being DHL's main partner for many of its operations across Mozambique. It is also proud of operating intercontinental flights. STA's challenges for the future lie in the development of the transport sector. In terms of geographical location Mozambique is very well situated and STA strives to increase its future activity.

Tap-Air Portugal

José M. Martins Moreira, General Manager for South Africa & Mozambique
Rua da Sé n°114, Centro Comercial do Hotel Rovuma, Loja n°28, Maputo
Tel: + 258 - 1 - 303915
Fax: + 258 - 1 - 303947
Website: www.tap.pt

Transportes Aereos Portugueses, also called TAP-Air Portugal, is the Portuguese national airline. It operates flights to 60 destinations worldwide. It started operations in Mozambique before the independence with a weekly flight. Slowly it increased its activity and today TAP-Air Portugal operates two flights a week and holds 60 of the intercontinental flights market. TAP-Air Portugal offers several flight services in Mozambique: Twice a week International Passenger Flights between Maputo and Lisbon; Freight/Cargo Services. TAP-Air Portugal has a code share agreement with Linhas Aéreas de Moçambique (LAM) which gives the company a leading edge on its competitors. In fact through various bilateral code share agreements with several major airlines, such as KLM and Continental Airways, it offers flight destinations across the whole of the globe. In addition, TAP-Air Portugal distinguishes itself from its competitors through its great experience in Mozambique, its punctuality, the quality of its services and its closeness to the local culture. This strength is reflected in the fact that TAP-Air Portugal accounts for 60% of the intercontinental flights from and to Mozambique. TAP-Air Portugal has managed to establish in Mozambique a strong and loyal client base. In fact TAP-Air Portugal has not only gained the trust of individual travellers but also that of the biggest corporations, which have chosen to fly their staff with tap. As tourism and business will increase in the years to come, TAP-Air Portugal will increase the regularity of its flights and strengthen its leading position in Mozambique.

Telecomunicações de Moçambique SARL (TDM)

Salvador Adriano, Managing Director
Rua da Sé, 2°
P.O.Box 25, Maputo
Tel: + 258 - 1 - 431921
Fax: + 258 - 1 - 323178
E-mail: sadriano@tdm.mz
Website: www.tdm.mz

Telecomunicações de Moçambique E.E. was created on the 10th of June of 1981, through the dissolution of "Correios, Telégrafos e Telefones (CTT)". It then became a public company on the 10th of September 1992. Today the Mozambican telecommunication sector is being liberalized and consequently TDM is in a phase of restructuring. TDM is Mozambique's main telecommunication operator and has for principal objective the establishment, the management and the exploration of Mozambique's telecommunication network. TDM offers the following services: Fix lines (main service); Broadband services; Infrastructure services; and International communications. TDM is also composed of several subsidiaries: M-Cel (Cellular Telecommunication); Teledata de Moçambique, Lda; TV Cabo (Cable Television); Televisa (Telecommunication Network); Listas Telefonicas de Moçambique; and Teleserve (Telecommunication Services). Although the telecommunication sector is being liberalized, TDM still has a social obligation and thus has to expand the telecommunication networks to all of the country. Also as new competition will be entering the market, TDM is actively preparing itself to receive them and to actually provide them with various services. In fact TDM sees the arrival of new competition as an opportunity to expand its activity. TDM launched in 1997 a successful mobile service in Mozambique. TDM is also the first telecommunication company in the SADC to have set up a full digital exchange system. Finally TDM has put in place an extensive fiber optic network that connects the south and the centre of the country. In the 5 - 10 years to come TDM strives to be present throughout the whole country offering various services, including infrastructure services, to all the telecommunication operators present in Mozambique.

TPM - Transportes Públicos de Maputo E.P.

Luciano Jaime Sitoe, President of the Board of Administration
Av. Filipe Samuel Magaia, N°1481
C.Postal 1060, Maputo
Tel: + 258 - 1 - 425793 / 428124
Fax: +258 - 1 - 424383
E-mail: ljsitoe@tvcabo.co.mz

The company first started as a private company in the 1930s. Later on, the Colonial Government decided to nationalize it and named it SMV (Serviços Municipalizados de Viação). In 1978, following the independence, SMV merged with "Companhia de Transportes de Moçambique", an urban-rural transport company, and formed TPU (Transportes Públicos Urbanos) a state-run company. In 1996, after the war ended, the government changed the company's name to TPM, which is today a public but functions under a management contract. TPM offers regular urban passenger transport services in the capital city of Maputo and neighboring city, Matola. TPM also offers special urban transport services to private companies. Transportes Públicos de Maputo strives to accompany both cities in the general growth consistently offering effective, regular, and safe urban transport services. This will be done through the establishment of new lines and the acquisition of the correspondent number of buses. TPM, in comparison wit the other city transport companies, offers professional and customer focused services. Its labour force is well trained and thus their services are safe and respectful. TPM is a public company and thus it plays a social role offering cheap and accessible transport services and in fact its fares are the lowest on the market.

CCC Transportes Urbanos

Luis Brazuna, General Manager
Av. Organizaçao de Unidade Africana n° 500
Maputo
Tel: + 258 - 1 - 407588 / 9 / 407590
Fax: + 258 - 1 - 405060
E-mail: lbrazuna@tu.mz
Website: www.ccc.pt

CCC Transportes Urbanos was incorporated as a Mozambican limited liability company in August 1998 through 100% foreign investment. It is part of the IPG Group. As a specialized removals company, they started with a 300 sqm warehouse. Throughout the years they have slowly grown and today they work with a premises of 2,500 sqm. CCC Transportes Urbanos is a removal company which offers the following services: Office Removals; International, Local and Fine Art Removals; Ware housing; Computer Center Removals; Technical Service and Renting of External Elevators; Outsourcing of Logistics Departments; Integrated Logistic Services for Technology; Distribution. The growth areas are to be determined in the lines of opening new branches in Tete and Lichinga, and the acquisition of fleet and other equipments. Transportes Urbanos is a well-integrated service company in the market with local knowledge, which collaborates with the biggest companies in Mozambique. Premises: warehouse 2,300 sqm + 800 sqm in Maputo; Open areas 1,800 sqm in Machava + 3,600 sqm in Marracuene; Group Headquarters 600 sqm offices in Maputo; Group offices in Beira and Nampula.

TOURISM

ebiZ guides

OVERVIEW

The potential of Mozambique in terms of natural resources with its extensive flora, animal wildlife and cultural diversity, and the interaction of all these elements early attracted the government's attention to turn Tourism in one of the driving forces for economic development and poverty reduction.

One notable feature of Mozambique's attractions is the presence of the big five, which include elephants, lions, rhinos, leopards and buffalos. Other major animals are also present such as giraffes, zebras, antelopes and gazelles. This natural presence of an extensive wildlife is complemented by a significant geographical diversity and the contrast of African cultures and habits together with Asiatic and European lifestyles.

Tourism was the most affected sector during the war as most of the tourist infrastructures were in rural and remote areas were the war was directly felt. Since then the government has become aware of the importance of tourism activities to the national economy. In fact, tourism in Mozambique aims to provide suitable conditions for the well-being and leisure of its citizens and to establish more affinity and cultural exchange with people of other nations. Tourism contributes to an increase in job opportunities. Decree n°1093 of 22nd June established the "National Tourism Fund" (Fundo Nacional do Turismo - FUTUR) in charge of the promotion and financing of tourism development. In 1996, the government also created the National Tourism Policy as the basis for the regulation and organization of tourism development, which put in place the necessary actions and priorities. Consequently the National Tourism Direction was created with the task of analysing and proposing tourism policies and development strategies, and assuring their execution, while approving, orientating and controlling all the public and private activities related to Tourism. The government also created the National Tourism Enterprise, which has for objective to manage the public tourism enterprises and its participation in joint ventures. Additionally the National Committee for Tourism Facilitation was established for the coordination and facilitation of tourism development through the inter-ministerial and inter-sector links. The separation of the Ministry of Tourism from the Ministry of Trade and Industry in 2000 was made in order to meet more effectively the growing demands of the tourism sector. Finally through international fairs, the government and FUTUR launched themselves in the promotion of Mozambique as a tourism destination and a reliable country for investments in such area.

Sunshine in Bazaruto

MOZAMBIQUE'S TOURISM

All these efforts have had strong positive results and the tourism sector has been steadily growing over the years and in 2002 its contribution to GDP grew to 2,22 per cent.

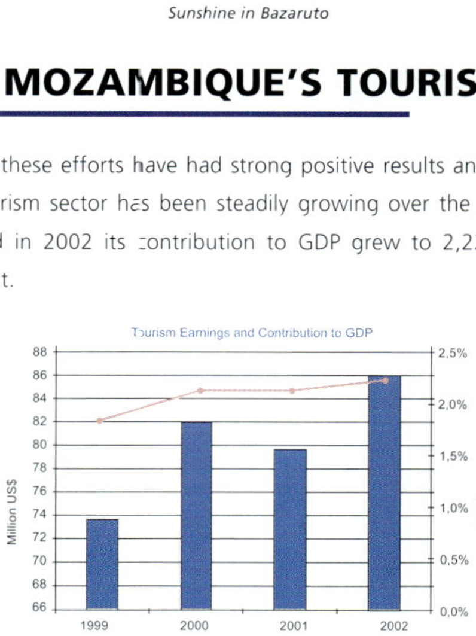

Source: National Statistic Institute

The number of visitors has also continuously increased over the last years, rising from an insignificant number during and just after the war (1992) to above 500,000 in 2002. Most of the visitors are from Southern Africa, notably South Africa, Zimbabwe and Malawi but the number of European and American tourists, as well as Mozambican, has strongly increased.

Origin of visitors, 2002 (%)

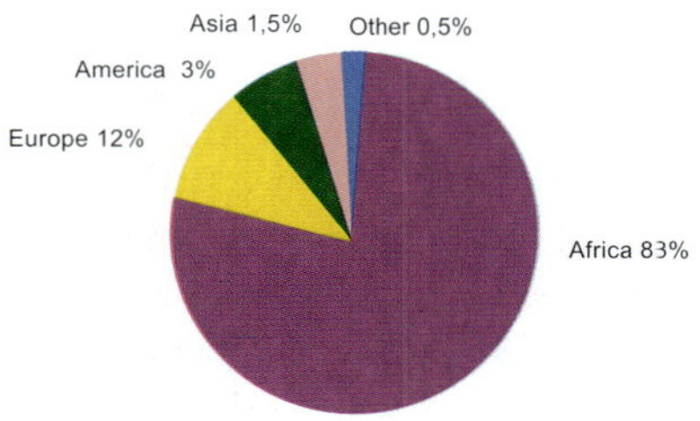

Source: National Statistic Institute

Increasing the average tourist's expenditure is the main challenge facing the government. The average tourist expenditure per visit in Mozambique is relatively low ranging approximately around US$172 per visit. This situation is such because most tourists arrive from South Africa, and they come on a three-day trip (US$ 57 per day) and tend to bring along all the provision they will need during their stay in Mozambique.

Tourist Expenditureper stay

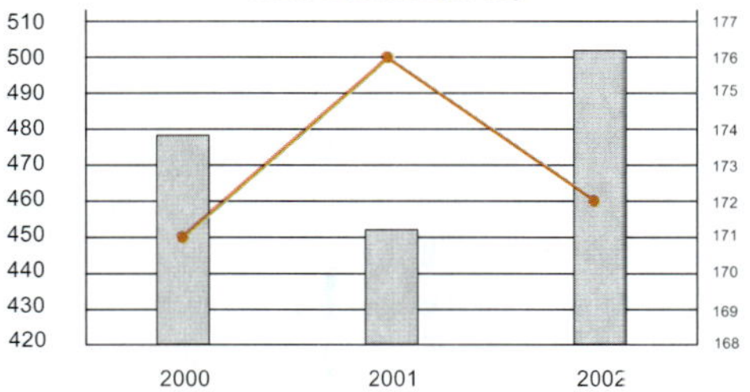

Source: National Statistic Institute

In order to improve this situation, the government and the private actors are creating new attractions and, rehabilitating and improving existing ones. The main objective is to make tourism in Mozambique more accessible to the general public.

The government has identified key regions for tourism development. These include: Ponta D'ouro including Ponta Malangane, Ponta Mamoli, the Maputo reserve and Santa Maria Cape; Maputo including Catembe, Xefinas and the Marracuene coast; Inhaca Island; Pomene and its natural reserve; Vilanculos including Bartolomeu dias, the Bazaruto archipelago and the Bazaruto National Park; Beira as well as the cities of Sofala and Songo, and the Savage beaches; The Gorrongoza National Park area including Gorrongoza ridge; The Pemba area, from the Lurio River to the Rovuma river mouth including the Quiriimba Archipelagos.

Mozambique aims at developing eco-tourism. In fact as various countries in the region, Mozambique wishes to have a non-massive tourism industry, which would respect its environment and people. Thus it aims to develop a number of diversified packages including resort holidays, safaris, trips to the coast, bird watching, scuba diving, fishing, and hunting among other activities.

Parks, Reserves and Enclosures

	Unities	Total area	% of the territory
Parks	**5**	27 170 Km sq	3.40%
Reserves	**5**	19 500 km sq	2.40%
Hunting enclosures	**12**	49 717 km sq	6.20%

Mozambique is still a virgin country, which has much to offer to the tourism industry especially with the emerging trend of eco-tourism. The country's main attractions are its beaches and parks. Mozambique possesses a coastal line of about 2,500 kilometres, which is mostly unexplored. Additionally it has an extensive wildlife and diversified landscape. Before the civil war, the Gorrongoza natural park was one of the world's most important conservation area. Today there is much to be done but the resources have remained.

On the 4th of October 2001, former South African President Nelson Mandela, following the process of creating the Great Limpopo Transfrontier Park (GLTP), opened the barred gate that separated Kruger National Park and Limpopo National Park. This new park will combine three conservation areas and national parks in three different countries: the Limpopo National Park in Mozambique, the Kruger National in South Africa Park and the Gonarezhou National Park in Zimbabwe. It was made official on the 9th of December 2002 with the signing of an International Tripartite Treaty. It will form one the biggest parks in the world and a demonstration of the potential that exists in Mozambique and the whole region.

Investment opportunities exist in the areas of accommodation, restaurants, entertainment, shopping, and others.

Would you like to be there?

MAIN COMPANIES

Avis - Rent a car

Paul De Almeida, General Manager
Praça dos Trabalhadores N° 21 R/C
Maputo
Tel: + 258 - 1 - 424144 / 5
Fax: + 258 - 1 - 431990
E-mail: pdealmeida@avis.co.za
Website: www.avis.com

Moçambique Car Rental, Lda, trading as AVIS Rent a car, was incorporated and commenced operating in Mozambique in 1989, offering local and international clients a short-term rental service. AVIS Mozambique is also the pioneer of a successful full maintenance-leasing product in the country. It is placed as the 51st largest company and the largest Rent a car company in Mozambique. Today is has almost 1000 vehicles in its fleet. Its major shareholder is Avis Southern Africa. The company is split in 2 main divisions: Rent-a-car and fleet services and Fleet Services. The company's activities include: Rent-a-car services (rental extending from 1 to 360 days); Professional chauffeur driver services; Used car sales, Fleet services, Full maintenance leases; Operational leases with managed maintenance; Maintenance contracts; Sale + leaseback contracts; Advance driving courses; Fleet accident management services. Avis strives to ensure that the rent-a-car and the fleet services business vehicles are, on average, always the youngest in the market and therefore Avis is continuously investing in new vehicles. Avis Mozambique is also planning on opening new branches in the Northern regions of the country. Their growth strategy is based on the youth, the mixture and the quality of its vehicles. It is also focused on the continuous improvement of the sales and marketing function as well as on ensuring constant customer satisfaction. Avis is mostly proud of having achieved the leading position in the rent-a-car market in Mozambique as well as having innovated with the full Fleet Service Business. Avis is committed to maintain and strengthen its position in the Mozambican market by exceeding their customers' expectations at every customer interface.

Atlas

Jaime Mora Barroso, General Manager
Av. 24 de Julho, n° 981 R/C
P.O.Box 167, Maputo
Tel: + 258 - 1 - 304600
Fax: + 258 - 1 - 304620
E-mail: j.barroso@atlas.co.mz
Website: www.atlas.co.mz

Altas Lda. is a well established Mozambican tour operator. It offers a wide range of services including the following: Plain Tickets; Rent-a-Car; Tours; Travel Insurance; Passports and Visas; Touristic Information; Hotel Reservations (in and outside Mozambique); Package Tours; Transfers; Conferences; and Rental and Buying of Properties. In fact Atlas Lda, with its professionally integrated team, is at your service to solve your every problem, through useful information, saving you time and money, anticipating all details in order to prevent all worries or set-backs. Their philosophy goes beyond a good service towards the client in a pro-active commitment to give the best service in the market. It has active partnerships with AVIS, the Pestana Group, and Lion Sands. Today, Altas Lda. offers high quality, paradisiacal and unique destinations in Mozambique. These include trips to the resort of "Quilálea", situated in the Quirimbas Island of the Coast of Cabo Delgado. Through this offer, Atlas has strengthened its leading position as the main tour operator for the Cabo Delgado region, especially in denominated "Packages" for Pemba.

Grupo Cotur Travel & Tours

Noor Mohamed, General Manager
Av. Karl Marx 1242
Maputo
Tel: + 258 - 1 - 427505 / 301924 / 324341
Fax: + 258 - 1 - 324151
E-mail: cotur@emilmoz.com

The creation of Grupo Cotur Travel & Tours arose from the need in the market for high quality service travel agents. Grupo Cotur Travel & Tours is a family business. It was created as a new concept to offer the public high standard ticketing and tourism services. Today it is one of the major travel agents in Mozambique. Grupo Cotur Travel & Tours offer the following services: Ticketing for local, regional and intercontinental flights; and Tourism packages in and out of Mozambique. The Grupo Cotur Travel & Tours has recently invested in the construction of a new three floors building in the centre of Maputo. Through this new investment the Grupo Cotur Travel & Tours has increased its capacity, to attend its customers in a more efficient way and to add new services to its activity line. The Grupo Cotur Travel & Tours is the leader in ticket issuing for the past years. GCT wants to innovate in the sector, and make Mozambique self sufficient in the ticketing service. Mozambique depends on other countries to issue international flight tickets but today Cotur's new infrastructure offers the major world airlines the capacity to have representation in Mozambique.

Pestana Hotels & Resorts Mozambique

Arturo Esposito, Area Director of Operations
A/c Pestana Rovuma Carlton Hotel, Rua da Sé, 114
Caixa Postal 4376, Maputo
Tel: + 258 - 1 - 305000
Fax: + 258 - 1 - 307288
E-mail: esposito@pestana.co.mz
Website: www.pestana.com

The first Pestana complex was built in 1962 in Lourenço Marques (now Maputo) but in 1974, all private property in Mozambique was nationalized. Twenty years later, the Pestana Group negotiated a long-term renewable concession with the new government for the property, and in 1998 the Pestana Rovuma Carlon Hotel reopened. In 1994 the Group also built two resorts off the coast of Mozambique: the Pestana Bazaruto Lodge and the Pestana Inhaca Lodge. Pestana Mozambique is a Hotel & Resorts company and thus competes in the tourism sector. It operates its four properties: the Pestana Rovuma Hotel; the Pestana Bazaruto Lodge and the Pestana Inhaca Lodge; and the newly built Pestana Kruger Park Lodge. The four properties offer a total of 415 rooms. Pestana Mozambique's growth strategy is based on the acquisition of management contracts of hotels situated in the whole of Mozambique. The Pestana Group's strategy in the region is to market holiday packages thanks to the Group's very strong presence in Europe with their tour operators and airlines: "Come and experience true African hospitality". Pestana Mozambique's major achievements these last years have been the acquisition of management contracts and concessions in Inhambane and the Kruger Park. The major challenge will be to strive in an increasingly competitive environment by gaining more management contracts.

Remember those dreams you used to have of African landscapes?
It's our Hotels you see there.
Pestana Rovuma
Pestana Bazaruto Lodge
Pestana Inhaca Lodge
AFRICA
There's nothing as an exotic environment for a memorable holiday. Pestana Hotels & Resorts provide you with a marvellous adventure in the african trcpics, with all the comfort and refinement that you deserve. Here you will be charmed by the beautiful landscape and the abundant wild life. In each of our 5 hotels in Africa, you will be delighted with our hospitality. Go on holidays with us and get back in love with this enchanting continent.
Pestana
HOTELS & RESORTS
A memorable moment
Pestana Rovuma Pestana Inhaca
Pestana Bazaruto Pestana Kruger Lodge Pestana Trópico
Reservas 808 252 252 e-mail:cro@pestana.com

Holiday Inn Maputo

Mr. Paul Norman, General Manager
Av. da Marginal
Caixa Postal 4354, Maputo
Tel: + 258 - 1 - 495050
Fax: + 258 - 1 - 497 700
E-mail: Pauln@himaputo.co.mz
Website: www.southernsun.com

The Holiday Inn Maputo is part of the Southern Sun Investment Group, the leading southern African hotel group ranked in size in the top 50 worldwide and a respected player in both the local and international hospitality industry. The Holiday Inn Maputo started operating in December of 2000 but was officially inaugurated by President Chissano himself in June of the following year. Holiday Inn Maputo represented the country largest investment in the tourism sector at that time. Today it has become the leading hotel in the Capital city. The Holiday Inn Maputo is a heaven for both business and leisure travellers. It stands as a symbol and a point of reference for the rest of the sector. The high standards of quality and services you expect from Holiday Inn worldwide are complimented with a welcome that is always warm and friendly. It is situated just 7 km from Maputo International Airport and is magnificently situated right on the beachfront. The Holiday Inn brand name always assures clients a high standard of quality and services, which continuously meet all their expectations even exceeding them. The Holiday Inn Maputo does not infringe this rule and on the contrary, reinforces it. Additional benefit such as loyalty programs and international reservation system give the hotel an even greater reputation. Holiday Inn Maputo is proud to have become a major player in the hospitability industry having built a strong reputation and consequently capturing an important share of the market. Holiday Inn will strive to strengthen its position as the leading hotel in an increasingly competitive industry where the number of hotels is augmenting.

Hotel Holiday Inn Maputo, a nice place to stay

Hotel Cardoso - Maputo

John A. Elliott, General Manager
Avenida Martires De Mueda, n°707
P.O.Box 707, Maputo
Tel: + 258 - 1 - 491071 / 5
Fax: + 258 - 1 - 491804
E-mail: info@hotelcardoso.co.mz
Website: www.hotelcardoso.co.mz

Hotel Cardoso is one of the Capital's oldest hotel as it was built in 1917. In 1990 it was bought by the Lonrho Africa Hotels Group, which possesses hotels across the African continent. This famous hotel offers an ideal venue for both business and leisure travellers. All bedrooms, lounge, bar and restaurants present a fresh, bright appearance and are fully air-conditioned. The restaurant, café and bar provide a wide variety of food from which you can choose. You can enjoy a fine a la carte dinner, a more informal buffet for lunch or dinner, a quick snack, or just a relaxing drink in the bar. A major feature of the hotel is the large outdoor pool, which is surrounded by spacious gardens and terrace that enjoys stunning views over the bay and city of Maputo. The Hotel Cardoso is 5 minutes by car to the business centre of Maputo and just 15 minutes from the Maputo International Airport. Hotel Cardoso's 131 bedrooms are all equipped with the Private bathroom, Air conditioning, Satellite TV, Mini bar, international direct-dial telephone, 24-hour room service, same day laundry, and dry cleaning service and Internet access points. The 12 Flamingo Rooms are larger, with a more spacious seating area and balcony. And The Luxury Suites have a large lounge and a separate bedroom. The lounge has both seating and dining areas. The long balcony runs the full width of the lounge and offers stunning views of the city and Bay of Maputo. Also the hotel has 4 meeting rooms of various capacities. The largest, Salão Bayete, is an ideal meeting venue with a capacity for up to 100 delegates. Main audiovisual equipment is available at the hotel and more specialized equipment can be arranged on request. These rooms as well as the spacious hotel gardens provide an ideal venue for wedding receptions, banquets and functions. Although the number of hotels in Maputo has strongly increased over the years, Hotel Cardoso has successfully managed to maintain high levels of occupancy notably thanks to the strong clients loyalty and their reputation for offering high standard conference centre services. Hotel Cardoso is actively working to maintain its position as a leading hotel in Maputo, especially focused towards satisfying the needs of businessmen.

Hotel VIP Maputo

Abdul Agige Gulamhussen, Administrador
Av. 25 de Setembro 692
Maputo
Tel: + 258 - 1 - 351000 / 312920
Fax: + 258 - 1 - 351001 / 312921
E-mail: hotelmaputo@viphotels.com

Hotel VIP Maputo is part of the International VIP Group from Portugal. In 1993, as Honourable Joaquim Alberto Chissano, President of the Republic of Mozambique visited Portugal he met with Mr. Sharaf Ali, owner of the VIP Group, and convinced him to open a hotel in Maputo. Consequently, the group invested in the creation of a brand new hotel in Mozambique, and the Hotel VIP Maputo was inaugurated by President Chissano, on the 28th of August 2002. Hotel VIP Maputo is a five star hotel that offers high quality accommodation and conference centre services. They dispose of 204 rooms, including 6 suites and 2 rooms for disabled persons, which are all equipped with private shower rooms, hair dryer, air condition, mini-bar, tea and coffee maker, cable TV, direct telephone lines and free internet access. The hotel also offers additional services such as swimming pool, dining room, and has several bars. Hotel VIP Maputo has been built on virgin grounds and thus is specifically adapted to today's needs in terms of accommodation. Their clients are mostly from the SADC region and are composed of tourists as well as businessmen. What differentiates the Hotel VIP Maputo from the rest of the hotels in Maputo is its location, as it is situated along one of Maputo's main avenues, its security, and its pleasant atmosphere. In fact Hotel VIP Maputo offers high quality services at accessible prices. In terms of investments, the group is planning to build a conference centre of 700 person capacity right aside the hotel, to build a health club as well as VIP executive apartments. Finally they have also decided to locate themselves in the province of Nampula.

Hotel VIP Maputo strives to offer increasingly high quality services in a country where tourism and business are bound to increase.

Mextur - Moçambique Expresso Turismo e Viagens

Bachir ADAM, General Director
Av. 25 de Setembro, 1226 r/c dtº Loja 10
CP 1222, Maputo.
Tel: + 258 - 1 - 428427 / 8 / 9
Fax: + 258 - 1 - 428430
E-mail: mextur@emilmoz.com

When Mextur was created in 1993 it was meant to be a Tour Operator but because of the security risks, tourism was very low in Mozambique and Mextur actually became a Travel Agency. When peace came to Mozambique, Mextur started operating as it was meant to do in the beginning, thus as a Tour Operator. Mextur has three shareholders: LAM (Linhas Aéreas de Moçambique); Banco Austral; and Austral Desenvolvimiento. Mextur's main clients are mostly from Europe especially from Portugal, Spain and the UK. Although Mextur is mostly active as a Travel Agency, it offers the following services: Business Trips; Travel Insurance; Tourist Packages; Rent-a-Car; Hotel reservations; Passports and Visas; Transport; Conference Organizations; and Excursions. Mextur strives to be at the forefront of the tourism development in Mozambique by strengthening their leadership in the market. They will do so through the continuous improvement of the quality of their services. Mextur is part of several international tourism organizations such as IATA, ASTA and RETOSA. Finally they represent various European and South African tour operators. Mextur is extremely proud of its position today. It has been able to maintain and strengthen it over the years, making it today one of the oldest and biggest tour operators in Mozambique. Over the years, Mextur has received several awards for the high quality of its services.

Mozambique Adviser Lda.

João Das Neves, Team Leader
Av. Ahmed Sekou Touré, 1034 R/C
Maputo
Tel: + 258 - 1 - 314041 / 303082
Fax: + 258 - 1 - 302054
E-mail: jneves@adviser.co.mz
Website: www.adviser.co.mz

Mozambique Adviser was created in 1999 with three shareholders. They started with 50 per cent of their activity focused towards tourism and the other 50 per cent towards consulting. Over the years Mozambique Adviser grew and past from 5 workers to over 14 today. Also the tourism section grew in importance and today it represents 80 per cent of the company's activity. They are members of IATA, SATSA and AVITUM. In the tourism activity line, Mozambique Adviser offers the following services: Tour operator, Visas/passports/insurance, rent a car, transfers, conference and event management, charter, aircrafts, hotel bookings, air tickets. In the consulting activity line, these are just a few examples of the services they offer: Organization of guided visits for investors, Identification & Recommendation of investment potentials for investors, Market surveys, Projects and Feasibility studies Licensing and authorizations for setting up a new company in Mozambique, Assistance. Mozambique Adviser differentiates itself from other companies through their unique combination of activity lines. They are actively investing in their labour force and are specializing their activity lines in order to offers even more unique services. Mozambique Adviser is proud of the services they offer. They are the only Mozambican Tour Operator specialized on Mozambique and that gives them that special hedge when it comes to business consulting. Combining tourism and business consulting services that cover the whole country is a difficult task which Mozambique Adviser strives to improve in the years to come.

Hotel Rovuma Carlton

TOP COMPANIES
(In alphabetical order)

1.- A Forjadora
2.- ABB Tecnel, Lda.
3.- Aberdare Intelec
4.- Academica Lda
5.- Açucareira de Moçambique
6.- Aero - Serviços
7.- Aeroportos de Mocambique
8.- Afco Mozambique LDA
9.- African Banking Corporation
10.- Africom, Lda.
11.- Agencia Nacional de Despacho E.E
12.- Agrifocus
13.- Agrimo - Companhia Agropecuaria de Moçambique
14.- Agro Alfa
15.- Aguas de Moçambique
16.- Alcatel Mocambique Lda
17.- Alexander Forbes Moçambique Limited
18.- Alfa - Segurança de pessoas e instalaçoes
19.- Angopesca
20.- Aquapesca Lda
21.- Austral Consultoria e Proyectos
22.- Auto Centre, Lda.
23.- Autovisa - Serviços Auto
24.- Avis Rent a Car
25.- Banco Austral
26.- Banco Central de Moçambique
27.- Banco de Fomento e Exterior S.A.
28.- Banco de Microfinanças - Novo Banco
29.- Banco Standard Totta de Mocambique
30.- BCI - Banco Comercial e de Investimentos
31.- BDC - Banco de Desenvolvimento e Comercio de Mocambique
32.- BIC Moçambique
33.- BIM - Banco Internacional de Mocambique
Blue Point, Lda.
34.- BMI - Banco Mercantil e de Investimentos
35.- BNP Nedbank
36.- BP Mozambique Ltd
37.- British American Tabaco
38.- Bytes & Pieces, Lda.
39.- C.M.C. africa austral lda
40.- Caltex Oil (Mozambique)
41.- Capafrica, Lda
42.- Centracontabil, lda.
43.- Ceres - Industrias Alimentares LDA
44.- Cervejas de Mocambique
45.- CETA Construçoes e Serviços
46.- CFM - Portos e Caminhos de Ferro de Moçambique
47.- CGSM - Companhia Geral de Seguros de Moçambique
48.- Chá de Magoma JFS
49.- Ciclomotores, Lda.
50.- CIMBETAO - Cimpor Betao moçambique
51.- Cimentos de Mocambique SARL
52.- Ciprel, lda
53.- Citrinos de Chimoio
54.- Citrinos de Maputo
55.- CNAA's
56.- Coca-Cola Sabco
57.- Colgate Palmolive Moçambique
58.- International Conference Centre
59.- Companhia da Zambezia, SARL
60.- Companhia da Zambezia, SARL
61.- Companhia de Moçambique de Serviços
62.- Companhia Agricola JFS
63.- Companhia de Pescas de Zambezia
64.- Companhia Comercial JFS
65.- Companhia Industrial JFS
66.- Complexo Sheik
67.- Comunicaçoes Timbila
68.- Confederation of Business Associations & Chambers of Commerces (CTA)

69.- Construa Lda.
70.- Construçoes Edgar Miller Moçambique (EKÁ)
71.- CONSTRUTORA DE TAMEGA, SA
72.- Consultec - Consultores Asociados
73.- Coopers & Lybrand
74.- Cooperativa de poupança e Crédito
75.- Cornelder de Moçambique
76.- Correios de Mocambique
77.- Cotur & travel Tours
78.- CPI. Centro de Promocao do Investimento
79.- Credicoop
80.- Crustamoz
81.- Dataserv
82.- Deloitte Touch Tohmatsu
83.- Delta Trading Company
84.- DHL
85.- DINAME, Distribuidora nacional de material Escolar
86.- Distribuidora Nacional de Açucar
87.- Domus
88.- EDM - Electricidade de Mocambique
89.- EFACEC Moçambique
90.- Efripel
91.- Electrotec
92.- EMAUTO, Empresa Moçambicana de Automoveis
93.- EMIL - Computer B. Centre
94.- EMAUTO, Empresa Moçambicana de Automoveis
95.- EMIL - Computer B. Centre
96.- Emocil
97.- Emopesca
98.- EMOSE - Empresa Moçambicana de Seguros
99.- Ernst & Young Mozambique
100.- FUTUR
101.- Gambeira Lda.
102.- Gapi
103.- Hotel Avenida
104.- Hotel Cardoso
105.- Hotel Holiday Inn
106.- Hotel Ibis
107.- Hotel Montecarlo & Hotel Terminus
108.- Hotel Mozaika
109.- Hotel Polana
110.- Hotel VIP Maputo
111.- King & Sons (Moçambique) Lda.
112.- Linhas Aereas de Mocambique, EE
113.- Manica Freight Services SARL
114.- Matola Cargo Terminal - MCT
115.- M-Cel
116.- Maputo Port Development Company
117.- Mextur
118.- Mogas
119.- Morgest
120.- Mozline
121.- NationalSugar Institute (INA)
122.- Pestana Group
123.- Pescamar
124.- Petróleos de Moçambique, PETROMOC
125.- Skynet Worldwide Express

ebiZ guides

TOURISM & LEISURE

INTRODUCTION

Mozambique is rapidly positioning itself at the forefront of the international tourism scene as one of the most attractive and intriguing tourist destinations in Southern Africa. Indeed it is considered as one of Africa's most fascinating countries, offering visitors a wide range of activities and experiences. Some call Mozambique, the wild west of Africa, as much of its beauty remains to be known. With its intriguing history, friendly and welcoming people, an exotic and vibrant cultural blend, a spectacular coastline and diversified landscape, Mozambique has much to give. Consequently an important number of new hotels, luxury lodges and resorts are coming on stream. Additionally the country's national parks and game reserves are gearing up to once again welcome wildlife enthusiasts. The establishment with neighbouring countries of cross-border wildlife reserves such as the Great Limpopo Transfrontier Park, also known as peace parks, are an important factor in this upcoming.

Mozambique's 2,500 kilometres-long coastline with white, palm-fringed desert beaches, lapped by the warm, crystal clear waters of the Indian Ocean is a key attraction for tourist. With its extensive marine life, including unique coral reefs which hosts a number of marine plants and animal species, and its countless beautiful islands, this amazing country offers numerous evasion opportunities. But Mozambique offers much more. The mainland with forest-clad mountains, mighty rivers, bubbling hot springs, vast inland lakes, grasslands and magnificent waterfalls is here to tempt adventurous travellers seeking new horizons and thrills. Indeed, for those who wish to escape the beaten track, the choice is extremely large.
The main fact is that the whole of Mozambique offers unforgettable experiences.
Northern Mozambique, with the mysterious mountains of Namuli and Unango, the historical settlements of Angoche, the World Heritage Site of Mozambique Island, the natural harbour of Pemba from which one can take a boat to Ibo Island, and the marine sanctuary surrounding the undiscovered Island of Quilálea, part of the Quirimbas Archipelago National Park, will surpass any expectations either of evasion or relaxation.

A place for peace in the Paradise Island, Bazarauto

Central Mozambique is a lively and vibrant place to explore. The city of Beira, within the Province of Sofala, is known as the heart of Mozambique and is one of the oldest cities in Southern Africa. From the arrival of Arab traders in the 10th century to these days, it has continuously attracted travellers' curiosities. Additionally with numerous national parks and game reserves, Central Mozambique will reach out to the most demanding of us.
Southern Mozambique, with the white sandy beaches of the Bazaruto Archipelago, the dynamism of the Capital city of Maputo built in colonial style, the resort of Ponta d'Ouro and the surrounding regions, propose a remarkable wealth of attractions.

Culturally, Mozambique provides a contrast to other countries in the Southern Africa region with its blend of African, Semites and Portuguese influence. This mix is especially noticeable in the Afro-Portuguese cuisine and the Latin beat of the music in the clubs and discos. The Mediterranean charm lives on within the fun-loving atmosphere that is unique within the region.

Visitors will warm to the liveliness and exuberance of Mozambique - the country of Smiles.

Mozambique is like...

MAPUTO

Maputo, previously called Lourenço Marques, is the sprawling capital of Mozambique with a population of about two million people and a large harbour. Several rivers spill into the sea around here and two islands - Inhaca and Portuguese Island - lie just off the coast. In 1898 central authority for the country was transferred from Mozambique Island to Lourenço Marques and the city quickly became established as the trade and industry centre and as a port to serve the gold fields of South Africa. In the early days transport riders made the perilous journey with ox and wagons, but when the rail link was constructed, transport became safer and more profitable.

Under Portuguese influence, Lourenço Marques became one of Africa's most beautiful and fashionable cities with an impressive skyline of tall buildings and a cosmopolitan Portuguese - African atmosphere attracting many visitors. Places like the Polana Hotel buzzed with the chatter of socialites and the nightclubs thumped until the early hours. The war in the 1970s and 1980s changed all that, and when it was over the once proud city was in terrible disrepair. Thousands of immigrants crowded the buildings; litter lay everywhere and major services including water and electricity were out of commission. A lot has changed since then and the city is now re-inventing itself and slowly recreating some of its former glory. Today with its wide avenues lined with red acacia and lilac jacaranda flowering trees, it is once again one of Africa's most attractive capitals and it offers tourists innumerable historical, cultural and scenic spots. The city lies alongside the estuary of the Rio Espirito Santo and Baia de Maputo in the far South of the country. In fact the city is set on a small cliff overlooking Maputo Bay and is swept by the cool sea breezes from the Indian Ocean. Numerous pleasant pavement cafes are scattered across the city contributing to its relaxed atmosphere. Maputo is a bustling place with colourful markets, diverse architecture, a lively and extensive cultural scene and it withholds one of Africa's best nightlife.

Rotonda: the major office, Maputo

With its rich blend of African, Portuguese and Oriental cultures, Maputo is a cosmopolitan and vibrant city characterized by the constant passing of overloaded chapas (mini-buses) and street vendors selling everything from tissues and plastic bags to batiks and paintings. International modern style high-rise buildings of the 1970s and more recent times dominate the skyline, creating sharp contrast with the more ancient and lower colonial buildings. While street names like Vladimir Lenine, Karl Marx and Mao Tsé

Tung are silent reminders of the country's experiment with socialism, Maputo has strongly developed these last few years and has become the Eastern terminus of the Maputo Corridor - an initiative for the regional economic development notably through the linkage of Johannesburg and the South African economy with Maputo's ports.

Buy it and bring it home, they will love it!

Maputo is the economic, educational and tourist centre of the country as it is home to the government of Mozambique, the Central Bank and most of the countries businesses, the University of Eduardo Mondlane, the Natural History Musuem and the National Library. In fact Maputo is the most economically developed city in Mozambique and tourists are offered a wide range of sites to visit and activities to carry out. It can be reached from South Africa via the Komatipoort / Ressano Garcia border (120 km from Maputo) on the EN4, or from Swaziland crossing the Namaacha border (80 km from Maputo). There are also daily flights from Johannesburg and others direct from Europe. Flights are also available from neighbouring countries. In terms of accommodation, the city has many hotels and boarding houses accessible to the whole range of travellers. For more information, see the following section "where to stay".

One sure thing: Maputo is a unique city within a unique country and is definitely worth the visit.

PLACES TO VISIT - MUSEUMS

National Art Museum (Museu Nacional de Arte)

Located at 1233 Avenida Ho Chi Min, half a block west of Karl Marx, this museum has an impressive and extensive collection of paintings and sculptures by Mozambique's finest and greatest contemporary artists including work from the painters Malangatana and Naguib and the sculptor Alberto Chissano. Exhibitions are also held from time to time. It is open from Tuesday to Sunday 15:00 to 19:00 and entry is free.

Natural History Museum (Museu da História Natural)

It is located near the hotel Cardoso on the Praça da Travessia do Zambeze in an impressive gothic style building and is surrounded by beautiful gardens, which include a mural made by Malangatana. This museum displays many of the animal species of Mozambique. As for most museums in the capital, it is open from Tuesday to Sunday 15:00 to 19:00.

Museum of the Revolution (Museu da Revolução)

Museum of the Revolution documents Mozambique's independence struggle during the 1960s and 1970s. Exhibits in Portuguese and a number of photos give visitors a good feel for those events that shaped Mozambique's recent history and which have made the country what it is today. The museum is located on avenida 24 de Julho and is open from 09:00 to 12:00 and from 14:00 to 18:00 daily, except Saturday morning when it is closed, and Sunday, when it is open from 15:00 to 18:00. Entry costs approximately US$ 1.

Chissano Museum (Museu Chissano)

Here you can see the work of the renowned sculptor Alberto Chissano. In fact this Museum in located within the sculptor's family residence in Matola, outside Maputo, on Rua Torre de Vale in Bairro Sial. It is open from 09:00 to 12:00 and from 15:00 to 17:00, Tuesday to Sunday. Entry costs US$ 1.5.

Money Museum (Museu da Moeda)

Situated on Praça 25 de Junho in a yellow house, which is one of the oldest buildings in the city as it housed the first colonial government. The Museum traces the history of money in Mozambique back to the days of barter trade. It is open on Tuesdays, Wednesdays, Thursdays and Saturdays from 09:00 to 12:00 and 14:00 to 16:30, as well as on Fridays from 09:00 to 12:00 and Sundays from 14:00 to 17:00.

Geology Museum (Museu de Geologia)

It offers visitors the possibility to see the various minerals and precious stones that can be found in Mozambique. It is located on avenida 24 de Julho. The building with its Manuelino architecture was once the Maputo synagogue. It is open Tuesdays to Fridays from 15:00 to 18:00, and Saturdays from 09:00 to 12:00 and 15:00 to 18:00.

Museum of natural history

PLACES TO VISIT - SPECTACLES

Teatro Avenida

It is Maputo's best-known theatre and is located at 1179 Avenida 25 de Setembro, close to the FACIM complex. It continuously holds plays in Portuguese, which usually run for several weeks.

Africa Bar

Situated on Av. 24 de Julho, this is one of Maputo's best-known bars. Quiet during the week, it becomes the centre of attention on Thursday night with its live music. Indeed a variety of famous musicians come to this bar. The atmosphere is friendly and joyful.

Concert in Africa Bar, can you feel the beat!

Franco-Mozambique Cultural Centre (Centro Cultural Franco-Moçambicano)

The centre is mostly known for the high quality of the shows it proposes. From classical music to Mozambican Rock, and from Shakespeare to Molière, all tastes are satisfied here. The centre also proposes foreign-language films.

Casa da Cultura

Situated on Avenida Albert Luthuli, near the intersection with Avenida Ho Chi Min, it houses Mozambique's excellent National Company of Song & Dance.

Café con Letras

Located on the Marginal, near the new Ministry of Foreign Affairs building, this club offers every Thursday night, the best Jazz Maputo has to offer. The setting is relaxed and drinks are mid-range.

PLACES TO VISIT - ART GALLERIES

National Art Museum (Museu Nacional de Arte)

It is Mozambique's main art museum. It regularly holds art exhibitions. For more information see section "Places to Visit - Museums".

Franco-Mozambique Cultural Centre (Centro Cultural Franco-Moçambicano)

Situated on Praça da Independencia in a beautiful red and blue building, it regularly accommodates art exhibitions and other activities. There is also a small bar, which serves light refreshments.

Portuguese Cultural Centre (Centro Cultural Portugues / Instituto Camões)

The centre proposes art exhibitions from all over Mozambique and Portugal, and is located on Avenida Julius Nyerere, opposite the restaurant Mundos.

Brazilian Studies Centre (Centro de Estudos Brasileiros)

Exhibitions of local and international artists are regularly held here. Located at 1728 Avenida 25 de Setembro, it is open Tuesdays to Fridays from 09:00 to 13:00 and 15:00 to 19:00.

Centro cultural franco-mozambicano in Maputo

Many local artists present their work during the week-end
in the colourful market, Mercado Artesanato, on Praça 25 de Junho.
It is full of crafts, batiks, paintings and wooden artwork
and is truly tourist's paradise.

Additionally murals are commonly found all the cities. In fact they are the most usual form of public art. They were mostly painted in the early years following independence. One of the most popular mural can be found along the Hospital Central. Another significant mural is to be found opposite Praça dos Heróis Moçambicanos, near the airport.

Artedif, a co-operative run by disabled people
is located on the Marginal and offers a variety of crafts,
including leatherwork,
ceramics and weavings,
as well as curios.
It is well worth the visit.

PLACES TO VISIT - NATIONAL PARKS

Maputo Elephant Reserve (Reserva Especial do Maputo)

On the road to Ponta d'Ouro, a two-hour drive from Maputo, is located the Maputo Elephant Reserve. The 50.000 hectares natural reserve was established in 1939 and extends from Baia de Maputo southwards to the southern tip of Lago Xinguta, but excludes the Machangulo peninsula. Its western boundary is partly formed by the Rio Maputo and the Rio Futi, while in the east the reserve is bounded by the Indian Ocean for almost 40 kilometres. It houses a variety of landscapes including lakes, floodplains, mangrove swamps, grasslands, bushy savannah, woodlands and forested dunes which sweep down onto unspoilt beaches. Like its name suggests, the reserve was once a sanctuary for large herds of elephant. In fact it was created to protect the local elephant population, rhinos and several other game species, as well as various species of turtles. Nevertheless due to war and poaching, animal numbers had considerably diminished. Today thanks to various international agencies, notably the Endangered Wildlife Trust, an important amount of efforts are being put in place to re-establish the reserves glorious past. Apart from the big game species, the reserve's other attraction is its birdlife. More than 300 bird species have been identified, including fish eagles, Rudd's apalis, Woodwards' batis, pink-throated twinspot, woodland kingfisher and many other wetland species. An additional attraction is the coast and the opportunities it offers for angling, diving, snorkelling, and spearfishing. Indeed the coast's reefs are still in pristine condition. Diving in the crystal clear Indian Ocean may lead to encounter whale sharks, mantas, large potato bass, scorpion fish and turtles.

You may be just there soon!

The Great Limpopo Transfrontier Park (GLTP)

This recently established park combines three conservation areas and national parks in three different countries:

the Limpopo National Park here in Mozambique, the Gonarezhou National Park in Zimbabwe and the Kruger National Park in southern Africa. It was made official with the signing of an International Tripartite Treaty on December the 9th 2002 in the Mozambican city of Xai-Xai, by the respective heads of state, Joaquim Chissano, Robert Mugabe and Thabo Mbeki. Stretching over 3.5 million hectares, it is one of the biggest parks in the world and a demonstration of the more recent world-scale tendencies in management of regional ecosystems involving country borders. Indeed the Great Limpopo Transfrontier Park made history when on October 4th 2001, the barred gate that separates Kruger National ark and Limpopo National Park (LNP) was opened by the former South African President Nelson Mandela, and a herd of 25 elephants was set free in the old Coutada 16 area in Mozambique. The park houses an important number of animal and insect species including the "big-five": elephant, rhinoceros, buffalo, lion and leopard. The Great Limpopo Transfrontier Park is truly on the verge of becoming the best park in the world.

CITIES NEAR THE CAPITAL

Catembe

It is a small town on the south side of Maputo Bay across the port channel, which offers a great view of Maputo's skyline. It accessible by ferry which can be taken in front of the Ministry of Finance and Planning building on the marginal or by car. There is not much to do in Catembe but it makes a good excursion and gives visitors a taste of upcountry atmosphere.

Accommodation and restaurants on Catembe are limited but of good quality.

Where to Stay
Catembe Gallery Hotel

Tel: + 258 - 1 - 380050 / 1 / 2

Fax: + 258 - 1 - 330003

Email: office@catembe.net

How many crocodiles do you see?

Where to Eat
Restaurante Marisol
Tel: + 258 - 1 - 495813
Seafood restaurant.

Motorboat charters can be arranged through any Maputo travel agency. Additionally local boats from the fishing village near Restaurante Costa do Sol will take you there much more slowly, but much cheaper.

View of Maputo from Catembe

Xefina island

Xefina Pequena, Xefina do Meio & Xefina Grande

At the mouth of the Rio Incomati a narrow sandpit extends southwards for several kilometres. On its landward side lies Xefina Pequena (Little Xefina), a small desert island. It is separated by a narrow gap from Xefina do Meio (In-Between Xefina). The third island is Xefina Grande (Large Xefina). It lies about 3 kilometres offshore from Costa do Sol and about 12 kilometres from the Catembe ferry dock. This island has a long history as a Portuguese trading base, prison and war garrison. Indeed it served as an ivory trading post, penal colony and a military installation. Of interest are the ruins of the old Portuguese fort and the rusty remains of the battery of heavy canons that guarded the entrance to the harbour during World War II. Built on a sand dune which has since been eroded by the lapping waves, the guns have slid down the dune into the sea. Visiting these ruins, swimming and picnicking are the main diversions. The beaches are nice but the water is not that attractive the same water way lead to the harbour. There are no facilities on the island, so you will need to bring everything with you, including water.

Inhaca Island

Inhaca Island (pronounced Inyaaka) is situated in the Bahia de Maputo, about 25 kilometres east of Maputo. The tropical island, which lies amidst the turquoise waters of the Indian Ocean, is an important marine research centre and a popular weekend gateway. Its offshore coral reefs are among the most southerly in the world, an parts of the island and surrounding waters have been designated a protected reserve. With a length of 12,5 kilometres and a width of 7,5 kilometres, the island owes its name to the Tsonga chief, Nhaca, whose chieftaincy extended from Maputo Bay southwards to St Lucia in south Africa's KwaZulu-Natal Province. Just across the island is situated the Portuguese Island (Ilha dos Portuguêses), part of the Inhaca marine reserve system.

There are very good beaches on Inhaca's north-eastern edge, and on Portuguese Island. On inhaca's south-western corner is a Marine Research Centre (Estação de Biologia Maritima) run by the Edouardo Mondlane University. The small museum has an interesting collection of coral, tropical fish and other marine species including the skeletal remains of a dugong. Bird-watching opportunities abound, with about 300 birds species recorded on the Island. Most of all Inhaca offers great diving and snorkelling opportunities with various shipwrecks and abundant marine species. Access by boat to the Island can be done thought the Club Maritimo in Maputo and flights can be arranged through the Rovuma Carlton Hotel (see "where to stay" section).

Inhaca Beach

Where to Stay
Inhaca Island Lodge
(part of the Pestana Group)

(see tourism section)

Tel: + 258 - 1 - 305000

Fax: + 258 - 1 - 305305

Email: helena.goncalves@pestana.com

Website: www.pestana.com

Where to Eat
Inhaca Island Lodge

Serves buffets and set menus.

Lucas Restaurant

Situated in the village, it is specialized in seafood dishes.

Pequenos Lebombos Dam

Pequenos Lebombos dam (Barragem dos Pequenos Lebombos), which impounds the Umbuluzi River, lies in the hills about 45 kilometres south-west of Maputo and supplies the capital's water. Going to visit the area makes a pleasant day trip if you have your own vehicle. The nearby Lebombo mountains offer wide views and pleasant cycling.

Macaneta

Macaneta is the closest open-ocean beach to Maputo and a popular weekend trip from the capital. It is located on a narrow peninsula divided from the mainland by the mouth of the Nkomati river and is reached via the small town of Marracuene, which lies about 35 kilometres north of Maputo along the EN1. Marracuene used to be the gateway for wealthy Maputo residents during colonial times, and the scene of some heavy fighting in the 1980s during the war.

Macaneta

Where to Stay & Eat
Complexo Turistico Macaneta

Tel: + 27 - 1 - 650006 / 309073

South Africa

There are two and four bed chalets and a popular restaurant.

Jay's Beach Lodge
Tel: + 27 - 82 - 300143, South Africa
Fax: + 27 - 1 - 330143, South Africa
Offers comfortable self-catering chalets for 4/6 people and a restaurant.

Nkomati River Camp
Email: nkomati@mail.tropical.co.mz

WHERE TO STAY - HOTELS

Pestana Rovuma Carlton Hotel
(see tourism section)
Arturo Esposito, Area Director of Operations
Pestana Rovuma Carlton Hotel, Rua da Sé, 114
Caixa Postal 4376, Maputo
Tel: + 258 - 1 - 305000
Fax: + 258 - 1 - 307288
E-mail: esposito@pestana.co.mz
Website: www.pestana.com

Girassol Bahia Hotel
Paulo Varela, President of the Administration Council
Av. Patrice Lumumba, n° 737 / 739
Tel: + 258 - 1 - 360350
Fax: + 258 - 1 - 360330
Email: girassolbahiahotel@visabeiramoz.co.mz
Website: www.grupovisabeira.pt

Hotel Avenida
Manuel Pereira, General Manager
Av.Julius Nyerere, n° 627
Maputo
Tel: + 258 - 1 - 492000
Fax: + 258 - 1 - 499600
Email: h.avenida@teledata.mz

Holiday Inn Maputo
(See tourism section)
Mr. Paul Norman, General Manager
Av. da Marginal
Caixa Postal 4354, Maputo
Tel: + 258 - 1 - 495050
Fax: + 258 - 1 - 497700
E-mail: Pauln@himaputo.co.mz
Website: www.southernsun.com

Hotel Cardoso - Maputo
(See tourism section)
John A. Elliott, General Manager
Avenida Martires De Mueda, n°707
P.O.Box 707, Maputo
Tel: + 258 - 1 - 491071 / 5
Fax: + 258 - 1 - 491804
E-mail: info@hotelcardoso.co.mz
Website: www.hotelcardoso.co.mz

Hotel Polana
David Ankers, General Manager
Av. Julius Nyerere, 1380
P.O.Box 1151, Maputo
Tel: + 258 - 1 - 491001 / 7
Fax: + 258 - 1 - 491480
E-mail: gen@polana-hotel.co.mz
Website: www.serenahotels.com

Hotel Tivoli
Av. 25 de Setembro, n° 1321
Maputo
Tel: + 258 - 1 - 307600
Fax: + 258 - 1 - 307609
Email: Tivoli@teledata.mz

Hotel VIP Maputo

(See tourism section)
Abdul Agige Gulamhussen, Administrador
Av. 25 de Setembro 692
Maputo
Tel: + 258 - 1 - 351000 / 312920
Fax: + 258 - 1 - 351001 / 312921
E-mail: hotelmaputo@viphotels.com

Ibis Maputo Moçambique

Av. 25 de Setembro, n° 1743
Maputo
Tel: + 258 - 1 - 352200
Fax: + 258 - 1 - 352220
Website: www.ibishotel.com or www.accorhotels.com

MOZAMBICAN FOOD - TYPICAL DISHES

Mozambican food is very rich with its strong Portuguese, European, Arabic and traditional influences. With the frequent use of hot pepper, called peri-peri, Mozambican dishes have a spicier flavour then elsewhere in Southern Africa. Local dishes generally consist of Xima, a maize or cassava-based staple, which is served with a sauce of beans, vegetables or seafood. Mozambique's seafood, especially its shrimps (camarões), has worldwide reputation. Indeed specialized seafood restaurants are common within Mozambique. The Portuguese influence is particularly evident with the use of wine. One such dish is Matata: clams cooked in port wine with finely chopped peanuts and tender young greens or fruits. A favorite dish of the interior is Frango a Calrial which means "Chicken, the African way." Chickens heavily rubbed down with Piri-piri are roasted over charcoals. They are so peppery that it would be impossible for us to eat them. There is also "Chicken, the Portuguese way," made with tomatoes and wine. Caril is the name for curries, also served very "hot" with Manga Achar, a special mango chutney that is one of the little dishes accompanying it. The other little dishes contain chopped peanuts, coconut, cucumber, bananas, etc. They are similar to the Sambals (relishes) of India. The fish of Mozambique and especially the shellfish-lobster tails, shrimp, and prawns are considered by many to be the most delicious in the world.

Boiled Crab: a dish speciality in Mozambique

Here is a list of recommended Mozambican dishes:

Sopa de Feijao Verde (String Bean Soup)

Yield: 2 quarts (8 cups)
In a 3-quart saucepan:
Bring to a boil 1 1/2 quarts WATER.
Add: 2 tsp. SALT
1/2 tsp. PEPPER
3 large POTATOES, cut in chunks
2 medium TOMATOES, cut in chunks
2 large ONIONS, cut in chunks.
Simmer for 30 minutes
or until vegetables are tender.
Puree through a sieve or food mill.
(It should be a thin puree.)
Add 1 lb. FRESH STRING BEANS, cut across in thin slices.
Simmer for about 10 minutes until beans are tender.
Correct the Seasoning
Serve in bowls.

It will take a little time to slice the fresh string beans in very thin (straight-across) slices. As an adaptation and for the sake of speed, here's the fast modern version of this lovely soup:

Combine: 1 cup INSTANT POTATOES
1 Tbs. ONION POWDER
1 1/2 quarts BOILING WATER
1 6-oz. can TOMATO SAUCE
No pureeing is necessary.
Cut 1 package FROZEN ITALIAN BEANS
(thawed) in thin slices.
Add to the mixture above.
Simmer until beans are done.
Serve in bowls or large soup plates.

Matata (Clam and Peanut Stew)

Yield: 8 portions

Matata is a typical Mozambique entree made with pumpkin leaves. We have used spinach as a substitute. This is one dish that wasn't influenced by the Portuguese cuisine. Imagine a combination like clams and peanuts and tender young greens! You may want to hold out the crushed red pepper. Start without it and add it gradually, with discretion.

In a 4-quart saucepan
Saute: 1 cup ONIONS chopped finely in
2 oz. OLIVE OIL until soft but not brown.
Add: 4 cups CANNED CHOPPED CLAMS
1 cup PEANUTS, chopped finely
2 TOMATOES cut in small pieces
1 Tbs. SALT
1/2 tsp. BLACK PEPPER
1 tsp. CRUSHED RED PEPPER.
Simmer gently for 30 minutes.
Add 1 1/2 lbs. FRESH SPINACH (young leaves)
chopped finely.
Cover tightly and, as soon as leaves have
wilted, Matata is ready to serve.
Correct the Seasoning
Cook:
2 cups WHITE RICE in
5 cups BOILING SALTED WATER until tender.
Serve over rice.

PIRI-PIRI (Hot Pepper)

Combine: 4 Tbs. LEMON JUICE
4 Tbs. OLIVE OIL
4 Tbs. COARSE RED PEPPER
1 Tbs. SALT
1 tsp. GARLIC POWDER.
Place in a small bowl.
Serve with a tiny spoon. Use sparingly.

SALADA PERA DE ABACATE (Avocado Salad)

Yield: 8 small salads

Canned peach slices may be added to the Avocado Salad- in which case use one slice of tomato and two to three peach slices. This Lemon Dressing is excellent on a tossed green salad or hearts of lettuce. It is light and easy to make.

Cut 1 head ICEBERG LETTUCE down in
3/4-inch round uniform slices.
Arrange one slice on each salad plate.
Alternate: 2 TOMATOES cut in 8-inch uniform
slices overlapping with
2 AVOCADOS cut in thick uniform slices
across the lettuce in a straight line.
Spoon 2 Tbs. of the following Lemon
Dressing over the avocado salad:
Lemon Dressing
Combine: 1 cup LEMON JUICE (bottled)

1 cup OLIVE OIL
Shake: 1 cup PEACH SYRUP (from a can or use any fruit syrup)
1 tsp. SALT
1 tsp. SALAD HERBS
1/4 tsp. PEPPER.
Serve as a side salad.

ANANAS CON VINHO DO PORTO
(Fresh Pineapple in Port Wine)

Yield: 8 portions

Peel 1 large RIPE SWEET PINEAPPLE
Cut in 1/2 inch slices and remove the core.
Sugar each slice lightly on both sides.
Place in a 2-quart glass or china bowl.
Cover with 1/2 cup RED PORT WINE.
Allow to stand for several hours.
Turn the pineapple in the wine from time to time.
Turn again just before serving on dessert dishes.
Serve with spoons and forks.

Cashew nuts are one of the major crops of Mozambique. It would be quite appropriate to sprinkle cashew nuts on the pineapple or to pass a bowl of cashew nuts with the dessert or as a snack later in the evening.

FRANGO A CAFRIAL
(Barbecued Chicken)

Yield: 8 half chickens

In Mozambique about 4 Tbs. of hot red pepper are used in the Cafrial. In this recipe, crushed red peppers may be substituted. 1 tsp. cayenne pepper will give quite a "bite" so if you prefer to hold the seasoning and add it after the chickens are cooked, cut down on the amount given.

Combine: 1 tsp. CAYENNE PEPPER
1 Tbs. SALT
1 tsp. GARLIC POWDER
1/2 tsp. GROUND GINGER
1 tsp. PAPRIKA and
1/2 cup SALAD OIL, and blend thoroughly.
Rub 4 2 1/2-lb. WHOLE CHICKENS with the seasoned oil on all sides thoroughly.
Roast, Broil, or Barbecue the chickens in your favourite manner, basting them from time to time with the seasoned oil
until chickens are done.
Cut chickens in half.
Serve with plenty of white rice
(allow 1 cup cooked rice per person).

SHRIMP AND SEAFOOD
THE MOZAMBIQUE WAY

In a 2-quart saucepan:

Place: 1 lb. RAW SHRIMP
(with or without shells)
3 cups WATER warm from the tap
1 tsp. SALT
1 tsp. CRUSHED RED PEPPER, or use a few drops Tabasco.
Squeeze 3 LEMON WEDGES into the pot and toss the lemon in it.
Bring the shrimp up to the boiling point and turn off the flame. Cover.
Allow to stand for 30 minutes. Shrimp will be thoroughly cooked.
Devein, wash in clear water and chill.
Serve with Piri-piri.

Note: how tender the shrimp become, cooked this way. And don't waste that water. Plan to use it in a chowder or in a sauce. Taste it. It's great! Other seafood may be prepared in this manner.

Bon Appétit !!!

MOZAMBICAN DRINKS

Drinking water from the tap is not recommended. Bottled water (água mineral) is available in all larger towns, but can be harder to find and more expensive in villages and rural areas. Soft drinks are available almost everywhere and is the best alternative to bottled water if not available. In cities and larger towns, there is a choice of local brand soft drinks or the more expensive international brand. Imported fruit juices are also available in cities and larger towns. Beer is also widely available. Local brands include Manica, Laurentina and 2M, and are sold by the bottle, by can or by pint within the western style bars. South African beers are widely available, including Castle, Black Label, Lion and Amstel, as are Namibian beers such as Windhoek Lager, and foreign beers such as Heineken and Kronenbourg. Portuguese and South African wines are available in all cities.

Many traditional societies in dry areas of the South brew their own beer (usually millet based). In rainy areas further up North, palm wine (sura) is the drink of choice. Other common traditional drinks are flour water and ginger juice.

WHERE TO EAT - RESTAURANTS

1908

Av. Edouardo Mondlane, n°560

Tel: + 258 - 1 - 424834

Upmarket Mozambican and Indian cuisine, and one of Maputo's most luxurious restaurants.

Clube Marítimo

Av. Marginal (next to the FACIM complex)

Standard Portuguese cuisine and excellent seafood.

Costa do Sol

Bairro Costa do Sol (20 mins drive from Maputo)

Tel: + 258 - 1 - 450115

Known as the best seafood restaurant in town. Particularly popular on Saturday evenings and Sunday afternoons.

Manjar dos Deuses

RECOMMENDED ebiZ Guides

Av. Julius Nyerere, n° 162

Tel: + 258 - 1 - 496834

Try their carvoatas of meat or shrimps, truly delicious and great for big meals with business partners or friends.

Miramar

Av. da Marginal (next to the Holiday Inn)

Standard Portuguese and Mozambican cuisine, and very good seafood.

Mi Casa

Av. julius Nyerere, n° 28

Tel: + 258 - 1 - 491130

Upmarket steakhouse, and great deserts.

Mimmo's

Corner of Av. 24 de Julho & Av. Salvador Aliende

Tel: + 258 - 1 - 309490 / 1

Standard, Italian and Portuguese Cuisine.

Mundos

Av. Julius Nyerere (in front of Cinema Xenon)
Tel: + 258 - 1 - 494080
One of the best places in town for a relaxed beer before a good standard meal. Try their pizzas, probably the best in Mozambique.

Restaurante o Escorpiao

Rua Belmiro Obadias Muianga (within the Feria Popular)
Economic Portuguese cuisine but probably one of the best restaurant in town.

Restaurante Sagres

Avenida da Marginal (next to the Holiday Inn).
Excellent Portuguese cuisine and delicious seafood. The service is very good.

Rodizio Real

Av. Julius Nyerere, n°794
Tel: + 258 - 1 - 497275
Upmarket Brazilian cuisine. The service is of very good quality.

Salsa Latina

Av. da Marginal (next to the Holiday Inn)
Standard cuisine and the possibility to eat with your feet in the sea.

Villa Italia

Av. Friedrich Engels, n°635
Tel: + 258 - 1 - 497298
Has a pleasant garden seating and serves upmarket Italian cuisine.

MOZAMBICAN MUSIC

Traditional Music is widely played all over Mozambique, particularly in villages and rural areas. The timbila orchestra are one of the best-known musical traditions in the country. Orchestra Marrabenta was the country's best-known band. Its music is bright, lively and up-tempo, with lyrics that celebrate life's pleasures. The guitar players were clearly influenced by the sounds emanating from Zaire, but they also seem to owe a good deal to the traditional timbila (xylophone) orchestras. The totality is a delightful dance music, made the more so by the call-and-response between guitars and/or vocalists and the brass section, who seem to have been listening pretty intensively to salsa and other Hispanic-American sounds, rather than those of Brazil, which might seem more a likely influence.

Mozambican traditional music is a mix of influences and differs very strongly from the South to the North of the country. Indeed in Mozambican music you can feel the Latin American influence because Latin music is mixed with African music like Rumba which happened years ago with slavery. Mozambican Marrabenta would be a beat most linked to Latin.

Astra Harris is regarded as one the real voices of Mozambique, exploring the different strands and directions in her county's music. She sings in the languages of her local regions Zambezia and Sofala as well as in Portuguese. Her music is recognised by its heartfelt, and innovative interpretations of traditional songs, and live people tell of mesmerising performances with an intense, soulful delivery.

Mabulu (dialogue in Shangana) is a new band from Mozambique that recorded its debut release Karimbo during the catastrophic floods of early 2000. It brings together musicians from different generations, Lisboa Matavel ('the troubadour of Mozambique'), born in 1938, to the young Chiquito, born in 1978, who represents the new Mozambican rap movement.

Eyuphuro is another internationally known band. It was founded in 1981 by Omar Issa, Gimo Remane and vocalist Zena Bakar (previously a fishing woman) and soon became the most successful music group from Mozambique. In 1989 - 91 their tours of Europe and USA garnered much critical acclaim and they recorded Mama Mosambiki, one of the greatest recordings ever produced from the region. The group comes from the island of Mozambique, in the north of the country. Their music reflects the island's role as a meeting point of African, Arabic and Latin cultures dating back to the eighth century, which has created a fusion of musical influences. Eyuphuro (meaning whirlwind in the Macua language) is also an important representative of traditional Mozambican rhythms such as tufo, namahandga, masepua, djarimane, morro and chakacha.

Local band

These are long-established rhythms from the northern province of Nampula, bordering Tanzania, and the homeland of most of the band members.

"In Mozambique there are many tribes who play different sounds and rhythms".

Modern music flourishes in the cities, and the live scene in Maputo is excellent. Do not hesitate to go around the cities' music stores and ask for the latest trends.

CITIES IN THE NORTH

Northern Mozambique is composed of the Provinces of Nampula, Niassa and Cabo Delgado with the cities of Nampula, Lichinga and Pemba, their respective capital, and several other major cities.

Mozambique Northern Provinces

Nampula

Nampula is Mozambique's third-largest city and the commercial centre of the north. Until recently, the city had little influence in the region due to the closeness of Ilha de Moçambique. The situation changed in the early 1930s with the construction of the rail link from the coast and the expansion of the port at Nacala in the 1940s. The city gained prominence as a rail junction and administrative centre.

Nampula has little to offer tourists, but is nevertheless an important transport hub and stocking-up point. The surrounding area is characterized by numerous striking inselbergs - large masses of volcanic granite, which intruded into the earth's crust aeons ago and were then exposed over the millennia by erosion of the softer surrounding rock. Some sore close to 1000 metres into the air.

Where to Stay

Hotel Brasilia

Rua dos Continuadores, n° 14ª

Tel: + 258 - 6 - 212127

Located in the southern part of town, this hotel offers clean double rooms with bathroom and has restaurant services.

Hotel Lúrio

Av. Paulo Samuel Kankhomba

Tel: + 258 - 6 - 212520

Has good rooms with bathroom.

Hotel Tropical

Near Av. Eduardo Mondlane

Tel: + 258 - 6 - 212232

Nampula's best hotel offers comfortable air-conditioned and good restaurant services.

Where to Eat

Almeida de Garrett

Av. Francisco Manyanga

Popular restaurant which serves good dishes.

Pinto's

Outside town

Simply Nampula's best dining

Quinta de Gallo

Several kilometres outside town

Very pleasant restaurant situated on a small lake.

Sporting Club

Near Av. Eduardo Mondlane

Mogincual

Mogincual is an old trading settlement 175 kilometres south-east of Nampula which sits near an estuary divided by a narrow finger of land from the sea. The surrounding areas are in fact extensive wetland systems, which offer good bird-watching opportunities.

Angoche

Formerly known as Antonio Ennes, Angoche is an old Arab-trading centre dating from at least the 15th century. It was one of the earliest settlements in Mozambique and an important gold and ivory trading post. By the early 16th century, it had been eclipsed by Quelimane as an entry port to the interior. However, Angoche continued to play a role in coastal trade and was an important economic and political centre in the region. Nevertheless the end of the 19th century saw the beginning of Angoche's downfall.

Today it is a quiet district capital with few reminders of its past. Despite this, Angoche has a particular charm and is worth a visit if in the region. It possesses beautiful beaches up north at Praia Nova. The island offshore are also very attractive and worth visiting.

Where to Stay & Eat

Casa Tipo Colonial

Tel: + 258 - 6 - 212722

A colonial-style house overlooking the ocean which offers either to rent the whole house, or double rooms.

Ilha de Moçambique

Arab, Indian and Portuguese architectural influences are blended in this part of Mozambique. Once a trading post on the sea route from Europe to the East Indies, Ilha de Moçambique was placed on UNESCO's World Heritage List in 1991.

The little island, which lies four kilometres off the coast of Africa just opposite Madagascar, was for hundreds of years a major centre of intercontinental maritime trade. It was occupied by Arab merchants from the tenth century until the end of the fifteenth, and in the sixteenth century became a port of call on the route from Europe to the East Indies opened by the Portuguese navigator Vasco de Gama. In 1507, the Portuguese built a fortress on the island where the Customs House stands today. A later fortification that has survived is the fort of St. Sebastian, which was built between 1558 and 1620 and is inspired by Italian Renaissance military architecture.

Ilha de Moçambique's harbour grew rapidly during the sixteenth and seventeenth centuries. Its business houses stood on the sea front, along a rocky belt where boats with a shallow draught could land at high tide. Over the years a town of twisting streets lined with flat-roofed houses took shape around a central square.

The town as it appears today has a strong architectural homogeneity which is largely due to the use over the centuries of the same building materials, mainly limestone from quarries in the south of the island and wood for beams and framework. The decorative style of the facades, with their cornices, high rectangular framed windows and rows of pilasters, is equally homogeneous. The flat roofs, designed to collect rainwater and compensate for the island's lack of freshwater springs, and a rectangular ground plan in which space is divided into six square rooms also uphold a general impression of unity which encompasses the smallest houses roofed with palm leaves the macuti that constitute around a quarter of the city as well as the most luxurious residences. The preponderant architectural influence is that of southern Portugal, although there are undeniable Arab and Indian elements.

The main motivation for visiting Ilha de Mozambique is to experience its rich history, architectural heritage and atmosphere. In fact, every street, every house, every brick has its own, faded history. The island is a huge open-air museum. You can feel yourself transferred 300 years back in time and imagine walking among the early settlers, soldiers, pirates, etc. It is living history.

Where to Stay

Omuhi'piti

Tel: + 258 - 6 - 526351

Fax: + 258 - 6 - 526356

This four-star hotel offers comfortable rooms with satellite TV.

Where to Eat

Reliquias

Tel: + 258 - 6 - 610092

The best restaurant on the island. It has a pleasant atmosphere and serves good food.

Nacala

Nacala is set on an impressive natural harbour and is northern Mozambique's busiest port, developed in the mid-20th century. The entire town evolves around the port activity and thus it is of little interest to travellers.

Nevertheless outside town there are some good beaches at Fernao Veloso in the north and Relanzapo to the east.

Where to Stay & Eat

Hotel Nacala / Maiaia

Bairo Mocone, n° 105 A

Tel: + 258 - 6 - 526350 / 1

Situated on the main road it has recently been renovated and offers good rooms.

Restaurante Sandokan

Tel: + 258 - 6 - 526740

Serves good meals.

Lichinga

Lichinga or Vila Cabral is the capital of Niassa Province, which is the most remote and the least visited of all. It has approximately 75,000 inhabitants and is located on the plateau of the same name. The city is surrounded with pine groves and distant hills which give it a nice atmosphere pleasant for walking or cycling. Indeed Lichinga is a relaxing place well worth spending a day or two on your way to Lake Niassa and the Sanga Reserve.

Where to Stay

Ponto Final

Rua Filipe Samuel Magaia

Tel: + 258 - 71 - 2912

One of the best accommodations in town.

Pousada

Town Centre

Tel: + 258 - 71 - 2232

Fax: + 258 - 71 - 2223

Offers simple but clean rooms.

Wimbi beach in Pemba

Where to Eat

O Chambo

Feira Exposiçao Niassa
Tel: + 258 71 3354
Lichinga's best restaurant.

Pemba

Pemba in the northern province of Cabo Delgado, was once known as Porto Amelia. Though the name may have changed, the unspoilt natural beauty of this coastal town has remained unchanged over the years.

Like so many towns and villages along the coast, Pemba developed as a trading station and later, as a colonial post under Portuguese rule. It is situated only 240 kilometres from the Tanzanian border, accounting for its warm, sub-tropical climate. The town is a bustling centre of shops and traditional markets, a treasure for shopping enthusiasts.

Pemba is also known as a prime destination for water sport and diving enthusiasts as the coral reef lies close to the shore. Prime fishing waters at St Lazarus Banks are also within easy reach. To the south, lie the beautiful islands of Ibo and Ilha de Mozambique. We strongly recommend you to some time on Wimbi Beach drinking cocktails and swimming in crystal clear water.

Where to Stay & Eat

Pemba Beach Hotel

Tel: + 258 - 1 - 301618
Fax: + 258 - 1 - 301625
Email: reserves@rani.co.mz
Website: www.pembabeach.com

A truly magnificent hotel built in old Arab style and situated on the beach, which offers great accommodation and restaurant services a well as a number of sport activities.

Complexo Nautilus & Complexo Caraçol

Tel: + 258 - 72 - 3520 / 2826
Fax : + 258 - 72 - 3717
Email : nautilus@emilmoz.com

Good rooms and apartments situated along the beach. This is the best place in town for water sports, scuba diving and fishing.

For restaurants and places to eat inquire at the hotels as these tend to change rather frequently.

Quirimba Archipielago

The Quirimbas Arquipelago consists of 32 coral islands stretching from Pemba (the capital of Cabo Delgado Province) to the Rovuma River, which forms the natural frontier between Tanzania and Mozambique. The area has never been developed and remains an unexplored tourist paradise. Quilálea Marine Sanctuary, consisting of Quilálea and Sencar Islands, lies 55 kilometres north of Pemba. Quilálea Island is 35 hectares in extent and is unique having a deep channel on the landward side, allowing protected mooring all year long and at all points of the tide. There are various beaches around the island. Seashells abound due to the high biodiversity of the zone. Sencar Island is 75 hectares in extent. It is O-shaped, with a coral rag exterior and a mangrove swamp interior. Water rushes in through a twisting, saltwater river at high tide. Sencar is a paradise for sea birds and has large areas of untouched coastal thicket. Samango monkeys made their homes on Sencar, though no one quite knows how they arrived there or how they stay alive in the absence of fresh water. Sencar has only rudimentary beaches.

Where to Stay & Eat

Quilálea Lodge

Tel/Fax: + 258 - 72 - 21808
Email: info@quilalea.com or quirimbas@teledata.mz
Website: www.quilalea.com

CITIES IN THE SOUTH

Southern Mozambique is composed of the Provinces of Maputo, Gaza and Inhambane with the cities of Maputo, Xai Xai and Inhambane, as their respective capital and several other major cities.

Mozambique Southern Provinces

Ponta D'ouro & Ponta Malongane

Ponta d'Ouro, the Point of Gold, at Mozambique's southern-most tip is known for its surfing, great beaches, and abundant marine life. Here lies a sandy headland covered in magnificent coastal dune forest which forms a sheltered bay that sweeps northwards for some 5 kilometres. It is one of the most frequented areas in Mozambique and is popular with South Africans and residents of Maputo as on weekends it can be easy to forget you're in Mozambique. The village is small and houses a few shops selling basic provisions. About 5 kilometres north of Ponta d'Ouro is the quieter Ponta Malongane.

Both areas offer very good opportunities for water activities such diving, snorkelling, boat angling, surfing, fishing, spear-fishing, and swimming. There are various operators based in the area.

The area between Maputo and Ponta d'Ouro was hard-hit during the war and heavily mined. Therefore it is recommended to be cautious before venturing off roads.

Where to Stay & Eat

Parque de Campismo

Tel/Fax: + 258 - 1 - 303177

Offers camping infrastructures and good chalets.

Motel do Mar

Tel/Fax: + 258 - 1 - 650000

It is a large complex on the beach with various self-catering chalets.

Blues Beach House

Tel: + 258 - 1 - 304098

Fax: + 258 - 1 - 421908

This is a private house with 3 double rooms 50 metres from the beach.

There are several other private houses along the beach available for rent. Inquire with Maputo travel agents.

Bilene

Bilene is a small resort town overlooking the large Uembje Lagoon. This beautiful turquoise water lagoon is separated from the sea by a narrow, sandy spit, and thus its waters are good for swimming. Indeed the lagoon is linked to the sea via a channel, which permits influxes of fresh water.

Historically, the area around Bilene served as capital for the first Gaza chief, Soshangane. Today Bilene's beach and pleasant weekend atmosphere make it a popular escapade for South African families and tourists.

Bilene beach resort

Where to Stay

Praia do Sol

Tel: + 258 - 82 - 319304

Website: www.pdsol.co.za

An eco-friendly resort situated on the beautiful shores of the Bilene Lagoon.

Pousada de São Martinha

Tel: + 27 - 59 - 002 (South Africa)

Offers good-vale doubles and four-person self-catering chalets.

Complexo Lagoa Azul

Tel: + 27 - 59 - 006 (South Africa)

At the southern end of town, this complex has self-catering four-person chalets.

Complexo Humula

Tel: + 258 - 1 - 415766

Fax: + 258 - 1 - 415769

This is Bilene's luxury option. It houses several comfortable self-catering chalets for two/five/six persons.

Where to Eat

All the places mentioned in the previous section offer restaurant services.

Estrela do Mar

It is located on the beachfront road not far from the market. It mostly serves seafood dishes.

Pavilhão Tamar

This restaurant is situated on the beach and is recommended for light meals.

Tchin-Tchin

Also located on the beach, it is a and pleasant small restaurant.

Xai-Xai

Xai-Xai (pronounced "shy-shy") is the capital city of the Province Gaza and was known during colonial times as João Belo, after the Portuguese Minister of Colonies in the mid-1920s. It is situated about 224 kilometres from Maputo along the EN1 and the nearby and very popular beach is at 10 kilometres from the city centre. Situated on the northern bank of the Rio Limpopo, Mozambique's second largest waterway and once navigable by coastal steamers as far as Xai-Xai, the town was developed in the 20th century as a satellite port to Maputo to serve the interior of the lower Limpopo region.

The wetlands around the lower reaches of the Limpopo are good bird-watching areas and are most accessible near Zongoene on the river's mouth. Nevertheless, Xai-Xai's main attraction is the beach at Xai-Xai beach, 8 kilometres off the main road and 10 kilometres from the city centre.

Where to Stay & Eat

Complexo Touristico Halley

Tel: + 258 - 22 - 35003

Situated on Xai-Xai beach, this complex offers double rooms, restaurant services and a disco.

Motel Concha

Tel: + 258 - 22 - 25099

The best choice in town. Located on the main road about 2 kilometres north of the centre near the beach turn-off. Double rooms are available here as well as restaurant services.

Inhambane

Inhambane, the capital city of Inhambane Province, is one of the most charming coastal cities in Mozambique. It is situated on the shores of a sheltered bay formed by two sandy headlands and is the springboard of some of the most popular resorts along the coast of Mozambique. Long before the colonial era it served as a stop for Arab traders and in 1534 the Portuguese established there a permanent settlement. Thus today it offers a number of interesting buildings to visit as well as a small but good museum. About 10 kilometres northeast of Inhambane in the bay are two islands, Ratos and Porcos, which make pleasant excursions.

There are various coastal towns around the city of Inhambane, which are very popular holiday destinations due to their attractive beaches and good game fishing. These include the villages of Tofo and Barra.

Where to Stay

Hotel Inhambane

Av. de Independência, n°438a

Tel: + 258 - 1 - 426074 / 6

Cell: + 258 - 82 - 300056

E-mail: hotelinhambane@tropical.co.mz

On the road to Inhambane

Hotel Inhambane is conveniently situated in the central business district of the city surrounded by cultural heritage building, and a few minutes drive from the prestine beaches. It offers 32 rooms comprising of 4 self-catering family apartments, 15 twin rooms, 6 double rooms, 5 deluxe, 2 suites spread on two floors. It has a pool, a conference centre, and a very good restaurant.

Barra Lodge

Tel: + 258 - 23 - 20561

E-mail: barra@pixie.co.za

Website: www.barralodge.co.za

There are 20 self-catering cottages, which can accommodate 6 people, 20 casitas for two, camping facilities, and a good restaurant.

White Sands (Barra)

Tel: + 258 - 82 - 490928

Located at the tip of the Barra peninsula, it offers self-contained chalets and camping, as well as diving and fishing arrangements.

Hotel Marinhos (Tofo)

Tel/Fax: + 258 - 23 - 29015

Pleasant hotel located on the Tofo beach.

Tofo Beach Cottages

Tel: + 258 - 82 - 864144

E-mail: willem.stapelberg@t-systems.co.za

Self-catering beachfront cottages, fully furnished and serviced to accommodate 6 people.

Pensão Pachiça

Tel: + 258 - 23 - 20565

E-mail: inhambane@africamail.com

This is a great place for backpackers and it offers clean private rooms.

Where to Eat

Maçaroca

Tel: + 258 - 23 - 20489

Pleasant place with delicious food.

Restaurante Tic-Tic

Near the market, this restaurant offers basic dishes.

Vilankulo

This is probably Mozambique's up-coming holiday resort. Indeed during the holiday seasons it fills up with tourist from South Africa and Maputo, and accommodation is often booked out. Vilankulos has great beach with crystal clear beaches with beautiful sites, but the main attraction is the nearby Bazaruto Archipelago (see the following section). Around town there are several interesting buildings to visit and decent walks to do. Snorkelling, diving and water sport activities are popular here.

Aerial view of Vilankulos

Where to Stay & Eat

Malibú, Travel and Business Centre Vilanculos

Tel: + 258 - 23 - 82291

Fax: + 258 - 23 - 82091

E-mail: malibutlagency@teledata.mz

This agency cover all the resorts in Vilanculos and the Bazaruto Islands.

Casa Rex

Tel: + 258 - 23 - 82048

E-mail: casarex@teledata.mz

Accommodation and restaurant.

Vilanculos Beach Lodge

Tel: + 27 715 7011

Fax: + 27 715 7971

E-mail: beachlodge@vilanculos.co.za

Website: www.vilanculos.co.za

An exclusive, private lodge, situated on mainland Mozambique, 5 kilometres from Vilanculos village. It offers 10 private chalets, built on ironwood stilts amongst the dunes - all situated for perfect sea views. Each chalet is luxury en-suite

Bazarauto Archipelago

The Bazaruto Archipelago, which is situated 10 to 25 kilometres offshore between Vilankulo and Inhassoro, is also called the "Crown Jewels of the Western Indian Ocena". It is a string of islands, which protrudes into the Mozambique Channel like five stepping stones. Indeed the Archipelago consists of five main islands: Bazaruto, Benguerra (formerly known as Santo António), Magaruque (Santa Isabel), Santa Carolina (Paradise Island) and tiny Bangué. Since 1971, the Archipelago has been protected as a national park. Its rich ecosystems provide a habitat for numerous bird species, reptiles and amphibian species, and an impressive marine life. There are also

Shhhhhhhh... listen the sound of the sea in Sta. Carolina

extensive coral formations. For visitors, the Bazaruto Archipelago, with its azure waters, sandy beaches and animal life, is a great holiday and relaxation destination.

Where to Stay & Eat

Bazaruto Lodge, Island Resort

Bazaruto Archipelago, Inhambane Province
Tel: + 258 - 1 - 305000
Fax: + 258 - 1 - 305305
E-mail: helenagoncalves@pestana.com
or reserves@pestana.com
Website: www.pestana.com
Robinson Crusoe never had it this good. Truly a recommended destination!!!

Pestana Resort, Bazarauto

Pestana hotel

Archipelago Sun resort
Bazaruto Archipelago, Inhambane Province
Tel: + 263 - 4 - 746532
E-mail: Sharon@sunvac.co.zw

Benguerra Lodge

Benguerra Island, Bazaruto Archipelago
Inhambane Province
Tel: + 271 - 1 - 4832734
E-mail: benguerra@icon.co.za
Website: www.benguerra.co.za

Indigo Bay Hotel, Island Resort

Bazaruto Island, Inhambane Province
Tel: + 258 - 1 - 301618
E-mail: reservas@rani.co.mz
Website: www.indigobayonline.com

Marlin Lodge

Benguerra Island, Bazaruto Archipelago
Inhambane Province
Tel: + 271 - 2 - 5432134
E-mail: reservations@marlinlodge.co.za
Website: www.marlinlodge.co.za

Sky and dunes, Bazaruto Island

CITIES IN THE CENTRE

Central Mozambique is composed of the Provinces of Sofala, Manica, Tete and Zambezia with Beira, Chimoio, Tete and Quelimane, their respective capital, and several other major cities.

Beira

Beira, the capital of Sofala Province, is Mozambique's busiest port and second-largest city. Despite its tarnished image, Beira is a pleasant place with a lively central area with numerous colonial-era buildings and a relaxed ambiance. The coastline is just an added attraction.

Although Beira is a fairly modern city, settlement in the area can be traced back at least to the 9th century AD with small fishing and trading settlements hankered nearby the coastline. The most important settlement was Sofala, which was once southern Africa's major gold-trading port. Then came the Portuguese and the British, which used Beira as a base for their expeditions to the interior and the development of the Mozambique Company. Today Beira is an important commercial centre and link to the neighbouring country of Zimbabwe.

Mozambique Central Provinces

Where to Stay

Hotel Embaixador

Tel: + 258 - 3 - 323121
Fax: + 258 - 3 - 323788

It is centrally located hotel and is one of Beira's oldest hotels. Rooms are pleasant and service is good. Rooms are air-conditioned and have satellite TV. There is a very cosy pub downstairs, with live music at the weekend. We strongly recommend you to try it!

Hotel Moçambique

Tel: + 258 - 3 - 329352
Fax: + 258 - 3 - 325060

Situated in the city centre, Hotel Moçambique offers good air-conditioned rooms but does not have a restaurant.

Hotel Tivoli

Tel: + 258 - 3 - 320300
Fax: + 258 - 3 - 320301

This is probably the best hotel is town although the room tend to be relatively small. Nevertheless service is good, and visitors have access to a bar and coffee shop.

Where to Eat

Clube Nautico

Tel: + 258 - 3 - 313093

It is an old Portuguese club on the beach with restaurant and pool. It is popular with families on weekend afternoons and from time to time a big barbecue is organized.

Clube Palmeiras

Tel: + 258 - 3 - 312947

Just off Avenida das F.P.L.M, this restaurant has a good selection of local and Portuguese dishes.

Oceano

Av. Mateus S. Mutemba

Tel: + 258 - 3 - 322919

Good pizzeria with a sports bar and a disco.

Restaurante Mira Mar

Av. Mateus S. Mtemba

Tel: + 258 - 3 - 322919

Located on the beach next to Hotel Miramar, it serves fare dishes.

Take Away 2 + 1

Rua 7, n°100

Tel: + 258 - 3 - 324569

Situated between Praça do Municipio and Avenida Samora Machel, it has meals to go and smarter dining upstairs.

Sofala

Sofala is situated about 40 km south of Beira and just south of the Búzi River is the site of the ancient gold-trading port of Sofala, dating from at least the 9th century AD. Sofala was an important city because of its role as a major link between the gold trade of the interior and the powerful sultanate at Kilwa in present-day Tanzania. By the 15th century, Sofala had become one of East Africa's most influential centres, with ties as far as Madagascar, India and even Indonesia. San Caetano, the first Portuguese fort in Mozambique, was built at Sofala in 1505 with stones shipped from Portugal. But trade routes shifted northwards to Ilha de Moçambique and Sofola's influence slowly declined. Today there is not much left of its former glory and the ruins of the fort have been completely overtaken by the sea. Nevertheless Sofa a remains an interesting city to visit especially due to the nearby "Gorongoza National Park" which used to be one of the greatest conservations areas in the world. The Park is being rehabilitated and it should soon regain it past glory.

Sofala still does not have good accommodation for visitors, thus we recommend you stay in the city of Beira.

Marromeu

Marromeu is mostly known as a sugar-growing centre dating back to the late 19th century when the Portuguese Sugar Society if East African began a plantation and sugar factory here. Today the factories have been rehabilitated under Mauritian ownership. About 45 km upriver from Marromeu is the town of Chupanga, where Mary Moffat, wife of the missionary and explorer David Linvingstone, is buried. She died here on the 17th of April 1862.

Chimoio

Chimoio is the capital of Manica Province and is Mozambique's fifth-largest city. Although Chimoio does not have any particular attraction, it is a nice town and its pleasant climate make it a good stop if you are in the area. It is just 95 kilometres from the Zimbabwean border. If you go 5 km northeast of the town, you will find Cabeça do Velho, a large rock that resembles the face of an old man at rest. We recommend you to climb up the rock with locals. Once at the top, it is customary to offer a prayer to the rock as it is associated with legends and traditions.

Where to Stay

Executive Manica Hotel

Tel: + 258 - 51 - 23135

Fax: + 258 - 51 - 23129

The best hotel in town it offers clean and comfortable rooms with TV, personal showers, a pool and a restaurant.

Residencial Flor de Vouga

Av. 25 de Setembro / Rua Dr. Araujo de la Cerda

Tel: + 258 - 51 - 22469

A pleasant hotel with nice double rooms. It is situated directly above Banco Austral.

Where to Eat

Elo 4

Av. 25 de Setembro

This is the best restaurant in town, and it serves excellent Italian food.

Restaurante Maua

Feira Popular

A good restaurant that serves local cuisine.

Manica

Manica is located 70 kilometres west from Chimoio. It was once the heart of the kingdom of Manica and an important gold trading area. About 5 kilometres from town are the Chinampere rock paintings (pinturas rupestres), which are considered sacred by local residents. Also recommended is the visit of the Chimanimani Mountains, with the Mt Binga, Mozambique's highest peak, on the Zimbabwean border that is a cross-border conservation area with great biodiversity of animals and plants.

Tete

Tete, the capital of Tete Province, was an important Swahili Arab trading outpost well before the arrival of the Portuguese and today remains a major transport junction. During the 16th and 17th century AD, it served as a departure point for trade caravans to the gold fields further inland. Today with the nearby Cahora Bassa Dam it has maintained its economic importance. With a population of over 50,000, it is one of the major towns in the Mozambique interior.

The suspension bridge that spans the Zambezi River is impressive at 538 metres high. Apart from this, Tete has little to offer visitors except its unique charm and atmosphere due to the hot climate, baobab trees and brown landscape. Tete is nothing like the other provincial capitals.

Where to Stay

Hotel Zambeze & Hotel Kassuende

These are the two best upmarket options in town.

Motel Tete

Tel: + 258 - 52 - 23467 / 23498

Situated along the river, it offers rooms with air-conditioning and TV.

Univendas

Tel: + 258 - 52 - 23198

Above a shop in the town centre, you will find here spacious and pleasant rooms.

Where to Eat

Motel Tete

The Motel has a good restaurant.

Restaurante Pemba

Along the river behind the old cathedral, this is the most popular restaurant in town.

Cahora Bassa Dam & Songo

About 150 kilometres northwest of Tete near the town of Songo is Cahora Bassa, the fifth-largest dam in the world. The dam, which was completed in 1974, is situated at the head of a magnificent gorge in the mountains and makes a good day trip from Tete. The Town of Songo is pleasant green place for a stroll. The main attraction is the visit of the dam and its impressive underground turbine rooms. For tours inquire at the office of HCB (Hidroelectrica de Cahora Bassa) in Tete.

Quelimane

Quelimane is the capital of Mozambique's densely populated Zambezia Province. It stands on the site of an old Arab trading settlement dating to at least the 15th century and built on the banks of the Bons Sinais (Qua Qua) River in the days when this was linked to the Zambezi. Today Quelimane is an important river port, and is known throughout the country for the affability and friendliness of its residents. The Portuguese cathedral on the waterfront is an attractive sight, as well as the nearby mosque. The attractive beaches around town make excellent excursions.
The town has a good nightlife and an active cultural scene.

Where to Stay

Hotel Chuabo

Tel: + 258 - 4 - 213181
Fax: + 258 - 4 - 213812
This hotel is probably the best in town and an institution. Large, comfortable rooms with TV, fridge and air-con are available here.

Hotel Zambeze

Av. Acordos de Lusaka
Offers good single/double rooms with bathroom, plus restaurant services.

Where to Eat

Quelimane has plenty of cafes and good restaurants. Here are our favourites.

Restaurante-Bar-Pizzeria da Estação

Located near the old train station, this restaurant serves great pizzas made in the oven and good-value Italian meals.

Coquinha

Located about 100 metres east of the Benfica cinema, you will be delighted here with Dona Guida's Zambezian dishes.

Mocuba

Mocuba is the junction town for travel from Quelimane to Nampula and Malawi. Not to far, about 40 kilometres north, in the Lugela district, visitors can enjoy the amazing site of hot springs and the cavernas do Monte Mulide, caves used during the war and considered sacred.

WILDLIFE

Mozambique's wildlife is very extensive. Indeed Mozambique has more than 200 mammal species, although most large mammal populations strongly diminished during the 1980s with the war.

Nevertheless important efforts are made for the recovery of wildlife populations. In fact Mozambique's game parks and reserves are now being re-stocked with wildlife, and their facilities restored, but by far the most exciting developments are on-going plans for cross-border wildlife reserves known as Transfrontier Conservation Areas (TFCs) - or Peace Parks - in the Southern African region. Large tracks of land in Mozambique are included in these two projects - The Great Limpopo TFCA and the Lubombo TFCA.
The Great Limpopo TFCA will constitute an area of 99,000 sq kilometres making it one of the largest conservation areas in the world. Much of it will be in Mozambique where it will incorporate the recently inaugurated Limpopo National Park, and the former Zinave and

Banhine National Parks, with the Kruger National Park in South Africa and Gonarezhou in Zimbabwe. Both the Kruger and Gonarezhou are rich in wildlife and the removal of border fences will allow game to move from these parks into Mozambique.

The Lubombo TFCA is planned to link Mozambique's Maputo Elephant Reserve with South Africa's Tembe Elephant Park and Khosi Bay Nature Reserve, and Swaziland's Hlane National Park and Mlawula and Mbukuzi Game Reserves, to create a major elephant stronghold along Africa's eastern coastline.

There is also an on-going wildlife relocation programme between Mozambique and South Africa which is expected to see 6,000 animals relocated from the Kruger National park to the Limpopo National Park over the next three years. Last year's movement comprised elephant, impala, warthog, waterbuck, wildebeest and zebra while plans for this year and next include eland, hippo, roan, sable, tsessebe and white rhino.

Looks like Bambi?

Banhine National Park

Located in the north of Gaza Province, between the Limpopo and Changane Rivers, this park, which is home to a rich variety of wildlife, is earmarked to become part of the Great Limpopo Transfrontier Conservation Area.

Bazaruto Marine Park

The park has recently been extended to cover the entire Bazaruto archipelago. This marine reserve with its 1,400 sq kilometres reserve is one of the largest in the Indian Ocean. In addition to humpback whales, turtles, manta rays and dolphins, some 100 dugongs survive here. It is one of the very few viable populations on the East African coast.

Gile Game Reserve

This wildlife conservation area, in Zambezia Province, is home to a great variety of mammal and bird species. Its former rhino population is now extinct but large numbers of elephant can still be seen and through relocation programmes populations of other mammal species are slowly increasing.

Gorongoza National Park

In Sofala Province, 150 kilometres from Beira, this used to be one of the great game reserves in Southern Africa. The park's wildlife is currently being re-stocked with animals and the fortunate will see lions, leopard, elephant, buffalo and hippo. There are said to be 500 species in the park including 300 large mammals.

Maputo Elephant Reserve

Situated 79 kilometres south of Maputo, via the ferry to Catembe, or 112 kilometres by road, this reserve is named for its large herds of elephant as well as huge flocks of flamingos that gather on the inland lakes.

Marromeu Buffalo Reserve

Also in Sofala Province, Marromeu is another park undergoing re-stocking of wildlife. The reserve used to boast 30,000 buffalo.

Niassa Reserve

Located in the north of Niassa Province, this reserve contains an estimated 9,000 elephants as well as large populations of buffalo, eland, giraffe, impala, kudu, wildebeest and zebra.

Pomene Game Reserve

Located on the coast of Inhambane Province, t is proposed to enlarge this terrestrial reserve to include some of the adjacent marine areas of ecological importance.

Quirimbas National Park

Lying off the coast of Cabo Delgado Province, within the Quirimbas Archipelago, this park embraces both marine and terrestrial habitats. The park covers an area of 7,000 sq kilometres and contains large mammals, bird-life, coral reefs and other marine fauna and flora. It also embraces four of the Global 200 areas of ecological importance.

Zinave National Park

Situated in Inhambane Province, on the border with Gaza and Manica, this is another park earmarked to become part of the Great Limpopo TFCA.

A mother rhino and her cub

SPECIAL INTERESTS, OFF THE BEATEN PATH AND TOP THREE ITINERARIES

Special Interests

Bird-Watching

The wealth of bird life in Mozambique is stunning. The varying habitats to be found, particularly those in central Mozambique, account for a rich variety of bird life - more than 900 species have been recorded.
On Inhaca Island alone, 300 bird species, including seven species of albatross, flocks of flamingos and pelicans have been recorded. Another bird paradise is Benguerra Island, which alone is home to 115 different types including the rare crab plover, olive bee-eater and green coucal. Other areas include Lake Chicamba with its waders and water-birds, the Chimanimani mountains (Mt Gorongoza and Mt Namúli) with its dappled mountain robin and chirinda apalis.

Cultural Heritage

Traditional ways of life are well preserved in Mozambique - varying from Province to Province. This cultural kaleidoscope provides visitors with a host of treasured experiences and memories. From the initiation rituals of the fearless Makonde people from the Cabo Delgado Province in the North, to the "timbila" dance and instrument of the Chope people form Inhambane Province in the south, passing by the painted faces of the Makua women from Nampula Province and the agility of the Nhau dancers from Tete Province, Mozambique offers many opportunities to learn about other cultures.

Dolphin Watching

Ponta d'Ouro, a resort to the South of Maputo, and the Bazaruto Archipelago are popular places for dolphin watching. Pemba is also a good location to watch these friendly mammals.

Dugongs

A family of 100 rare dugongs, also called "sea cows", live in the waters surrounding the Bazaruto Archipelago Marine Park and represent one of the largest populations along the East African coast. Other places along the coast where dugongs have been spotted include Inhambane Bay, Angoche, Ilha de Moçambique, Nacala and the Quirimba Archipelago.

Flora Enthusiasts

Mozambique hosts an abundance of flora, including numerous endemic species although much of this richness remains poorly documented. More than 5,600 plant species have been recorded in the country, with the actual number likely to be much higher. Of these, an estimated 250 may be endemic.
Cycads and other indigenous plants can be admired in Maputo's Tunduro Gardens, designed in 1885 by the English gardener, Thomas Honney.
Ancient baobab trees, sometimes known as the "upside down tree", are to be found in Tete, Cabo Delgado and Inhambane Provinces.

Two areas notable for their plant biodiversity are the Chimanimani mountains, with at least 45 endemic species, and the Maputaland Centre of Plant Diversity, south of Maputo.

Rock Paintings

Ancient rock paintings are found in the Provinces of Manica, Tete and Zambèzia.

Whale Watching

At certain times of the year whales can be seen off the coast of Inhambane and in the Quirimbas Archipelago which serves as an important nursery are for Humpback whales and their calf.

Off the Beaten Path

Bazaruto Archipelago Marine National Park

Nestled in the warm Indian Ocean and brushed with gentle tropical breezes lies the island of Bazaruto. An ecological paradise, its waters teem with glistening marine life, offering endless opportunities for sea-loving enthusiasts. Situated about 10 kilometres off the coast of Vilankulo, the archipelago consists of 5 islands: Bazaruto, Benguerra (formerly known as Santo António), Magaruque (Santa Isabel), Santa Carolina (Paradise Island) and tiny Bangué. Since 1971 the archipelago has been protected as a national park, with funding and management provided by various bodies including the Worldwide Fund for Nature. Today it is one of the most beautiful places on the continent, complete with azure waters, sandy beaches, palm trees, pristine coral reefs, plus tropical fish to goggle at and big game fish to catch.

Lago de Cahora Bassa

The Barragem de Cahora Bassa dams the Zambezi River approximately 150 kilometres north-west of Tete in the Tete Province. Completed in 1974, this is the fifth-largest dam in the world and is one of the largest civil engineering projects of its time in Africa. Lake Cahora Bassa, lake created by the dam, stretches for 270 kilometres and pushes back to the confluence of the Zambezi and the Luangwa Rivers on the border with Zambia. The setting and surrounding scenery is beautiful with a magnificent gorge in the mountains.

Lake Niassa (Lake Malawi)

Lake Niassa is Africa's third largest lake with a width of 75 kilometres and length of 550 kilometres, and a depth of 700 metres in parts. Lake Niassa was visited and named by Scottish missionary and explorer David Livingstone in 1859. The Lake presents, from an ecological point of view, an exceptional diversity of fish with over 500 species identified, including more than 350 endemics. Additionally it contains one-third of the world's known cichild (freshwater fish) species. The Lake District (Distrito do Lago), area bordering the lake is extremely beautiful with narrow sandy beaches surrounded by mountains and steep hills rising directly from the lakeshore, endless forest and bush, and beautiful waterfalls.

Quilalea Island

In the 1500s Portuguese and Arab traders passing through Quissanga on the Mozambican coast discovered an island refuge in the Indian Ocean and called it Quilálea. In fact its name comes from "lala", the Swahili word for sleep. This peaceful island sanctuary is now part of the Quirimbas Archipelago Marine National Park and protects life and ecology as it was created. The spectacular archipelago stretches from Ponta Diabo to the Rovuma River, the frontier with Tanzania. Quilálea and neighbouring Sencar are in the shelter of Montepuez Bay, a marine sanctuary that protects turtles, whales and shy dugongs. Quilálea and the other islands offer great escapade and relaxation opportunities.

TOP THREE ITINERARIES

Maputo to Ponta D'ouro

RECOMMENDED ebiZ Guides

Distance: 230 km
Time: 3 hours to 1 day depending on the weather
Road Conditions: Gravel and sandy tracks which require 4X4

The easiest and quickest way to reach Catembe, on the southern bank of the Rio Espirito Santo, from Maputo is by ferry, as by road it is a 120-kilometre journey. The ferry trip is an experience in itself. The ferry operates from the terminal on Avenida 10 de Novembro and leaves Catembe at 05:00, 06:00, 07:00, 08:30 and then every two hours. Tickets can be bought at the kiosk at the entrance gate to the pier. Although the trip only last 20 minutes you will enjoy unique views of the Maputo skyline and the harbour. About 100 metres south of the Catembe ferry terminal you will join the EN201. Turn left here and continue for 42 km along a gravel road, which is in fair condition, before joining a tar road quite unexpectedly. The road joining in from the right is the route from Namaacha on the Swaziland border and the road from Maputo and Boane. After about 3 km you will reach a turnoff to Bela Vista, situated on a bank overlooking the Rio Maputo; its name is translated as "beautiful view". Just over 1 km on there is another turnoff to Bela Vista. The tar road continues for another 14 km until you reach the bridge over the Rio Maputo and the rather elaborate Temple Shree Ram. After the checkpoint at Salamanga, the road surface deteriorates and about 8,8 km beyond the checkpoint you will reach a bridge over the Rio Fruti. About 200 m beyond the bridge turn left and travel 2,6 km to a T-junction where you turn left again. On reaching the park headquarters of the Reserva Especial do Maputo 500 m further, turn right. From the park headquarters, where entrance and camping fees are payable, follow the signposted track of Miradouro de Changas for 300 m and then keep left. About 4,5 km further keep left, following the track signosted to machangulo and Chlombane. The track traverses several forested dunes, alternated with grassy plains and extensive seasonally inundated reed-covered pans. About 20,6 km from the park headquarters a major track joins in from the right; turn left and after about 2,4 km you will have a stunning view over Lago Munde. Keep right where a small track splits off to the left to Machangulo and a short way on you will be at the northern shores of the lake. Ignore another small track turning off to the left and after 1,2 km you will pass a small lake on your left. For the remaining 6,8 km to Ponta Milibangalala the track traverses undulating grass-covered dunes.

From Milibangalala, backtrack for about 10,4 km; Ignore the road to the park headquarters to the right and continue south. A short way beyond the junction the track heads up a steep dune with deep loose sand and 14 km on the Lago Piti comes into view to the left. Take a breath, enjoy the view. About 400 m further you will reach an old Portuguese trading store at a major junction; the track to the left ends at a small fishing settlement on the lake shore, while the faint track to the right heads to the park headquarters via Lago Xingute. Keep to the main track south and after 5,1 km you will reach the park's southern entrance gate. From here continue south until you reach a sign post to Ponta Mamoli. When you reach Ponta Mamoli head south for Ponta Malongane. Here follow the signposted sandy track to Ponta d'Ouro for about 6 km until you join a tar road where you turn left for Motel do Mar and the Ponta d'Ouro Holiday Resort. There you go you have reached Ponta d'Ouro where you should enjoy the beautiful beaches and the various sport activities.

Maputo to Inhambane

Distance: 740 km
Time: 7 hours to 2 day depending on the weather and rush
Road conditions: Tar, except sandy tracks when heading to the coastal resorts

To get to the EN1 from the city centre, travel westwards along Avenida 24 de Julho to the circle at Praça 16 de Julho. Continue along Avenida da Oua for 1,4 km to a traffic light where you turn right into Avenida de Moçambique. After about 13,2 km you will pass the Marbor factory with an enormous metal and concrete statue, the work of renowned Mozambican artist Malangatana.

About 37 km north of Maputo you reach the village of Marracuene, which lies on a high bank overlooking the Incomati floodplains. The village is the gateway to Macaneta and the Incomati mouth, the closest resorts to Maputo. As you enter Marracuene, look out for a tree-lined road on your right.

To reach the Marracuene Camping Park and Chalet or the Macaneta Beach turn right and follow the rather potholed road for about 600 m until it curves to the left. To reach Macaneta it is necessary to take the ferry, which operates on regular basis.

From Marracuene the EN1 winds inland to avoid the extensive floodplains of the Rio Incomati. About 48 km beyond Marracuene the road winds through the town of Manhica with its neat reed houses and 6 km after passing through Xiavane you cross the Rio Incomati into Inhambane Province. Further along the road winds through cashew nut plantations and 19 km after crossing the Rio Incomati you reach the turnoff to Bilene at Macia.

To reach Bilene turn right here and follow the road, which has been rehabilitated and is in excellent condition, for 33 km to the circle at the entrance of the town.

Back on the main road, the EN1, cross the Limpopo River to reach the town of Xai-Xai, formely known as João Belo. Xai-Xai, the capital of Gaza Province, is a sprawling city with a population of 50,000. A signpost on the eastern outskirts of the town indicates the 15 km tar road to Praia Xai-Xai, a small resort with a large tidal pool, formed by a proeminent reef, offering safe swimming.

Continuing on the N1, the road traverses gently undulating countryside dotted with clumps of coconut palms and pleasant coastal bush. At Chidenguele a turnoff indicates the track to Praia do Chidenguele.

North of Chidenguele the EN1 winds further inland and then crosses into Inhambane Province. You then reach the town of Quissico, on a high hill overlooking the lagoon of the same name. Another 42 km on the road crosses the Lago Poelela and then reaches the town of Inharrine. As you continue north along the EN1, the coconut palms become increasingly dominant. At the roadside village of Lindela a signpost to the right indicates the road to Inhambane, the capital of Inhambane Province. Save for the potholes, the 33 km road is drivable.

Now you have reached the end of the journey. Just before entering Inhambane, a signpost opposite a fish factory indicates the turnoff to various resorts along the coast south of Inhambane, namely Tofo Beach (Praia do Tofo), Barra Beach (Prai da Barra), Coconut Bay (Baia dos Cocos), Guinjata Bay, and Paindane. All is left now is for you to choose either staying at Inhambane or head for the resorts, the latter being our recommendation.

Quelimane to Ilha de Moçambique and Pemba

Distance: 1,270 km
Time: 3 days
Road Conditions: Mostly tar roads but alternating with gravel roads

From Quelimane, the capital of Zambézia Province, head for 37 km to Nicuadala where you turn right; continue for 32 km along a tar road to Namacurra. From here the EN104 heads north along the valley carved by the Rio Licungo; the first 28 km is gravel and 5 km after joining the tar road you reach the abandoned Portuguese settlement of Malei. The remaining 52 km to Mocuba is on a good tar surface. At Mocuba the road swings northeast, ascending steadily through miombo woodlands to the Planalto Moçambicano. The first 100 km of the road from Mocuba to Alto Molócuè is tar in good condition, while the remaining 87 km alternates between gravel and tar.

Beyond Alto Molócuè a gravel road traverses undulating countryside. The next large settlement, Alto Ligonha, is reached 77 km beyond Alto Molócuè and the interesting castle-like building as you leave town is unlikely to be missed. About 34 km after leaving Alto Ligonha you cross the Rio Ligonha, the southern boundary of Nampula Province. Here you join a good tar road and 22 km further on pass through the village of Murrupala. The road then ascends gradually towards Nampula, the capital of Nampula Province. Nampula is a pleasant, bustling city of some 200,000 people and an important railway and road junction. Encircling the city are striking granite outcrops that rise abruptly from the plains.

From Nampula the main road continues north for 87 km to the village of Namiola where the EN 106 branches off to the north, while the road to Nacala and Ilha de Moçambique continues straight. After about 38 km you pass the turnoff to Monapo, which lies at the railway junction to Nacala and has a factory where cashew nuts can be bought. About 2,4 km on you turn right onto the EN 105, a good tar road, to Ilha de Moçambique.

If you are interested in history after 24 km you will pass a signpost to the settlement of Mossuril, which lies on a peninsula to the north of Baia de Moçambique. The settlement is reached after 21 km along a gravel road and once there ask for directions to the Igreja de Nossa Senhora de Remedios (Church of Our Lady of Remedy), a beautiful church built by the Portuguese at the settlement of Cabaceira in the 18th century.

Back on the EN 105, continue for about 25 km to the 3,5 km-long bridge linking the mainland with Ilha de Moçambique. Now you have reached one of the country's most fascinating destinations. Enjoy!!

Once ready to continue towards Pemba, backtrack for 89 km to the village of Namiola, where you turn right onto the EN 106. The road traverses moimbo woodlands with baobabs and magnificient star chestnut trees conspicuous as you continue north. Villa Nacaroa is reached after 65 km and the village of Alua is another 56 km further on. Beyond Alua the scenery is dominated by fascinating granite outcrops, baobabs, chestnut trees and groves of cashew nut trees. About 31 km beyond Alua you reach the Rio Lúrio which forms the southern boundary of Cabo Delgado Province.

Continuing north, you reach Metoro after 73 km. The settlement lies at the junction of the roads to Pemba and this is also where route 11 (Lichinga to Pemba) joins in. Turn right here to reach the turnoff to Macomia and Mocimboa da Praia 12 km further at the village of Sunate (also known as Silva Macua). From here, continue straight along the EN 106, a patched tar road in fair condition, except for a few bad sections at bridges. After about 17 km you will enjoy your first glimpse of the coastal plains and a few kilometres on the road begins its descent to the plains. As you approach, keep an eye out for the Makonde Co-operative under the trees to the right of the road, a short way beyond the turnoff to the airport. Pemba is reached 80 km beyond Sunate. Welcome to the largest city north of Nampula, and one of the up and coming holiday destinations. Head to the beach, lay down and enjoy the view.

LISTING

Reviews

Mozambique "Africa's Hidden Treasure"

By the Lonely Planet
1st Edition, October 2000
Very Useful tourist guidebook.

African Adventurer's Guide to Mozambique

By Willie & Sandra Olivier, Struik.Book Publishers,
2nd Edition, 2000
Good for planned itineraries and advice on activities.

A lot of Information is available from different Tourist Association, including FUTUR.

Resorts

Pestana Hotels & Resorts Mozambique

(see Tourism section)
A/c Pestana Rovuma Carlton Hotel, Rua da Sé, 114
Caixa Postal 4375, Maputo
Tel: + 258 - 1 - 305000
Fax: + 258 - 1 - 307288
E-mail: esposito@pestana.co.mz
Website: www.pestana.com

The group proposes great resorts on Inhaca Island and on the Bazaruto Island. Strongly recommended by Ebizguides.

Archipelago Sun resort

Bazaruto Archipelago, Inhambane Province
Tel: + 263 - 4 - 746532
Email: Sharon@sunvac.co.zw

Barra Lodge, Beach Resort

Strongly recommended by Ebizguides.

Barra Beach, Inhambane Province

Tel: + 258 - 23 - 20561
E-mail: barra@pixie.co.za

Barra Reef Resort

Barra Beach, Inhambane Province
Tel: + 271 - 2 - 3485838
E-mail: info@barrareef.co.za
Website: www.barrareef.co.za

Benguerra Lodge

Benguerra Island, Bazaruto Archipelago, Inhambane Province
Tel: + 271 - 1 - 4832734
E-mail: benguerra@icon.co.za
Website: www.benguerra.co.za

Casa Barry Beach Resort

Tofo Beach, Inhambane Province
Tel: + 258 - 2 - 329007

Guinjata Bay Resort

Guinjata Bay, Inhambane Province
Tel: + 271 - 3 - 7412795
E-mail: reservations@guinjata.com
Website: www.guinjata.com

Indigo Bay Hotel, Island Resort

Bazaruto Island, Inhambane Province
Tel: + 258 -1 - 301618
E-mail: reservas@rani.co.mz
Website: www.indigobayonline.com

Marlin Lodge

Benguerra Island, Bazaruto Archipelago, Inhambane Province
Tel: + 271 - 2 - 5432134
E-mail: reservations@marlinlodge.co.za
Website: www.marlinlodge.co.za

Mchenga Nkwichi Lodge

Lake Niassa, Niassa Province
E-mail: mdw01@bushmail.net

Palm Grove Lodge

Praia da Barra, Inhambane Province
Tel: + 258 - 82 - 459997

Pemba Beach Hotel

Pemba, Cabo Delgado Province
Tel: + 258 - 1 - 301618
E-mail: reservas@rani.co.mz
Website: www.pembabeach.com

Ponta d'Ouro Beach Resort

Ponta d'Ouro, Maputo Province

Tel: + 271 - 1 - 3397275

Pomene Lodge

Pomene, Inhambane Province

Tel: + 258 - 82 - 7118161

E-mail: bookings@pomene.co.za

Website: www.pomene.co.za

Praia do Sol Beach Resort

Bilene, Maputo Province

Tel: + 258 - 82 - 319304

Website: www.pdsol.co.za

Quilalea Island Lodge

Archipelago das Qurimbas, Cabo Delgado Province

Tel: + 258 - 72 - 21808

E-mail: info@quilalea.com

Website: www.quilalea.com

Vilankulos Beach Lodge

Vilankulos, Inhambane Province

Tel: + 258 - 23 - 82388

E-mail: beachlodge@vilanculos.co.za

Website: www.vilanculos.co.za

White Sands Beach Resort

Barra Beach, Inhambane Province

Tel: + 258 - 82 - 490928

Zongoene Lodge

Limpopo River Mouth, Gaza Province

Tel: + 258 - 82 - 305628 or + 258 - 22 - 42 000

E-mail: zongoene@satis.co.za

Website: www.satis.co.za/zongoene

There are many more resorts across Mozambique which offer high quality services and great holiday destinations.

Airlines

LAM - Linhas Aereas de Moçambique

(see Transport and Communications section)

Aeroporto de Maputo

P.O.Box 2060

Maputo

Tel: + 258 - 1 - 465074 / 465075

Fax: + 258 - 1 - 465134

E-mail: jrviegas@lam.co.mz

Website: www.lam.co.mz

SAA - South African Airways

(see Transport and Communications section)

Rua Fernao Melo e Castro, n° 287

P.O.Box 323, Sommerschield

Maputo

Tel: + 258 - 1 - 498097 / 498223

Fax: + 258 - 1 - 499546

E-mail: femiesaa@teledata.mz

Website: www.flysaa.com

TAP - Air Portugal

(see Transport and Communications section)

Rua da Sé, n° 114, Centro Comercial do Hotel Rovuma, Loja n° 28

Maputo

Tel: + 258 - 1 - 303927 / 303928

Fax: + 258 - 1 - 303947

Website: www.tap.pt

STA - Sociedade de Transportes Aéreos

(see Transport and Communications section)
Rua de Tchamba, n° 405
P.O.Box 665, Maputo
Tel: + 258 - 1 - 491765 / 492022 / 495107
Fax: + 258 - 1 - 491763
E-mail: sta.tta@tvcabo.co.mz
Website: www.sta.co.mz

Metavia

Maputo Airport
Maputo
Tel: + 258 - 1 - 465487 / 465089

Transairways

Maputo Airport
P.O.Box 1599, Maputo
Tel: + 258 - 1 - 465108
Fax: + 258 - 1 - 465011
E-mail: transairways@virconn.com

Car Rentals

Avis Rent-a-Car
(see Tourism section)
Av. Angola, n° 22
P.O.Box 1816
Maputo
Tel: + 258 - 1 - 467007 / 15
Fax: + 258 - 1 - 466512
E-mail: avismoz@avis.co.za

Avis is also present at the Maputo International Airport as well as the Beira International Airport.

Europcar

Av. Julius Nyerere, n° 1418
P.O.Box 4233, Maputo
Tel: + 258 - 1 - 497337 / 8
Fax: + 258 - 1 - 497334
E-mail: europcar@virconn.com

Europcar is also present at the Maputo International Airport. Strongly recommended by Ebizguides.

Hertz Car Hire

Av. 24 de Julho, n° 2006
P.O.Box 905
Maputo
Tel: + 258 - 1 - 494982
Fax: + 258 - 1 - 326077
E-mail: hertz.reservations@tropical.co.mz

Hertz is also present at the Maputo International Airport and the Polana Hotel.

Imperial - Car Rental

Av. Mao Tsé Tung, n° 591 R/C
Maputo
Tel: + 258 - 1 - 493545
Fax: + 258 - 1 - 493543
E-mail: imperial.mpm@virconn.com

Imperial is also present in the cities of Beira and Nampula.

TRAVEL AGENCIES, TOUR OPERATORS, SAFARI COMPANIES

Atlas

(see Tourism section)
Av. 24 de Julho, n° 981 R/C
P.O.Box 167 - Maputo
Tel: + 258 - 1 - 304600
Fax: + 258 - 1 - 304620

E-mail: j.barroso@atlas.co.mz
Website: www.atlas.co.mz

Expresso Tours Lda

Rua Joaquim Lapa, 95 R/C, Baixa de Cidade
Maputo
Tel: + 258 - 1 - 424738 / 431663 / 4
Fax: + 258 - 1 - 431665
E-mail: malo@virconn.com

Grupo Cotur Travel & Tours

(see Tourism section)
Av. Karl Marx 1242
Maputo
Tel: + 258 - 1 - 427505 / 301924 / 324341
Fax: + 258 - 1 - 324151
E-mail: cotur@emilmoz.com

Malibu, Travel and Business Centre Vilankulos

Vilankulos, Inhambane Province
Tel: + 258 - 23 - 82291
E-mail: malibutlagency@teledata.mz

Mextur - Moçambique Expresso Turismo e Viagens

(see Tourism section)
Av. 25 de Setembro, 1226 r/c dt° Loja 10
CP 1222, Maputo.
Tel: + 258 - 1 - 428427 / 8 / 9
Fax: + 258 - 1 - 428430
E-mail: mextur@emilmoz.com

Mozambique Adviser

(see Tourism section)
Av. Ahmed Sekou Touré, n° 1034
Maputo
Tel: + 258 - 1 - 309477
Fax: + 258 - 1 - 302054
E-mail: mozambique@adviser.co.mz
Website: www.adviser.co.mz

Some indicative prices

Bottle of Beer: $1 - 2
Bottle of Water: $ 0.75 (1.5 litres)
Pack of Cigarettes: $1 - 2
A meal: $7 ordinary restaurants, $10 - 12 in international ones
One night in a 5 stars hotel: min $100
Rent a car: $50 per day
Gas: $0.7 per litre
Rent a house: min $1,000 for a 3 bedroom flat
Office rent:
prices range from US$ 1 to US$ 8/m2
Decent hair cut: $10 - 12
Police officer salary: $50 per month
Taxi fare: $1 per km
Bus from Maputo to Matola: $0.2
Return flight to Beira: $350
Rent a DVD: $1,2
Local Newspaper: $0.4
Security guard: $60 - $80 per month
Housekeeping: $40 per month
(but you are welcome to increase it a bit! To have your people around happier)

Basic Portuguese Vocabulary

Basics

Hello = Olá

Goodbye = Adeus

How are you? = Como Estas?

Fine = Bem

Please = Por Favor/ Faz favor

Thank You = Obrigado

Yes = Sim

No = Não

Mr. = Senhor

Ms. = Senhora

Infant = Criança

Elder = Velho

Time

What time is it? = Que horas são?

Today = Hoje

Tomorrow = Amanhã

Yesterday = Ontem

Saturday = Sabádo

Sunday = Domingo

Monday = Segunda - Feira

Tuesday = Terça - Feira

Wednesday = Quarta - Feira

Thursday = Quinta - Feira

Friday = Sexta - Feira

Numbers

0 = Zero

1 = Um

2 = Dois

3 = Trez

4 = Quatro

5 = Cinco

6 = Seis

7 = Sete

8 = Oito

9 = Nove

10 = Dez

Getting Around

Where is the ....? = Onde Esta...?

How much? = Quanto custa...?

Is there ....? = Tenho....?

I'm lost = Estou Perdido/a

Money = Dinheiro

Bank = Banco

Hotel = Hotel

Restaurant = Restaurante

Telephone = Telefono

Police Station = Posto de Policia

Post Office = Correios

Tourist Office = Centro de Informação Touristica

Market = Mercado

Food and Drink

Water = Agua

Juice = Sumo

Soda = Soda

Beer = Cerveja

Wine = Vino

Glass = Copo

Soup = Sopa

Beef = Beef

Chicken = Galínha

Fish = Peixe

Potatoes = Batatas

Rice = Arroz

Vegetables = Vegetais

Bread = Pão

Fruit = Fruta

Plate = Pato

Tea = Chá

Coffee = Café

Milk = Leite

Sugar = Açucar

Fork = Garfo

Spoon = Colher

Knife = Faca

Health

I'm ill = Estou Doente

Doctor = Doctor

Medecine = Medecina

Drugstore = Farmacia

Pills = Comprimidos

Fever = Febre